And My Children
Did Not
Know Me

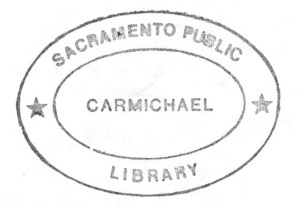

Minorities in Modern America

———

Editors

Warren F. Kimball
David Edwin Harrell, Jr.

And My Children
Did Not
Know Me

A History of the Polish-Americans

John J. Bukowczyk

INDIANA UNIVERSITY PRESS
Bloomington and Indianapolis

To my parents,
Stella Węgrzyn and Joseph Bukowczyk,
and
to my grandparents,
Mary Węgrzyn and John Węgrzyn,
and to my second cousins, Louie and Lily Rose,
Greek/Irish/Polish-Americans,
or just plain Americans?

The poem "When I Journeyed from America" is reprinted from
Merrily We Sing: 105 Polish Folksongs, edited by Harriet M.
Pawlowska, ©1961, by permission of Wayne State University Press.

©1987 by John J. Bukowczyk

Manufactured in the United States of America.

Library of Congress Cataloging-in-Publication Data

Bukowczyk, John J., 1950–
    And my children did not know me.

    (Minorities in modern America)
    Bibliography: p.
    Includes index.
    1. Polish Americans—History. I. Title.
II. Series.

E184.P7B84 1986	973'.049185	85-45888

ISBN 0-253-30701-5
ISBN 0-253-20391-0 (pbk.)

  2   3   4   5 90 89 88

When I Journeyed from America

When I journeyed from America . . .
And the foundry where I labored,

In pray'r my hands thanked our Father,
Hands that never shirked their labor.

Soon I came to New York City,
To the agent for my passage.

And the agents asked me if I
Had three hundred dollars with me.

"Ask me not such foolish questions.
For I carry gold and silver."

When I crossed the ocean midway,
No land could I see, sweet Virgin.

Our ship's captain was right busy,
Seeing, cheering all the people.

When I laid my eyes on Hamburg,
I thought I saw God Almighty.

When at last I landed safely,
"Lord," I prayed, "I thank thee for this."

"O how grateful am I, dear God,
That I've crossed the ocean safely."

Berlin came next after Hamburg,
"Barmaid, I will have some good wine."

Then I left Berlin for Krakow;
There my wife was waiting for me.

And my children did not know me,
For they fled from me, a stranger.

"My dear children, I'm your papa;
Three long years I have not seen you."

CONTENTS

Illustrations follow page 51.

MAPS

PREFACE

In the last, rootless decade families, neighborhoods, and communities have disintegrated in the face of gripping social, economic, and technological changes. This process has had mixed results. On the positive side, it has produced a mobile, volatile, and dynamic society in the United States that is perhaps more open, just, and creative than ever before. On the negative side, it has dissolved the glue that bound our society together and has destroyed many of the myths, symbols, values, and beliefs that provided social direction and purpose. These effects have touched every American. Today we are freer to do and to be, to act and to live as each of us chooses; less hindered by social constraints and community sanctions. Yet individual freedom has proven a difficult thing to bear. The free individual can become a purposeless and lonely creature, prey to anomie and anger, anxiety and frustration.

Ethnic Americans, with their cohesive families and strong communities, have had much to lose from disintegrative social changes. Thus, much recent ethnic history has been a sad story of decline. Ethnic cultures have been eroded by assimilation. Ethnic neighborhoods have succumbed to enemies from without—urban renewal and re-industrialization—as well as enemies from within—suburban diaspora. The shock of loss that these developments entailed has been variously expressed by ethnic Americans over the past fifteen years. Some, unfortunately, have responded through the bitter backlash of political reaction. Others have fashioned a more positive response to these social changes: they have begun to embrace their own history.

The search for history—for roots—has become a compelling preoccupation among many ethnic Americans. They have been touched deeply by their journeys of discovery into the past, journeys that have helped guide them through a chaotic contemporary world. Individuals have traveled many directions while seeking their roots. Genealogical searches have recovered family lineages anteceding living memory or oral tradition, and thus have bridged oceans and centuries. Cries of Ethnic Power have been an antidote to the ethnics' nagging sense of powerlessness, while invocations of Ethnic Pride have nurtured a healthy self-respect among ethnic peoples. The celebration of folk culture has revealed a newfound appreciation of a world we had almost lost, the world of our immigrant forebears. Through these manifestations, ethnic Americans have embraced their own ethnic identity. They

ix

have also shown that we cannot know who we really are without knowing our own history.

In some ways, this book is a personal journey of discovery that closes a circle. The circle began with a New Jersey boyhood, which was not considered particularly "ethnic"; daily lived, ethnicity was taken for granted. Farther afield, avenues of education broadened perceptions, altered political consciousness, and awakened new ambitions. Ten years later, via alien country—graduate study in history —the circle traversed other country that was enticingly familiar yet more alien still. In 1974 came a backpacking trek across Europe to Poland—sleeping on straw mattresses, cutting grain with a scythe, seeing factories rising in verdant countryside and a pile of broken shingles where a cottage once stood, a grandfather's birthplace. The circle then led to a dozen years of historical research; papers read, articles published, and this book written. And now the circle finally closes with the question: can one ever go home again?

Clearly the present study holds personal meaning, yet it possesses significance for the general reader as well. First, the 2.5 million immigrants who came to the United States from Poland in the late nineteenth and the early twentieth century were part of one of modern history's epic events—mass migration. During the period of mass migration, 55 million Europeans left their homelands, and of these, roughly 33 million came to the United States between 1820 and 1920. The Polish immigrants' story sheds light on an important saga in world history. Second, America's Polish immigrants thrived in their adopted country. By 1972, between 5.1 and 6 million Americans would claim a Polish heritage. In the 1980s, Polish-Americans remain one of America's larger ethnic groups. For this reason alone, understanding the Polish-American experience is necessary in order to understand fully the ethnic dimension of twentieth-century American society.

Too often, the search for personal history and the study of ethnicity have been romantic, myth-making exercises. By keeping the broader historical themes in mind, however, it is possible to sidestep myth and sharpen an analytical perspective while exploring the Polish-American experience of yesterday and today. If ethnicity seems romantic now, to the millions of men, women, and children who migrated it was immediate and real. Ethnicity was not only a matter of culture to these people, but of power and powerlessness. We can learn much from their view of ethnicity. In exploring ethnicity in America, we must examine power relations within immigrant and ethnic enclaves, and between those enclaves and the dominant society. We must also look at issues of class. Only by doing so can we escape the pitfalls of myth and nostalgia, and come to a deeper, sharper understanding of flesh-and-blood people. That is the aim of this volume.

In writing this book, I have incurred a number of professional debts that I would like to acknowledge with gratitude. Warren Kimball conceived the idea for this volume and, along with David Edwin Harrell, Jr., bore editorial responsibility for the manuscript. I am deeply grateful for their patient nurturing of this project. My thanks, however, also go to several friends and colleagues who commented on the manuscript, including Alan Raucher, Mary Cygan, Stanislaus Blejwas, Thaddeus Radzilowski, and Victor Greene, and to those who helped in other ways. John W. Brennan, Jr., and Jeff Alderman of the American Broadcasting Company (ABC) News Polling Unit furnished me with election statistics; John David Kromkowski of the National Center for Urban Ethnic Affairs shared his perceptive insights on ethnic political behavior and greatly influenced the conclusions drawn in chapter 7 of this book; Dolores Antosiak cheerfully made the clippings in the Hamtramck Public Library available to me; and the Office of Research and Sponsored Programs Services at Wayne State University granted me a summer Research Award that enabled me to finish revising the manuscript. Finally, a veritable legion of people assisted me in gathering photographs for the book. They include Alice Dalligen, Judy Barmatoski, and Joan Gartland of the Detroit Public Library; Stanley Mallach and Allan Kovan of the University of Wisconsin–Milwaukee Library; Kathy Koehler of the Bentley Library; Anne Steinfeldt of the Chicago Historical Society; Brother Michael Grace of Loyola University, Chicago; Rev. Anthony Kuzniewski of the College of the Holy Cross; Rev. Leonard Chrobot of St. Mary's College, Orchard Lake, Michigan; Tom Featherstone of the Walter P. Reuther Library of Labor and Urban Affairs, Wayne State University; Albert Juszczak, Rebecca Gola, and Elizabeth Koszarski of the Kosciuszko Foundation; Elizabeth White of the Brooklyn Public Library; Judith Kiefer of the International Institute in Detroit; Thomas Dietz of the Detroit Historical Museum; Linda Seidman of the Archives at the University of Massachusetts–Amherst; Deborah Moran and Pat Proscino of the Balch Institute for Ethnic Studies; Bill Falkowski of the *Polish American Journal;* Jim Martin and Dominic Pacyga of Columbia College, Chicago; Sister Mary Claver, C.S.S.F., and Irv Rabideau of Madonna College; Krystyna Włodarska-Baker of New York City; Steve Meyer of the University of Wisconsin-Parkside; and my graduate student Sarah Rutkowski. I thank you all.

There are some personal debts of gratitude that I also wish to acknowledge here. Christa L. Walck repeatedly provided examples of how to be a better writer. Many others gave me their friendship, support, and sometimes their advice at a time when I needed them. They include, in no particular order, Sandra VanBurkleo, Ed Wise, Tom Klug, Rosanne Hostnik, Carla Anderson, Saundra St. James, Harry and Deborah Smallenburg, Ed and Reba Pintzuk, Jacqueline Heymoss, Fred Cooper, Jane Burbank, Chris Clark, Margaret Lamb, Kimberly Volckaert, Kathleen Pascoe, Tyrone Tillery, Charles Hyde, Marta

Wagner, Nancy Kozlowski, Sam Scott, Marc Kruman, Mel and Sarajane
Small, Chris and Lois Johnson, Bob and Gay Zieger, Pat Pilling, Susan
Affleck-Childs, and William Siemers. I would like to single out for special thanks my dear friend and colleague Nora Faires for her critical
advice and moral support during the final months of work on the manuscript. To all of them, and to others too numerous to name individually,
I extend my warmest appreciation.

Finally, two words of apology must be extended to the reader. First,
the history of Polish-Americans told here is principally that of Poland's
Catholic emigrants and their descendants. The histories of the myriad
religious and ethnic minorities that migrated from the territories of Old
Poland could not receive the justice they deserve within the confines
of a short survey, and within ethnic America "Polish" came to imply
"Catholic." That pairing will be a subtheme of this work.

The second apology concerns this work's completeness. The cultural
and aesthetic life of the Polish immigrants, the reader may note, re-
ceives relatively little stress in this volume, in large part because this
area still remains little explored in the secondary literature. But even
for the themes that have received their fair share of attention—power,
politics, social issues, and economic life—there remain unavoidable
gaps. The history of Polish-Americans is still being written. Each year
exciting new articles and monographs appear that extend our understanding of this challenging field, and ethnic lives continue to be led.
Thus, while it relies upon both original research and the existing secondary literature, this book does not claim to be definitive. If it provokes
as it informs, however, it will have been successful.

Detroit, October 3, 1985

PRONUNCIATION OF POLISH NAMES

The accent in Polish always falls on the penultimate syllable. For aid in the pronunciation of Polish words and names, please consult the following key:

c is always pronounced as ts
ch very nearly like a gutteral h
cz as ch
g is always a hard sound, like g in get
i as ee
j as y
rz like French j, as in *jardin*
sz as sh
szcz as shch, with both sounds enunciated
u as oo
w as v
ć as ch
ś as sh
ż, ź both as zh, the former of higher pitch, the latter deeper
ó as oo
ą, ę as French en
ł as w
ń changes -in to -ine, -en to -ene, and -on to -oyne

Americanized Polish names and terms typically have dropped Polish diacritical marks, for example, Pułaski would become Pulaski. Parts of this pronunciation key were taken from M. Haiman, *Polish Past in America, 1608–1865* (Chicago: Polish Roman Catholic Union Archives and Museum, 1939).

And My Children
Did Not
Know Me

1

FROM HUNGER, "FOR BREAD"

Rural Poland in the Throes of Change

> While in Zbaraz [Galicia] I visited a school
> for peasant children. Its sessions were held
> in a rustic little one-room building with the
> conventional thatched roof. . . . [F]or my
> especial benefit, the prize scholar was
> asked where was America. He hesitated a
> moment, then he said he did not know, ex-
> cept that it was the country to which good
> Polish boys went when they died. . . .
>
> Louis E. Van Norman, *Poland
> the Knight Among Nations* (1907)

The history of Polish America begins abroad, for it is the story not only of why Polish men and women came to the United States but why they left their Polish homes. Rural Poland was a turbulent place in the nineteenth century, when large numbers of Poles first began to emigrate, looking for work and "for bread." But the turbulence in Polish rural society that produced the mass migrations did not begin in that period. It had its roots in the preceding three hundred years of Polish history, stretching back to the 1500s.

For Poland, the 1500s were a "golden century." The largest and perhaps the most powerful state in Europe, Poland was the "knight among nations" in western Christendom during those luminous years and stood as the eastern bulwark against tsarist, Tartar, and Turkish incursions.[1] Poland's position, however, was fragile, its power ephemeral. Repeatedly invaded by Sweden in the early 1600s—a period aptly termed "the Deluge"—the Polish state had entered a period of irreversible decline that lasted through the next two centuries.

The causes of Poland's decline were complex. Faced with the rise of strong, centralized states on all sides—the Russian Empire in the east, Brandenburg-Prussia in the north and west, and the Austrian Em-

1

pire ringing its southern border—the Polish state, which encompassed
the Duchy of Lithuania and the Ruthenian borderlands, also suffered
from internal weaknesses that exacerbated its dangerous international
situation. Like western European countries, Poland experienced not
only the Protestant Reformation, but also a highly successful Roman
Catholic Counter-Reformation, events that rent the fabric of Polish society. Ethnically, the expansive Polish state was seriously divided. The
perennial succession crises that followed the deaths of Poland's elected
monarchs produced chronic political instability in the Polish state and
quixotic vacillations in policy.

The political instability that plagued Poland was symptomatic of a
fundamental internal problem: decentralization of power. Poland's
aristocratic families held a tight grip on their domains and jealously
guarded their rights and privileges against infringement by would-be
absolute monarchs. The source of the nobility's power was control over
the land. Polish aristocrats derived status and wealth from their vast
landed estates, which gave them sweeping political influence at the expense of the monarchy and the state. The central position of landed
property in Polish society, however, produced two additional detrimental effects. First, social status in Poland was equated with dominion
over the land which deterred Polish nobles from engaging in commercial pursuits. This depressed the development of manufacturing and
trade in Poland precisely when such enterprise was becoming the backbone of Europe's modern, centralized states. The largely neglected
nonagricultural sphere in Poland therefore devolved on the country's
ethnic minorities—Germans, Gypsies, and Jews—whose efforts were
rewarded with low social status. Second, the Polish nobility monopolized the country's forests and agricultural lands. These were operated through the institution of serfdom, which doomed Poland's
peasantry to permanent deprivation and exclusion from the political
life of the nation. Amidst aristocratic splendor, the condition of Poland's
serfs was bleak. The questions of the peasants and land reform would
remain perpetual sources of trouble for Poland.

Poland entered the eighteenth century after a period of decline that
sometimes bordered on chaos. Its population decimated by the warfare
of the preceding hundred years, by the mid-1700s the exhausted Polish
state appeared defenseless to her acquisitive neighbors. The country
now faced dismemberment. Undermined by domestic intrigues at the
hands of leading Polish families who were more interested in protecting
their own interests—as individuals and as a class—than those of the
nation, in 1772 Poland was forcibly reduced in size by its rapacious
neighbors, Russia, Prussia, and Austria. This First Partition delivered
Poland's West Prussian territory to Prussia, lopped off the eastern tier
of Polish provinces for Russia, and bestowed Galicia, in the south, on
the Austrians. The partition of Poland was not destined to end with

Map 1. Partitioned Poland, circa 1870.

Source: E. Kantowicz, *Polish-American Politics in Chicago, 1888–1940*
(Chicago: University of Chicago Press, 1975), p. 4.

these modest annexations, however. Polish liberals, under French Revolutionary influence, promulgated the reformist Constitution of the Third of May in 1791; Russia and Prussia leapt to quell what they perceived as nascent Polish Jacobinism. The Second Partition, which was imposed in 1793, left Poland territorially unviable. An insurrection in 1794, led by Tadeusz Kościuszko, briefly challenged the will of the three dominating empires, but was brutally suppressed. In 1795 a Third Partition divided up what was left of the Polish state, and, as a result, Poland disappeared from the map of Europe. During the Napoleonic years a Duchy of Poland was briefly formed only to be dissolved by the victorious Holy Alliance of the three empires. In 1815 the empires once

Map 2. Administrative Divisions of Poland, 1912.

Source: C. Golab, *Immigrant Destinations* (Philadelphia: Temple University Press, 1977), p. 76.

again tightened their hold on Poland through what became, in effect, a fourth partition: Prussia and Austria acquired no new territory, and Cracow fell under tripartite jurisdiction (a status that lasted from 1815 to 1846, after which time it became the capital of Austrian-held Galicia), and Russia gained control of the lion's share of Poland. Lithuania was permanently severed from Poland and reconstituted as a separately governed territory under Russian tutelege, while the vast stretches of central and eastern Poland were organized into the Congress Kingdom (named after the Congress of Vienna), also under tsarist stewardship. (See Maps 1 and 2.)

Patriotic segments of the Polish aristocracy and middle class did not rest easily after Poland's bitter losses. The history of nineteenth-century Poland is remembered for a succession of uprisings that vainly sought to throw off the yoke of foreign oppression. In November 1830, Poles in the Russian partition rebelled against the tsar but were quashed ten months later. An 1846 uprising by Polish aristocrats was suppressed by the Austrian government with the assistance of the peasants, who harbored bitter grievances against their Polish landlords. Two years later, in 1848, an insurrection took place in the Prussian-held territory of Poznania. One result of Europe's "Springtime of Nations," the Prussian Polish uprising, was crushed also. The last armed insurrection in Poland took place in January 1863, in the Russian-held Congress Kingdom. By 1865, however, the January Insurrection was spent.

In terms of altering Poland's divided and subject status, this series of uprisings was an abysmal failure. Yet the insurrections underscored one fact expressed in the Polish national anthem, popularized during the Napoleonic period: "Poland is still living while we are still alive."[2] The November Insurrection of 1830, in particular, produced the core of Polish romantic nationalist ideology. Gifted writers and poets such as Adam Mickiewicz, Julius Słowacki, Sigismund Krasinski, and August Cieszkowski were all inspired by the uprising. Mickiewicz and Słowacki were instrumental in creating the new doctrine, which came to be known as Polish Messianism. A mystical doctrine, it claimed that Poland was a martyred Christ figure, crucified by the partitioning powers. Unlike Christ, Poland suffered for real sins, but like Him, a resurrected Poland would one day bring universal redemption to the nations of the world. Polish Messianism burned brightly in the hearts of a generation of Polish patriots sacrificed on the altar of insurrectionary politics.

After the failure of the January Insurrection of 1863, political temperaments moderated as more and more Poles accepted the partitions, and influential Poles sought an accommodation with their overlords. Polish positivists coined a new political slogan, "organic work," which sought to strengthen their country not through force of arms but through education, work, and industry. At the same time, they sought to make the best of a bad situation by advancing their own private economic and political interests.

Into the eighteenth century, the two points of relative stability in Polish society were the institution of serfdom and the manorial system from which Poland's estate-holding families derived their power. Serfdom in Poland developed only between the fifteenth and early sixteenth centuries, when that country became Europe's granary (serfdom was established earlier in western Europe). Once in place, however, Polish serfdom replicated many of the devices of western European feudalism—feudal dues and compulsory labor, tillage- and use-rights, peasant bondage to the land, and mutual duties and obligations between classes. More important, despite the fact that large surpluses of grain were extracted from peasant serfs and funneled into the international cereals exchange, peasant households in much of Poland remained shielded from the market economy. Into the eighteenth century, Polish rural society was, in short, insular and static. This would change with the breakdown of serfdom and the collapse of the manorial world that it supported.

In the late eighteenth and the nineteenth century a veritable revolution was taking place in Poland's social and economic systems. In the nineteenth century, Polish rural society became a cauldron of social and economic change in which a population increase, the expansion of commercial agriculture, and the growth of transportation, industry, and urban markets would forever disrupt the manorial world. The dissolution of the ties that bound the rural populace to the land and the creation of a large pool of surplus labor would later impel the mass migrations of the late nineteenth and the early twentieth century. How did these changes occur?

Divided into separately administered partitions, the lands of Poland experienced growth of population and commerce not simultaneously, but in sequence. These developments were affected by the separate experiences of the three partitioned areas and were influenced by the varying policies of the partitioning powers. Thus, the history of nineteenth-century rural Poland is not a single history at all, but three distinct histories.

The sweeping changes that transformed Polish rural society in the nineteenth century first occurred in the German-held° lands of western Poland. The Regulation Reform of the Napoleonic era ended serfdom there between 1807 and 1823, but left the majority of the peasants landless, stripped of their former feudal rights, and burdened by a system of taxes established to compensate their former masters. A thin stratum of well-to-do peasants did manage to fare reasonably well despite the meager terms of the emancipation, but the large landholders, or Junkers, still retained control over most of the land.

In the aftermath of emancipation, German Poland experienced a radical polarization of classes. The Junkers bought out the small holdings of an indebted and increasingly hard-pressed peasantry and consolidated their already large estates into vast commercial farms. By the latter part of the century, this powerful class monopolized about half of the best land in the German-held territories of Poznania and Pomerania. The other classes in German Polish rural society were less successful. Well-to-do peasants still survived as an important social group. The swelling ranks of landless agricultural laborers, who were systematically impoverished in the decades following emancipation, formed the new rural proletariat, which became an increasingly important element in German Polish rural society. By 1880, fully 80 percent of the

°In 1871, Prussia unified the German states and created the Second Reich (empire); Prussian Poland then technically became German Poland. The names will be used interchangeably in this text, as was the popular usage among Polish immigrants.

rural populace in Poznania and Pomerania fell into this distressed category.

Large landowners were supported by the German government in their efforts to transform the rural economy into a system of largescale commercial agriculture. The policy of Poland's German overlords encouraged the development of commercial agriculture and actively sought to make German Poland into "Germany's granary."[3] The state kept taxes on the great estates low and erected a banking and credit system that helped finance commercial agriculture. It also established a system of subsidies that protected German Polish landowners from competition by American wheat producers. Government policy also encouraged agricultural improvement in German Poland. The scientific farming techniques that were introduced—such as the use of improved seed and mineral fertilizers, crop rotation, and the diversification of crops, which saw the substitution of cattle and clover for grain cultivation—caused German Polish agricultural productivity to skyrocket. It also rendered superfluous the labor of increasing numbers of German Polish agricultural laborers. Mechanization of agriculture in the 1880s enhanced this harsh effect.

Higher productivity in German Polish agriculture might have led some to pronounce the commercial program a stunning success, but it produced staggering social costs. Emancipation of the German Polish peasantry was accompanied by widespread evictions, the expansion and consolidation of large estates created a vast pool of landless agricultural laborers, and the scientific revolution in farming techniques, which increased efficiency, exacerbated rural unemployment. For inhabitants of the countryside, the net effect was at best disruptive, at worst disastrous. Literally pushed off the land, German Poles entered other trades but found opportunities for employment severely limited. Bismarck's *Kulturkampf* in the 1870s, which was an attempt to erase Polish culture, and, in the subsequent decade, the colonization of German settlers on the German-held lands, further constrained the Poles. For Poles with some resources, however, one avenue of escape remained—emigration.

While the partition of Poland served to stimulate commercial agricultural development in the German-held territories, in Austrian Poland the partition resulted in economic stagnation. Partition boundaries interrupted river traffic on the Vistula, blocking Galicia from its western European grain markets. With no accessible market, the development of commercial agriculture was arrested. Galicia remained poor and very backward. Outmoded agricultural techniques continued, such as burning manure for fuel instead of using it as fertilizer, and the inefficient, three-field crop rotation system, which was practiced into the late-nineteenth century. Maldistribution of land—the prevalence of large estates—underlay the nagging poverty of rural Galicia and caused sharp class antagonisms. In addition, Galicia's population of Poles, Ukrainians, Moslems, and Jews generated ethnic and religious tensions.

In 1848, the Austrian government abolished serfdom in its Polish province, but emancipation brought little improvement to the mass of the peasantry. Under the terms of emancipation, the Austrian government forbade peasant evictions, endowed emancipated peasants with strong tillage- and use-rights, and allowed partible inheritance without setting a legal limit below which a farm could not be divided. This was done mainly to exacerbate class tensions between peasants and large landowners, rather than to protect the Galician poor. For the rest of the century struggle would continue between peasants and landowners over control of the soil and use of the rich forest lands. By driving a wedge between the Polish peasantry and their Polish landlords, Galicia's Austrian rulers cleverly sought to forestall the development of a broadly based Polish nationalist movement.

The political effects of Austrian policy were as predicted, but its social and economic results came as a grim surprise. If the policy of the German state had proved disastrous for the inhabitants of the German Polish countryside, Austrian policy in rural Galicia was catastrophic. Many Galician peasants acquired fewer than four acres as a result of emancipation, far too little for subsistence farming. These small landholdings, moreover, consisted of widely scattered plots "so small, as the saying ran, when a dog lay on a peasant's ground, the dog's tail would protrude on the neighbor's holdings."[4] They were inefficient because of size, shape, and difficulty of access. The Galician nobility continued to hold 43 percent of the arable land and fully 90 percent of the forests, and extracted a thirty-year land tax from the oppressed peasantry in order to compensate themselves for emancipation. This pattern would change little by the century's end.

In 1866, rapprochement between the Galician Polish landlords and the Austrian government delivered a large degree of local autonomy to the landowners. They used this newly won political influence to tighten the screws on the peasantry. By 1900, Galician statistics were truly depressing. In that year, the nobility held 37 percent of the arable land; forty-five estates consisted of over 15,000 acres each. Among the rest of Galicia's rural society, a pattern of small holdings obtained: 84 percent of peasant holdings were smaller than 12.2 acres; 48 percent were smaller than 5 acres; 700,000 peasants were completely landless; and a mere 5 percent of the peasant population achieved self-sufficiency. For good reason people coined the term "Galician misery."

As miserable as the Galician peasantry may have been because of the inequitable landholding system, other factors made their situation worse. Illiteracy and alcoholism were rife throughout Austrian Poland, while disease was a veritable scourge. Between 1847 and 1849 a typhus epidemic claimed 400,000 lives, while cholera killed over 100,000 between 1852 and 1855, 35,000 in 1866, and 120,000 between 1872 and 1877. Hunger also afflicted the province. Like Ireland, Galicia was hit by a potato blight between 1847 and 1849, and 1855 became tellingly known as the year of the Great Hunger. As if these calamities were not enough, a meteoric population increase over the course of the century multiplied the woes of the Galician peasantry.

The rural labor surplus and poverty created by imposed and natural causes found little relief into the twentieth century. With little industrialization, nonagricultural employment for the distressed peasantry was unavailable in Galicia. Neither did the penetration of railroad lines into rural Galicia in the late nineteenth century provide any direct aid. In fact, by carrying manufactured goods into the region, the railroad served to undercut cottage industry, which had provided the precarious peasant household an important source of supplementary income. The railroad did offer some hope to the distressed, for it allowed Galician peasants, rooted to their tiny plots of land, to search farther afield for bread and for work.

The economic development of the Russian Polish territories differed markedly from that of German and Austrian Poland but left no less rural distress in its wake. As in German Poland, the breakdown of the old manorial system began as early as the Napoleonic period. At that time peasants were legally freed in parts of central Poland, but they were left without land and were still under obligation to perform compulsory labor. Subsequent peasant evictions, coupled with the widespread devastation of the Napoleonic military campaigns of 1815, impoverished large numbers of Russian Polish peasants and transformed them into a landless rural proletariat.

The early disruption of Russian Polish rural society was furthered by tsarist policy during the remainder of the century, which determinedly promoted commercial agriculture in the Russian Polish provinces. Wheat, wool, and sugar beet production were encouraged, and landlords converted compulsory labor dues into cash rents in order to increase productivity and force their peasants to produce goods for the market. The emancipation of the serfs in 1864 hastened their entrance into the market economy. According to the terms of emancipation, peasants lost their feudal use-rights and left serfdom either landless or burdened by stiff land taxes intended to compensate their former masters. Thus, emancipated serfs did not usually enter the market economy as small producers but as agricultural laborers.

The pressure on the Russian Polish peasantry was intensified by a series of misfortunes, including crop failures, bad harvests, and epidemics of cholera and typhus between 1846 and 1856. The introduction of improved agricultural techniques such as new methods of tilling; better fertilizers; crop rotation; mechanical sowers, reapers, and threshers; and the use of horses and steam-powered machinery had a profound effect. Because efficient operation required larger farming units, these innovations spurred estate expansion and consolidation, increasing peasant landlessness. Because agricultural innovations heightened efficiency, they inflated rural unemployment rates.

The twists and turns of the international economy, which affected commercial agricultural development in Russian Poland, wreaked their share of social havoc. After the Napoleonic wars, the British government enacted a system of grain tariffs, known as the Corn Laws, that protected British agriculture from foreign competition. This closed an important market for Russian Polish grain exports. The resultant grain surpluses were diverted into liquor production, which produced a legacy of alcholism in the Russian Polish countryside. The landlords' other responses to the crisis—raising sheep and cultivating sugar beets instead of cereals—were no less damaging to the peasantry, as they intensified the rural surplus labor problem. The peasants' plight worsened with the abolition of the Corn Laws in 1845, when the foreign demand for Russian grain increased. Between 1865 and 1914 Russian Polish landlords cut down 1.75 million acres of forest land, which was essential to the peasant household, converting it to grain cultivation. Landlords also reduced the peasants' land allotments. The cereals boom, however, was short-lived. As a result of competition from American grain, the demand for Russian cereals collapsed in the 1880s and 1890s, throwing landless agricultural laborers out of work.

In Russian Poland an industrial revolution offset the landlessness, proletarianization, unemployment, and rural poverty that accompanied the expansion of the commercial agricultural sector. From 1815, tsarist policy toward the Polish territories encouraged commercial agriculture and sought to make the region into the industrial heartland of the Russian Empire. That policy was successful. By the end of the nineteenth century, coal mining, iron, steel, textile manufacture, and sugar refining had become mainstays of the Russian Polish economy. As a result, Warsaw was transformed into one of Europe's major urban centers, while Łódź, which grew from 31,000 inhabitants in 1860 to 314,000 in 1897, was nicknamed the Polish Manchester.

Industrialization in the Russian-held Congress Kingdom absorbed much of the surplus labor from the surrounding countryside throughout the nineteenth century. This was soon changed by politics and policy. The Russo-Japanese War in 1904 closed off the eastern markets for goods manufactured in the Russian Empire and caused a severe industrial depression in Russian Poland. The strikes and lock-outs of the 1905–1906 Revolution, which the depression had helped spawn, deepened distress in Polish industrial centers. In addition, tsarist policy since the late nineteenth century had begun to shift industrial production from the Congress Kingdom to Russia proper. That movement was now strengthened in an effort to reduce the possibility of future disruptions. The economic result of the move was to render permanent the industrial recession in Russian Poland. The massive industrial unemployment that followed forced both industrial workers and the rural unemployed to enter the stream of international migration.

While the peasant population of Russian Poland was being uprooted, the territory's Jewish inhabitants, who had occupied the middle commercial and trade strata in Russian Polish society, encountered special incentives to emigrate. Under the Russian May Laws of 1882, Jews were expelled from Moscow, St. Petersburg, and Kiev. An 1897 tsarist decree abolished the state monopoly in the liquor trade, in which many Jews were employed. Faced with restricted economic opportunities; civic, social, and political sanctions; a rising wave of anti-Semitism; and pogroms, many Jews fled.

The effects of the transformative process in each of the three partitioned areas were strikingly similar, although the combination of causes and timing differed. The transition to commercial agriculture and the development of a market economy—sometimes augmented by a population increase and the growth of transportation systems and industry—abruptly ended the isolation and stability of the Polish countryside. Partitioned Poland now experienced a sweeping social and economic revolution as a surplus labor pool was formed, and vast numbers of primarily rural Poles were literally pushed off the land. Because the nonagricultural sector of the Polish economy was not sufficiently developed to absorb them, their search for employment led them to migrate.

The economic emigration from Poland between the 1870s and the First World War, often called the emigration *za chlebem* (for bread), occurred in three phases, each of which involved different segments of the Polish population. Emigration from the German-held territories began in earnest in the 1870s and crested between 1880 and 1893. Those leaving included artisans, intellectuals, scions of the lower gentry, and agriculturalists. After 1893, economic depression in the United States and improving conditions in the German Polish countryside caused the number of emigrants to dwindle. By then, however, Poles had begun to leave the Russian-held territories. Most Russian Polish emigrants were small holders and agricultural wage laborers, but this emigration also included small-town dwellers and nonagriculturalists. Emigration from Austrian-held Galicia also began in the 1880s, its rate increasing rapidly after 1900. The Austrian Polish emigration was most depressed in terms of social composition. Of the Austrian Poles, with known occupations, who came to the United States between 1902 and 1911, about 33 percent were independent farmers (peasants), 43 percent agricultural day laborers, 17 percent servants, and only 7 percent skilled tradesmen. In all, between 1870 and 1914, approximately 1.2 million people emigrated from Prussian Poland, about 1.3 million from Russian Poland, and about 1.1 million from Austrian Poland. These figures include not only ethnic Poles, but Ukrainians, Ruthenians, Jews, Kashubians from German Poland, and other ethnic minorities.

If changes in their homeland—the so-called push factors—bulked largest in the Poles' decision to emigrate, developments abroad—pull factors—determined their destinations. Three generalizations can be made about Polish population movements in the late nineteenth and the early twentieth century: (1) migrants left depressed rural areas for commercial agricultural areas and industrial centers, (2) migrants moved from rural to urban areas, and (3) migrants moved from areas of labor surplus to areas with labor shortages. In short, since migrants moved in search of work, industrialization and urbanization abroad determined their destinations.

Within this general schema, however, great variations existed. For years, German Poles had been seasonal migrants traveling to grain harvests in Prussia, Saxony, and Denmark. Others migrated to the industrial centers of Silesia, the Saar, and the Ruhr for longer periods of employment. In fact, from the outset many of the latter were immigrants in the true sense of the word. Landless, politically persecuted, and with little stake in the society they left behind, these Poles migrated as family units because they considered their move to be permanent. Jews who left Poland during these years also left for good. For Poles with undersized parcels of land—many Russian Poles and most Galicians—temporary migration became a way of life. Single men and sometimes single women would sojourn abroad in order to earn money to assist the fragile household economy to which they planned to return eventually. They journeyed into Russia, Hungary, or German Poland (working for lower wages, they filled places left vacant by migrating German Poles), and farther afield to France, Canada, Argentina, or Brazil—wherever economic opportunity beckoned. In the late nineteenth and early twentieth century, enticing economic opportunity also beckoned from America. There, rapid expansion of coal mining, iron and steelworks, meatpacking plants, and other industries created a Second Industrial Revolution with an insatiable appetite for cheap, immigrant labor.

The migration process seems to have moved inexorably, but amidst the bloodless statistics and cold economic detail, migration had a human face as well: the migrants were people. Rural Poles who chose to leave their homeland did not fit the stereotype of *homo economicus,* "economic man," who made tidy calculations of the possible profits and losses from migrating and mechanically acted upon them. Migration would not have happened had the ties that bound Poles to the land not been loosened by the social and economic changes of the nineteenth and early twentieth century. The actual decision to emigrate was complex.

Foreign labor shortages were not the sole determinant of Polish migration patterns. Steamship ticket agents in Polish towns and villages sold transatlantic passages to those with sufficient funds, and so affected the rate of migration from Polish country districts; shipping routes directed the flow. Immigrants exerted a compelling influence on migration and settlement patterns in their correspondence to friends and loved ones. Immigrant letters often described urban amenities, job opportunities, and the excitement of a new life. Sometimes letters carried steamship tickets or passage money. Those Poles who accepted the invitation to join their countrymen and countrywomen abroad forged a continuous link between the Old World and the New in a process known as chain migration.

Though economic dislocation may have been a necessary precondition for mass migration, an individual's decision to leave was often precipitated by noneconomic factors. Poles, Ukrainians, Ruthenians, Kashubians, and Jews all had ample reason to seek freedom from political persecution, religious prejudice, and class oppression. Young Polish males faced a special incentive to emigrate. Subject to conscription into the armies of the partitioning powers, many migrated in order to escape foreign military service.

The actual decision to emigrate was always in the context of Polish rural culture. Most temporary migrants did not consider emigration an opportunity for "upward mobility" but a sacrifice necessary to preserve their culture and elements of life they held dear—family, farm, household, village, and community. Emigration was a big step, one that often seemed to endanger the very things it sought to preserve.

In order to make emigration seem less threatening, rural Poles established myths and beliefs that would justify their departure: the ideology of migration. This ideology legitimized actions, such as travel outside the village world or separation of families, that would normally have been considered a violation of culturally acceptable behavior. In part its myths were composed of elements borrowed from existing rural popular culture. One legend that circulated in isolated Russian Polish villages during the emigration to Paraná, Brazil, in 1910–1912, for example, held that until then Paraná was an unknown land, covered in mist. When the Blessed Virgin Mary saw the misery of the Polish peasants she "dispelled the mist and told them to come and settle." A variant of the legend introduced more detail:

> When the mist was raised, all the kings and emperors of the earth came together and drew lots to decide who should take the new land. Three times they drew, and always the Pope won. Then the Pope, at the instigation of the Virgin Mary, gave the land to the Polish peasants.[5]

Sanctioned by religion, emigration abroad might become a spiritual duty, safe from earthly criticism.

The ideology of migration incorporated newly created myths and beliefs into Polish rural culture. This was true of popularly held attitudes about the United States, a favorite emigrant destination. In the early 1850s, stories of America's "golden mountains," possibly originating in rumors of the California gold rush, had already gained currency in Prussia's predominantly Polish territory of Upper Silesia. Letters sent back to Poland from the United States inflated these wild myths. Treated like "religious relics" in Polish villages, they electrified the countryside and gave rise to the seeming obsession with emigration popularly known as "America fever."[6]

Of all three partitioning powers, Prussia and later Germany followed the most uniform policy toward Polish emigration in the late nineteenth century. Government authorities, ever mindful of the fragility of their hold on the Polish provinces, became obsessed with the need to colonize German settlers there and Germanize the Poles. Bismarck's emigration policy grew from this strategic imperative. Despite the agricultural labor shortage that its policy would cause, the German government encouraged the emigration of Polish agricultural laborers and restricted the immigration of seasonal migrants from Russian Poland and Galicia.

Whereas German policy, on the whole, encouraged Polish emigration, Russian policy was ambiguous. Russia's desire to industrialize Russian Poland in the early nineteenth century was accompanied by policies that endorsed both the immigration of foreign labor and, later, the migration of the indigenous Polish rural population to the cities. At the turn of the century, when Polish industrialization was no longer favored, Russian emigration policy changed accordingly. Russia did establish a Peasant Bank, which helped colonize eligible Polish peasants on their own farms. To the extent that this satisfied the peasantry's boundless hunger for land, this policy may have discouraged emigration, but the forced Russification of these Polish settlers often negated the colonization program's intended effect. Migrant Poles were urged toward industrial centers within Russia, and especially to the Siberian frontier.

Austrian policy, in contrast, concentrated on restricting the emigration of those young Poles who had not fulfilled their military service obligations. Repeated attempts were made to draft a comprehensive emigration law, but none was enacted. The semi-autonomous Galician legislative body steadily sought to block rural emigration by preserving those ties that bound peasants to the land, holding them to their contract or service obligations. The labor-intensive agriculture practiced on the large estates required an abundant supply of cheap labor. After the agricultural strikes of 1902 and 1903 in eastern Galicia, lawmakers began to look more favorably upon the emigration of the volatile surplus labor force. Eventually, as emigration increased, they simply tried to control its flow.

Polish opinions on emigration revolved around labor and national security considerations. The specific attitudes of individual Polish observers were largely colored by their social position and political perspective. The conservative landed gentry, for example, welcomed the departure of the politically volatile urban proletariat but bemoaned the loss of cheap agricultural labor. In their eyes, peasant emigration was a "disease" or a "plague" that they blamed on the "conspiratorial" activities of German and Jewish emigration agents and the political and religious oppression of the partitioning powers. Populists and some middle-class liberals, like Polish National Democratic Party leader Roman Dmowski, viewed emigration less harshly. He believed that emigration offered an "improvement of the fortunes of the masses who are leaving Europe," although others conceded that it also represented "an irretrievable loss to the national cause." Nationalist critics and other practical progressives suggested land reform and industrialization as perennial solutions to emigration. Meanwhile, they focused public attention on the welfare of the peasant migrants, in particular criticizing the ill-considered flight to Brazil. When it became apparent that the money emigrants brought back or mailed home was becoming a crucial prop of the capital-poor Russian Polish and Galician rural economies, anti-emigration sentiments generally softened. Colonization societies, formed in the late 1890s, reflected this change. Concerned with the welfare of the emigrant and with labor market issues, the societies no longer sought to check but only to control rural emigration.[7]

The rural exodus from the Polish countryside between the 1870s and the 1920s, however, was not caused by "conspiracy," nor did it result from poverty alone or from "hysteria." Rather, it was a by-product of the changes sweeping Polish agricultural society during that period. The effect of private opinion and governmental policy on Polish emigration would prove negligible. Polish peasants and agricultural laborers could not be deceived about their living conditions or dislodged from their resolve to try to better their lot. One Silesian Pole seemed to epitomize popular attitudes: "Whether we rot here or there, it's all the same to us. At any rate, we want to try our luck."[8]

Emigration tapered off in the second decade of the twentieth century. World War I interrupted the emigrants' routes and killed off a large part of Poland's "surplus" population. Postwar reconstruction and industrialization provided new sources of employment for many of the survivors. Yet before the exodus diminished, well over three million Poles journeyed from their homeland. Our story follows the more than two million who migrated *do Ameryki*—to America.

2

To Field, Mine, and Factory

Work and Family in Polish America

> What people from America write to Poland
> is all bluster; there is not a word of truth.
> For in America Poles work like cattle.
> Where a dog does not want to sit, there
> the Pole is made to sit, and the poor
> wretch works because he wants to eat.
> (Brooklyn, New York)
>
> —Anonymous letter (undated),
> *Listy Emigrantów z Brazylii i
> Stanów Zjednoczonych*,
> edited by W. Kula

Antique photographs give us a frozen glimpse of the immigrant passengers who journeyed across the Atlantic to America at the turn of the century. These men and women differed sharply from the first Polish settlers depicted in early American portraits—men as distinguished as Olbracht (Zaborowski) Zabriskie of colonial New Amsterdam; Revolutionary War heroes Casimir Pułaski and Tadeusz Kościuszko, who joined Washington's army; or the small band of political exiles who sought refuge on American shores in the 1830s and 1840s. Unlike their illustrious predecessors, the Poles who migrated "for bread" owned no large tracts of land, wore no military decorations, and received not a single accolade. Instead, their photographed images show them clad in bulky sheepskin coats or kerchiefs and fringed shawls, huddling together on the chilly decks or crouched in the crowded steerage quarters of the oceanic steamers that carried them to the United States.

To the ships' crews, the photographers, the immigration officials, and the native-born Americans who watched immigrants debark in places like Boston, Philadelphia, New York City, or Hoboken, they were little more than anonymous aliens. But if we look closely at the faces on those faded photographs, we see real people expressing their fears, hopes, regrets, and often unspeakable joy—the joy of having made safe landfall in the *nowy świat,* the New World, America. Whose lives are hidden behind the silent photographs? Who were these anonymous Polish passengers? What did they hope to find in the United States? What set them apart from other immigrants who arrived at American ports during the years of mass migration?

Contrary to the familiar inscription on the base of the Statue of Liberty, these immigrants were not Poland's wretched refuse. However much they may have wished to escape the grinding poverty into which they had sunk, the most distressed peasants lacked the resources to leave Poland. Polish emigrants were, therefore, upwardly mobile peasants and laborers or, more often, those not entirely impoverished men and women who chose migration as the best of their dwindling economic and social options. Polish migrants were neither as literate as Jewish and Scandinavian immigrants, as endowed with resources as the Scots, nor as desperate as the impoverished Irish who flocked to America in the 1840s and 1850s, contrasts that would color the Polish experience in America. Unlike the persecuted Jews and the very poor Irish, many Poles believed they had a homeland to which they could return. As a result, Poles more often considered themselves temporary sojourners and were slower to adopt America and act as though they had a stake in its society.

Whatever their socio-economic background and regardless of whether they had had previous experience as seasonal migrants, Polish emigrants began their journey to America at the muddy outskirts of country villages or on dusty Polish streets. Proceeding on foot or by wagon, migrating Poles headed for the nearest railhead or river where they traveled by trains or barges to a major transatlantic embarkation point: Bremen or Hamburg for most Poles, Trieste for some who traveled from the south. With the growing influx of transients, emigration ports literally teemed with people. Emigrants waited, sometimes for weeks, for an America-bound vessel, spending their precious cash reserves on food and housing and increasing their fund of facts and myths about their journey and its destination. Lodging was in short supply, food prices soared, and infectious disease ran rampant. For the most part, migrants stayed in waterfront boarding houses. With worsening congestion, sanitation, and contagion, facilities similar to barracks were constructed in some ports to house the polyglot crowds as they waited for their ships to depart.

From the 1850s to the period of mass migration, the transatlantic voyage taken by Polish migrants differed little. Peasant travelers booked passage in cramped steerage quarters located deep in the bowels of dark, airless ships. Until the 1870s, the trip to America took about two months, but as steam replaced sail, travel time fell to about two weeks and ticket prices dropped accordingly. Conditions on board remained spartan. Throughout the monotonous voyage, steerage passengers ate smoked, dried, or salted foods served communally from the ship's galley, which they supplemented with foodstuffs they brought aboard with them. Their cramped accommodations were downright unsanitary. As a result, passengers were sometimes afflicted with disease, always with boredom, and often with seasickness in the rough North Atlantic crossing.

Immigrant passengers survived their voyages (except on the occasional vessel stricken with typhus or cholera). Their first real view of America might have been the Jersey beacons in the approaches to New York harbor, a smoky haze hanging over the city's factory districts, and the arching stone towers of the newly built Brooklyn Bridge. Closer to them still, they could have spied the structures that symbolized New York City's status as an immigrant port—the lonely Statue of Liberty, the immigrant pavilion at Castle Garden on the tip of Lower Manhattan, and, after 1892, the red brick processing compound on Ellis Island. At Ellis Island, Polish travelers had their first brush with American officialdom. They were asked their names and destinations, and their physical condition was assessed (those judged unfit were forced to return to Poland). The earliest arrivals from Poland may have known not a soul in their strange new world. Latercomers might have clutched railroad tickets sent to them by their kin, been met by friends or relatives, or joined up with labor recruiters who would hasten them by ferry or railroad to their final destinations.

The migration process from point of departure to point of arrival was a homogenizing and disorienting experience which—in nineteenth-century parlance—threw together the "races of Europe." But immigrants did not allow themselves to become indistinguishable statistics absorbed in a faceless mass of humanity-in-motion. They clung to their traveling companions and naturally gravitated toward other migrants from their region or, at least, sought out passengers who spoke their language. On the way to America, and after their arrival, immigrants gradually replicated the ethnic, religious, and linguistic mosaic that had characterized southern and eastern Europe in the late nineteenth century. Highly localistic groups, like the southern Italians, clustered with fellow villagers so that even adjoining city blocks became very separate places. For the less parochial Poles, however, colonies of Polish-speaking Roman Catholic coreligionists were formed. Except for migrants from the Tatra highlands of Galicia, who preserved a regional identity, most Polish migrants shed strong village attachments. Since they came from three separate partitioned areas of Poland administered for a hundred years by Germans, Austrians, or Russians, they did retain some cultural traits, political opinions, and national identities associated with their partition of origin.

Usually Poles clustered near other Poles but broader settlement choices were shaped not by ethnic, religious, linguistic, and cultural ties, but by economic considerations. Polish immigrants are generally associated with industrial labor, but many of the first settlers from Poland in the 1850s sought opportunities on the agricultural frontier. In 1854, the first band of Poles who migrated "for bread" left the Prussian territory of Upper Silesia and, urged on by letters from their countryman, the missionary Franciscan Rev. Leopold Moczygemba, struck out for East Texas. There, sixty miles southeast of San Antonio, they founded America's first Polish colony, which they named Panna Maria after the Virgin Mary. A string of other Polish farming settlements grew up in the vicinity of Panna Maria. Poles also went on to settle in the Texas Panhandle and to found Krakow, Missouri.

Polish farming colonies grew in Ohio, Indiana, Illinois, Arkansas, Oklahoma, and Minnesota. German Poles also farmed in Parisville, Michigan, in the 1850s, and rural Michigan drew seasonal Polish agricultural laborers from the immigrant neighborhoods of Detroit throughout the nineteenth century. Other German Poles established the rural settlement of Polonia, Wisconsin, in 1858 and took up farming in the state's Trempeleau and Portage counties. In the East, Poles began to take over abandoned or worn-out farm lands by the end of the century. In the Connecticut Valley of western Massachusetts, Poles worked as agricultural laborers on old Yankee farms, and Polish enclaves grew up in the villages of Northampton, Greenfield, Hatfield, South Deerfield, and Sunderland. In New Jersey and on New York's Long Island, Polish settlers took up truck-farming, supplying the nearby urban market. Most of these were secondary settlements.

Polish immigrant farmers faced the challenge of life in a new land with the inevitable pain of culture shock and adjustment to alien surroundings. The Silesian Poles who landed in Texas traveled inland behind ox carts whose Mexican drivers had unfamiliar "swarthy complexions, broad sombreros and striped blankets. . . . "[1] In Panna Maria, they found abundant opportunity and a hard life on the scrubby East Texas plain. Sheltered in rough-hewn pole cabins and sod houses, the Silesian immigrants withered in the dry Texas climate and faced the constant perils of grasshopper plague and hostile Indian attack. Breaking the tough virgin soil proved an arduous chore, especially given a shortage of draft animals. The farmers' first task obviously was self-sufficiency, food for survival. The Silesians quickly learned to rely upon wild game and an unfamiliar cereal known to them as "Turkish wheat," corn. How fascinating it must have been for a farming people to encounter a wide diversity of new fauna and vegetation! Polish settlers discovered curious new crops such as sweet potatoes, "like our cucumbers," one Pole wrote back to Poland, but with a "sweetish taste."[2] The Poles' food preferences remained unchanged. The Polish Texan diet included traditional Polish dairy products, and one Silesian immigrant sent back to Poland for some beans. Few Polish newcomers grew cotton until after the Civil War, but Polish farm products did include corn, vegetables, cattle, oxen, pigs, and chickens. Incidentally, none of these Polish immigrants owned slaves; some Poles did fight on the side of the Confederacy with the coming of the Civil War.

While crops varied according to local conditions, Poles elsewhere on the frontier very much resembled the Texas Silesians. Indeed, in economic terms, Polish farmers very much resembled other immigrant farmers during the period. Some Polish frontier farmers and most Poles who farmed in the East, however, did differ markedly from others, native-born or immigrant, who farmed their own land. Oklahoma Poles, for example, purchased small parcels of land and began as part-time farmers, part-time urban workers. Gradually, they saved enough money to leave their part-time city jobs and increase the size of their farmsteads. The typical Polish agriculturalist in the Connecticut Valley in the 1870s was not, strictly speaking, a farmer at all but an agricultural laborer who worked growing vegetables or tobacco on a tired, Yankee-owned farm. This was the only way that Poles who wanted to try their farming skills could get a foothold on the land: Massachusetts land prices simply exceeded Polish resources. Through underconsumption and thrift, these Polish agricultural laborers became renters and eventually land owners. Farming for themselves, many of these Poles reached a level of prosperity that far surpassed that obtained by Yankee farm owners. Practicing a labor-intensive agriculture unknown to Yankees, Connecticut Valley Poles throve by coaxing onions and tobacco from the nearly barren New England soil.

According to an Immigration Commission report published in 1911, fully 10 percent of foreign-born Poles pursued agricultural occupations; this was probably a low estimate. Compared to other immigrant groups, Poles were underrepresented in agricultural callings. In contrast to the Poles' 10 percent, 50 percent of foreign-born Norwegians, 32 percent of the Czechs, 30 percent of the Swedes, 27 percent of the Germans, and 14 percent of the Irish made their livelihood at agriculture. The low level of Polish participation in agriculture is not surprising because it reflected the nature of Polish migration. Many German Poles, who accounted for most of the Polish immigration between the 1850s and 1880s, took up farming because they arrived when land in the West was still cheap, they possessed enough money to buy it, and, as they considered themselves permanent settlers, they wanted to put down roots in America. Unlike these German Poles, the Russian Poles and Galicians, who soon formed the great bulk of Polish immigrants between the 1880s and the World War, confronted inflated land prices, high capital requirements, and low market prices for farm commodities like grain and cattle. Under the best of circumstances few of these Poles could have shouldered the burden of farming under such conditions. Since most viewed their migration as temporary, they eschewed marginal agricultural occupations and the long-term commitment of farming. Instead, they joined the ranks of unskilled workers who toiled in the burgeoning mines and factories of America's Second Industrial Revolution.

Generally speaking, Poles did not randomly enter factory jobs but were funneled into those large industries that needed huge numbers of cheap, mostly unskilled laborers. Poles did not enter all such industries in equal numbers for, like other minority groups in the period, they fell victim to the racist attitudes that were growing in late nineteenth-century America. Whereas the Polish political émigrés of the early nineteenth century had enjoyed the sympathy and admiration of an American citizenry caught up in a heady republicanism, later peasant migrants ran into a harsher climate of opinion. They found that Gilded Age industrialists used attitudes on "race" to decide how to employ different groups of immigrant workers. In Pittsburgh, for example, industrialists preferred Poles and other Slavs for heavy industrial work because of their reputed "habit of silent submission, their amenity to discipline, and their willingness to work long hours and overtime without a murmur." "Give [Slavs] rye bread, a herring, and a beer," one Pittsburgh foreman remarked, "and they are all right."[3] Race stereotypes such as these encompassed most groups in the work force. Italian immigrants, for example, were considered "less robust than the Slavs, less hardy than the Irish," and were rarely used in the rolling mills "because of their physical lightness, or . . . lack of nervous strength."[4] Making such fine distinctions, employers established the pecking order of their workers on the basis of race, ranking white native-born Americans at the top; Irish, Scots, English, Welsh, and Germans below but near them; Poles, Magyars, Italians, Slovaks, and Russians next, in various orders; and Black Americans in the bottom category. This pervasive system of stereotypes weighed heavily upon immigrant workers because it depressed their chances for upward mobility and blocked access to cleaner and safer jobs. The system served the interests of capitalist employers remarkably well. However arbitrary the racial classifications, they increased managerial efficiency by lending order to personnel decisions. Moreover, by pitting group against group, they balkanized the work force and thus impeded labor organization.

Hiring policies dictated by race were carried out with the help of labor recruiters, who often took charge of newly arrived immigrants, sometimes to sign them up as "scabs," strikebreakers. But within the broad structural contours of the labor market, Polish immigrants themselves tried to choose where they worked. For cultural reasons, male Galician and Russian Polish migrants steered away from callings like the ubiquitous needle trades, which they considered "women's work." Dirty, hard, and dangerous jobs, however, did not scare them off. As temporary migrants, they looked for immediate and steady employment, regardless of the risks. They soon found that the worse the job, the greater the opportunity, and accordingly descended into bottomless mine shafts, or ventured into the smoky depths of factory compounds. Unlike Italians, Poles never developed the method of ethnic labor contracting known as the *padrone* system. Often at the urging of their employer Polish immigrants would write to relatives and friends in Poland, bidding them to come to America. Because the Second Industrial Revolution was built upon iron, coal, steam, and steel, the opportunities they dangled before fellow villagers and kin were located in America's heavy industrial heartland—from Milwaukee, Chicago, Detroit, Cleveland, and Pittsburgh through eastern Pennsylvania's grimy anthracite fields, from Buffalo down the old Erie Canal to New York, and in peripheral industrial locations like southeastern Connecticut, Brooklyn, and northern New Jersey. New Polish immigrants flocked to these places.

In 1910, a story in a Progressive magazine offered its readers a sketch of immigrant working people. Entitled "Jan,° the Polish Miner," the piece described a hard-working Polish collier and his bewildered, immigrant child-bride inching their way toward social and economic progress in the anthracite fields of eastern Pennsylvania. Undeniably, the magazine took a sympathetic slant toward its immigrant subjects. Yet, despite the best intentions, it conveyed only a caricature of immigrant working-class life, one in which the immigrants were more victims than participants. Indeed, were it possible to follow a real Jan and Maria Kowalski, immigrant worker and wife, one would have found resilient men and women who strove to hold onto the good in their lives, to improve conditions for their loved ones, and to shape their own destinies as much as possible.

Whether they lived in a Pennsylvania coaltown like Nanticoke, or in the congested factory districts of Buffalo or Chicago, the hypothetical Jan and Maria Kowalski would have faced many of the same difficulties in coping with industrial America. Through it all, they would remain Poles, would become—in a sense—more consciously Polish as they banded together with other Polish newcomers to form a network of institutions that would cushion, and often postpone, their entry into American society and the American economy. The institution on which they relied most heavily while adjusting to the new indus-

° Polish for "John."

trial environment was their family. Family members cooperated as much from a sense of duty as for daily survival in the new land.

Not all immigrants had families. While most German Poles immigrated as family units because they intended to remain here, Galician and Russian Poles were characteristic of temporary migrants—they were largely young, single, and male. Even the migrant who arrived alone sought out Polish households—often those of co-workers, fellow villagers, or kinsmen—and gained entrance as a boarder or lodger. For relatives, immigrant families provided human contact, moral support, and social shelter in often hostile surroundings. They provided much the same services for transient nonrelatives as well. In fact, boarding and lodging became the principal—if temporary—social support for the bulk of Polish newcomers until they either sent for wives who had remained abroad, returned to Poland, or married and formed families of their own in the United States.

The family of the hypothetical Jan and Maria Kowalski was more than just a social institution; it was also an economic unit. As head of an immigrant household, Jan Kowalski would have tried to find jobs for offspring, friends, and relatives, often with the support of his factory boss or mine foreman. Racism in the workplace cut two ways. While the industrious Black worker was considered an exceptional member of his race, Poles were stereotyped as racially suited for heavy industrial labor. Thus, while most Blacks were not considered for industrial jobs, Polish workers could pass jobs to friends and relatives. Industrialists relied upon immigrant family connections as a labor recruitment device. This ability to pass along jobs produced ethnic clustering in the workplace and strengthened the already sturdy intrafamilial bonds that Polish immigrants brought from Poland. As head of the family Jan Kowalski would have expected all family members to contribute their earnings to the household economy and to have deferred to his judgment in the workplace.

Jan Kowalski headed the immigrant household in its external economic relations and in the process developed a facility in dealing with the English-speaking world. Maria presided over affairs within the home, which afforded her little opportunity to become familiar with the English language. In this respect she resembled women in many other immigrant working-class groups during the period. Probably a younger bride than she would have been in Poland, since America had freed her from familial and economic constraints on early marriage, Maria Kowalska° bore weighty responsibilities. Thanks to the rising interest and new research in both ethnic studies and women's history, it is possible to begin reconstructing the story of the Maria

° Feminine form of Kowalski.

Kowalskas who held immigrant families together during the difficult years of migration.

While her husband may have worked over twelve hours a day in mine or factory, Maria Kowalska's toil would literally never have been done. For a woman, the workday began well before dawn. She would have lighted a fire in the wood stove, after emptying out the ashes from the previous day, and cooked breakfast before she roused her husband and the male lodgers. Maria tended the children who had awakened as the sound of voices rose in their cramped dwelling. After the men left for work, Maria would have turned her attention to the daily and weekly round of household chores. If her house or apartment did not have indoor plumbing yet, hauling water for cooking and washing was by far her most arduous task. If it did, trying to keep her home clean in a neighborhood that may have had dirt sidewalks and streets monotonously occupied much of her time. Once a week, this immigrant wife scrubbed laundry by hand in a steaming tub set on a chair in the kitchen and ironed next to the crackling stove. She might have made a weekly trip to the farmers' market and the corner store—where she had to negotiate credit—for goods she could neither make nor grow. More regularly, she would have tended the family's vegetable garden—canning produce in the summer—and looked after the ducks and chickens the family probably kept in a shed behind the house. As the afternoon wore on, she might have had time to mend or sew—perhaps on a sewing machine if the family had prospered. By then it would have been time for her to serve the evening's pot of soup, which had simmered all afternoon, and wait on the men as they returned at dusk, dirty and tired from a day in the mines or mills.

An immigrant wife like Maria Kowalska would have worked long and hard, the strain on her body increased by frequent pregnancies. Polish women who obeyed the Church resolutely foreswore birth control; those few who followed haphazard home techniques or sought contraceptive charms and potions from fortune-tellers or Gypsies probably fared no better. As a result, Maria Kowalska could have expected to bear five to ten children during her fertile years—possibly even more. Even with the assistance of a midwife, each pregnancy imperiled both mother and baby. Rudimentary living conditions and inadequate maternal nutrition helped produce Polish infant mortality statistics that exceeded those for Black Americans during the period and often killed the mothers as well. Most, of course, survived. They found that pregnancy and childbirth were just the beginning of their labor: caring for a succession of offspring multiplied the already heavy workload. With men at work most of the waking day, women reared their children virtually single-handedly. When whooping cough and measles, influenza and typhoid raced through crowded immigrant districts, as they did each year, they could only watch, pray, and cry, unable to help their often undernourished young.

In addition to domestic chores and child-rearing, immigrant women like Maria Kowalska made more direct economic contributions to the immigrant household economy. Though employment opportunities for Polish women were limited by the occupational structure—distribution of jobs—of the manufacturing cities (whose heavy industries required principally male labor) where most Poles settled, Maria probably would have worked outside the home at domestic service or light manufacturing until she bore her first child. Unlike her Italian counterparts who frequently seem to have worked long after marriage, the Polish immigrant wife soon succumbed to Polish cultural expectations, left her job, and became a full-time mother and housewife. Even so, her economic role in the Polish household would not have diminished. Since Polish wives kept the household accounts, Maria Kowalska would have "made" money for the family by saving it. Moreover, any money collected from boarders and lodgers was, in effect, her "wage" since she washed their clothes, cooked their food, and cleaned up after them.

The economic role of women like Maria Kowalska in America seems greater than what it had been in rural Poland; her authority within the home seems to have grown accordingly. Peasant women in Poland had had to shoulder full responsibility for rearing children, running households, and managing farms when married men became seasonal migrants. In America, with their husbands at work most of the day or night, the social importance of these women continued to rise. As kinship ties and friendship networks increasingly followed female lines, Polish immigrant families took on the matrifocal form common to other migrant, working-class groups, such as Blacks and Italians. Was an expanding role within immigrant households that important? It must be remembered that the household was one of the few areas in which the average immigrant working-class person could enjoy much authority. In the home, migration seems to have affected basic relations between Polish men and women. This probably often caused substantial tensions within immigrant families, doubtless even violent physical confrontations at times, but immigrant wives were gradually coming into their own.

In some ways the Polish immigrant man was out of place in the household he headed; as the woman's place of work, the immigrant home was "woman's space." Men had their own world—the corner saloon, where immigrant males could meet their friends and drink away the tiredness of the day. But men did not spend most of their

time talking, smoking, and drinking. Jan Kowalski was a miner, foundryman, still-cleaner, cooper, or sugar refiner. He spent his days—and
often his nights—in the hot factory, noisy mill, or dank mine where
he earned his wages and most of his family's livelihood.

His wife labored within and around their home, but an immigrant
worker like Jan Kowalski entered intimidating new surroundings
when he went to work. Despite seasonal migration within Europe,
few Polish newcomers had labored in industry before coming to the
United States. Of the Galician emigrants, with known occupations,
arriving between 1902 and 1911, for example, about 33 percent had
been independent farmers (peasants), 43 percent agricultural day laborers, 17 percent servants, and only 7 percent skilled tradesmen.
Similarly, only about 20 percent of the emigrants from the Congress
Kingdom in a sample year (1912) had either craft skills or factory experience. Working in America entailed an abrupt change in the kind
of work the immigrant performed.

For a man who had worked outside all his life, that change was often literally killing; it broke his health and often proved fatal. If Jan
Kowalski were a foundryman, he would have sweltered beside the
noxious molten metal in a smoking crucible—work considered fit
only for a Black man or a Pole. If he were a still-cleaner in an oil
refinery, he would have spent his days chipping out "cokes" inside
the 250-degree refining stills, his padded clothing sometimes
catching on fire due to the extreme heat. After a stint in the stills, one
doctor commented, immigrant workers looked like "boiled meat."[5] If
he were a miner, he would work his life away in damp, gaseous mine
shafts where, if a cave-in did not get him, eventually black-lung disease would.

The toll from dangerous industrial work in the early twentieth century was staggering. In a 1910 survey of industrial accidents in the
heavily immigrant city of Pittsburgh, one investigator concluded that
each year the district produced "45 one-legged men; 100 hopeless
cripples; . . . 45 men with a twisted useless arm; 30 men with an
empty sleeve; 20 men with but one hand; . . . 70 one-eyed men—500
such wrecks in all."[6] The grotesque nature of some accidents intensified their horror. There were also work-related deaths. A New York
Department of Labor annual report listed the particulars of fatal accidents that befell industrial workers in the state during 1902–1903. For
the Schenectady locomotive works alone, the partial list of casualties
reads like a bizarre litany:

> Pobish, Michael; helper in paint shop, 26 years of age; married; . . . in-
> stantly killed on December 21, 1902, while painting runway of electric
> traveling crane in erecting shop; crane crushing body so badly so as to
> expose heart to view. . . .

Brown, William; floor helper; 28 years of age; married; two children; . . . fatally injured, November 5, 1902, in machine shop; in attempting to jump on a transfer table Brown fell between two tables, one of them passing over him as he lay between the ties, causing a rupture of the bladder, a broken pelvis bone and bruises on the right hip and over the left eye; death resulted next day. . . .

Walazinovice, Simon; floor helper; 38 years of age; married; five children; . . . fatally injured on April 7, 1903, in the tank shop; while helping unload boiler plate, clamp slipped off plate which was suspended in air by lifting crane, and fell on Walazinovice, badly crushing abdomen and lower portion of body; death resulted almost immediately. . . .

Push, Chas.; laborer; 23 years of age; single; . . . instantly killed on July 15, 1903; while standing at end of crane car, was struck by swinging locomotive crane crushing breast bone and ribs and cutting neck half off from base of skull. . . .

William Quinlan; fireman; 25 years of age; married; two children; . . . fatally injured May 20, 1903; deceased was throwing coal into furnace when flue of boiler burst; the escaping steam and boiling water throwing him on coal heap and badly scalding face, top of head, shoulders, hands and arms; death resulted same day. . . .

Baker, Tony; helper; 32 years of age; single; . . . fatally injured February 17, 1903, in the erecting shop; while attempting to fix electric light wire, Baker was caught on line shafting and whirled around until his mangled and torn body fell to the floor, both legs being taken off below the knees, two ribs fractured over the heart, and head, chest and side badly bruised; death resulted two hours after the accident. . . .[7]

Death recognized neither ethnicity nor sex. Young Polish women faced similar conditions in the mills where they worked until they married or had children.

Moving from rural to industrial labor was only one of the changes that immigrant workers like the hypothetical Jan Kowalski faced; their work became more impersonal and their workpace quickened dramatically. If he had not farmed his own land in Poland, Jan Kowalski might have worked for board, payment in kind, or without pay for a relative. In America he invariably became a wage earner who experienced a new and more distant relationship to his English-speaking employer. He no longer brought special skills or personal qualities to his job; for an hourly wage, he simply sold undifferentiated commodities: his time and his strength. These were squeezed from him to the fullest measure by the ever tightening work discipline he encountered in the American factory. As historian Herbert Gutman has shown, immigrant workers like Jan Kowalski had followed an intermittent workpace when they toiled on the land, a natural work rhythm set by daylight, weather, the life cycle of lifestock and crops, holidays, holy days, and the alternating seasons. In the factory Jan Kowalski worked to the pace of unrelenting machines and twenty-four-hour production schedules, beginning and ending his day to the tick of the time-clock and blast of the factory whistle. In order to enforce this regimen, industrialists sometimes bribed their workers with bonuses, more often punished them with fines. They beat home the rules in English language lessons that taught workers simple yet pointed phrases: "I hear the whistle. I must hurry."[8] Industrialists tried to eradicate elements of immigrant rural culture that interfered with the factory order. In their place, they sought to instill habits of cleanliness, self-control, temperance, and obedience.

Immigrants found themselves pushed in conflicting directions by the industrialists' practice of sometimes reinforcing, sometimes repressing their ethnic identities. Factory managers often hammered home the ethnic differences of the immigrant workers, segregating workers of different nationalities by department, shop, or craft, impeding cross-cultural communication or organization. Managerial strategy thus reinforced the separate ethnicities. At the same time managers sometimes sought to efface ethnicity completely. Immigrants found that homogenization in the workplace attacked their identities more thoroughly than any other aspect of the migration process itself. As a group, Poles lost self-esteem when industrial managers transformed the name they called themselves, *Polak*, into an opprobrium. As individuals, Poles sometimes ceased to exist. How did a Brooklyn cordage worker, Stanisław Malecki, feel in 1897, for example, when a company official gave him the name "John Mullen" for "convenience of identification"? The change was thorough enough that the name stuck, and thirty years later he changed it legally.[9] The treatment accorded this one Polish worker illustrates how inexorably the process of deculturation advanced during the mass migration years. Yet paradoxically, the name that Malecki acquired from his foreman was itself *Irish*-American, a curious twist indeed. It is glaring testimony of how much America's earlier immigrants had forgotten their own pasts and themselves now colluded in the anti-immigrant drama.

American factories not only mass produced manufactured objects; they transformed immigrant workers into factors of production, nameless digits in an industrial army. How did Jan Kowalski respond to his industrial experiences? Despite all obstacles, he fought back and in doing so learned that he was not alone in his travail. He discovered that there were many Jan Kowalskis of all nationalities in industrial America. Together they resisted the humiliation, the atomization, and the killing workpace of the American factory system. In the process they underscored who they were, what they wanted, and what they shared in common.

As American factories affected immigrant workers in contradictory ways—reinforcing their rural ethnic identities while at the same time trying to obliterate them—the immigrants also responded contradictorily. Immigrant workers often fought against the relentless deculturation they faced in the workplace, flatly refusing to be stripped of their identity and robbed of their culture. Because they wanted to preserve customs that defined them as rural Poles, immigrant workers might protest work on Easter Sunday or a ban on drinking beer in the workplace, as Brooklyn's Polish sugar refinery workers did in a 1910 strike. Because they insisted upon a measure of ethnic respect, they might condemn their foremen's bigoted, abusive treatment as Bayonne's Polish still-cleaners did in their 1915 walk-out.

When Polish workers made conventional demands like higher wages, shorter hours, and better working conditions, their protests invariably bespoke their Polish identity. Polish societies and clubs rallied around immigrant strikers, as did friends, neighbors, and relatives—men, women, and children. Strikes by Polish workers usually mobilized the entire Polish working-class community; shared culture gave meaning to their strikes. If Jan Kowalski had been present in 1910 when Indiana steelworkers knelt before a crucifix and flickering candle as each in turn swore not to scab on the others, he and his fellows would not have questioned who they were or why they had come. Immigrant workers like Jan Kowalski expressed their grievances through transplanted cultural forms and used shared cultural values and symbols to legitimize their strikes.

Perhaps it was only logical that striking Polish workers should have underscored what was culturally important to them as a group; they worked in a world that seemed determined to homogenize them. When Polish immigrants realized how their cherished culture could be used to set them at odds with other groups of working people, they sometimes overcame their ethnic particularism to discover that working-class immigrants, regardless of language and culture, shared many of the same problems in American mines and factories.

Poles came to appreciate the commonality of immigrant workers because, as a group, they were steadily changing during the prewar years. Lattimer, Pennsylvania's striking Polish miners in 1897 illustrated that change. As they marched toward the mines the small clot of men bore no Polish signs or placards. Instead, they carried an American flag. These were not the "pauper laborers" whom American trade unions had feared and long considered "unorganizable." By the early 1900s the Poles had learned trade union principles, militant slogans, and radical ideology—some learned in America, some in the Socialist or Populist movements in rural Poland. Often the striking workers were immigrants who had acquired a stake in American society, temporary migrants who had decided to remain in America permanently. Such men and women staunchly resolved to stand up for themselves and demand their "rights," rights previously claimed only by American working people.

The immigrants changed at an auspicious moment, at a time when industrial America was also changing. In the years before the Great War, immigrant workers faced ever tighter factory discipline. At the same time, they found a broadening industrial union movement, belatedly interested in organizing them. Immigrant workers quickly chose sides. Overlooking ethnic differences—if briefly—Poles joined with other working men and women—Italians, Blacks, Hungarians, Slovaks, and Jews. Together they launched a wave of strikes and protests that ended their "docile" image.

Between 1900 and 1919, Polish immigrant workers instigated or joined most of the epic strikes that erupted during this period of labor turmoil—Brooklyn (1907, 1910, 1917), Chicago (1910), Lawrence (1912), Bayonne (1915, 1916), and the celebrated 1919 steel strike. Through each successive outbreak, Polish strikers made a simple yet apparently unacceptable point. We are not mechanical extensions of your factory machinery, Polish workers insisted repeatedly, but human beings. Treat us "like men" and give us a decent standard of living.

Other more radical Polish immigrants pushed forward their own vision of social justice and economic equality. One such man was Leon Czolgosz, the Polish anarchist who assassinated Republican President William McKinley in 1901. Other Poles, although no less radical than Czolgosz, advanced their claims for social justice through more conventional—and peaceful—political channels. In 1896, for example, Chicago Polish radicals founded the newspaper *Robotnik Polski* (The Polish Worker, headquartered in New York after 1907), while in 1907 Polish Socialists in New York published *Dziennik Ludowy* (The People's Daily). A few thousand Poles belonged to the Alliance of Polish Socialists, founded in New York City in 1896, while others supported the Polish Socialist Party in America. A handful of Poles rose to prominence in the militant and colorful Industrial Workers of the World (IWW), and IWW organizers played a vital role in organizing several major Polish strikes. Rather than altering to suit America's factory owners, rather than begging hat in hand for better wages, these radical Poles wanted to change capitalist America into a real economic and social democracy with liberty and justice literally for all.

Immigrant workers won higher wages and better conditions by striking for them, but their actions never came close to making the revolution that radicals among them had sought. The strikers' actions so shook the sensibilities of middle-class Americans that they touched off a wave of anti-labor and anti-immigrant sentiment throughout America's towns and cities. As xenophobic tempers rose during the World War and the Red Scare of the early 1920s, Poles and other immigrant strikers found themselves beset by public officials, industrial managers, and sometimes their own priests who vowed to stop the "un-American" strikers squarely in their tracks. At the outset, civic and industrial authorities used blunt force to break work stoppages, beating men, women, and children indiscriminately and firing shots into crowds of unarmed strike supporters. Later they found that less violent means were as successful. In the workplace, factory managers relied upon complicated systems of surveillance and espionage— agents provocateurs, informers, company spies, and private guards— to root out "troublemakers" before trouble could start. Of all industrial concerns, the Ford Motor Company most perfected such antilabor techniques; other corporations did nearly as well. Industrialists also sought to coopt immigrant working-class dissent through "welfare capitalist" measures like pension funds, sick-leave programs, and employee stock options, which lasted until many were discarded as too expensive during the cost-conscious late 1920s. Since public and industrial officials determined that "foreignness" itself was dangerous, they strove to Americanize the immigrants.

It is not clear how many Polish immigrants saw through the industrialists' schemes or how many bought the corporate line. Most learned a lesson in double standards from their middle-class Anglo-Saxon Protestant employers. That lesson was aptly summarized in the caption that appeared under the newspaper photograph of a slain 1919 steel striker:

> Casimir Mazurek, who fought on foreign soil to make the world free for Democracy, was shot to death by hirelings and thugs of the Lackawanna Steel Co. because he fearlessly stood for industrial Democracy on American soil.[10]

Though they might carry the flag and even fight for it, Poles were not considered Americans no matter how much they were "Americanized."

During these turbulent years not all Polish workers struck; compared to other immigrant groups, such as the Jews and the Germans, few had actually become radicals. While their fellow Polish immigrants stood on the picket line, more self-effacing men and women dutifully worked, avoided labor troubles, and found solace in family, parish, neighborhood, and community. Curiously, once immigrant strike activity foundered, the number of such people grew. Defeated —and often blacklisted—strikers might look elsewhere for work, perhaps moving from primary areas of Polish settlement and employment, like the anthracite fields of eastern Pennsylvania, to secondary areas, like the auto factories of Detroit. Others returned to Poland. Indeed, the high rate of return migration—up to 30 percent of those who arrived between 1906 and 1914—not only included returning temporary migrants, but men and women profoundly disillusioned with the life they had found in the United States. Most defeated strikers, however, chose a third option. They retreated back into the security of their own ethnic settlements and focused their attentions on family concerns and affairs within the Polish ethnic enclave—the immigrant community.

From an economist's point of view, Poles showed little upward mobility in their insular ethnic world. Greeks, Italians, Rumanians, and Jews all climbed the "ladder of success" on the rungs of small business, but most Poles settled into far less aggressive callings. Despite significant resources and advantages, only some German Poles became skilled workers, professionals, or small-business proprietors. Galician and Russian Poles did more poorly. Most of the more recent Polish arrivals filled America's unskilled or, at best, semiskilled jobs and stayed there throughout their entire working lives.

Anti-immigrant attitudes did submerge Polish mobility aspirations, but Poles attained little social mobility primarily because they did not seek it. The temporary migrants among them chose to forego risky business ventures or low-paid white-collar jobs even though they may have offered greater mobility potential. Instead they elected steady, well-paid blue-collar work. Temporary migrant and permanent settler alike shared what could be termed an antimobility work ethos. Catholic to the core, they valued humility, prayer, and otherworldly rewards. Peasant to the bone, they treasured security, stability, and steady work. Such people yearned neither for money, status, nor power in the "land of opportunity." What they sought was contentment in the the things they prized: family, faith, and fatherland.

Given their goals and expectations, America's Polish immigrants succeeded amply in their insular ethnic enclaves despite their modest economic achievements. Through hard work, underconsumption, and frugality, Poles saved money, brought relatives over, and—surpassing the record of most other ethnic groups—won the domestic security and social status of owning their houses. In these modest homes, Poles preserved their culture, prayed for their homeland, and practiced their faith. Best of all, they kept alive the Polish identity they had transplanted to the alien soil of America.

Polish immigrants lived their day-to-day lives and built the institutions that lent permanence to the settlements they planted in the United States—the parishes and religious groups, the political clubs and mutual aid societies, and the sprinkling of small businesses. In those varied institutions they grappled with weighty issues that concerned only themselves—religious disagreements, factional disputes, and the turbulent Polish nationalist controversy. They also pondered perplexing questions with wider ramifications. What was "Polishness"? How would they relate to Poland? What did it mean to become a "Polish-American?"

3

HANDS CLASPED, FISTS CLENCHED

Unity and Strife in the Immigrant Community

The physical parish, comprising the church
edifice, the school building, rectory and
convent is not truly THE parish. *The parish
is a faithful Catholic people, organized
spiritually and continually fed on the truth
of Christ's Gospel, obediently partaking of
His Sacraments at the hands of His appointed shepherd. A true parish then is a
spiritual entity.*

—*Golden Memorial Journal
of Our Lady of Consolation
Parish, 1909–1959* (Brooklyn,
New York)

When Poles retreated into their communities, in a sense they were
trying to move backward in time. While the immigrant community
was a place, it was also a way of life. There Poles prayed with other
Poles, drank and danced with them. They loved and married other
Poles and, when they died, were buried next to their countrymen and
countrywomen. To ordinary Polish working people, most with rural
roots, the Polish immigrant community was an urban village—a face-
to-face, day-to-day world of kinship and friendship; common values,
attitudes, language, and traditions; and a shared set of living and
working conditions.

The immigrants who settled in America—and the many who returned home—learned soon enough that they could not turn back
the hands of the clock. The changes sweeping rural Poland, including
the massive exodus of peasants who emigrated "for bread," were
eroding Polish village communities. The mere fact that many of the
immigrant Poles—as many as 40 to 60 percent in the early twentieth

century—who paused in any given urban neighborhood would be gone ten years later—returning to Poland or searching for cheaper housing, higher wages, friends, or kin in America—suggests that immigrant communities in America too were not as stable, insular, or traditional as many immigrant Poles, buffeted by harsh urban, industrial conditions, may have wanted them to be.

In order to render their settlements less fragile and immigrant life less tenuous, Poles created a string of durable immigrant institutions —small businesses, voluntary associations, and parishes—which became the structures that held the immigrant community together and into which transient Poles could fit themselves. Even though immigrants quickly christened their communities "Polonia" (Latin for Poland), as if to pretend that individually and collectively they were a replica of their homeland, Poles soon plainly discovered how much their "urban villages" differed from the Polish villages they had only recently left.

In the eyes of many young, restless, immigrant Poles, social structure and social relations in Polish villages had seemed oppressively fixed. This was not so in America, the land of ceaseless "progress," where, one newspaper remarked, "the smokestack is as sacred as the steeple."[1] As Polonia pulsed with events in distant Poland, Poles soon found that it also throbbed with the tempo of the large American economy of which it was a part. Poles in America were trading their past for an uncertain, yet dizzyingly hopeful future. In the New World they were creating their own new world and remaking themselves, whether they always knew it or not.

To understand what Poles were creating and remaking, it is necessary to recall the circumstances that brought them to America. An economic revolution—some historians termed it modernization; others, the rise of agricultural and industrial capitalism—had wrenched rural Poles from the soil and set them on the move. Some had joined the migratory industrial workforce whose strength powered mines and factories in places like Silesia, the Ruhr, Warsaw, Łódź, Chicago, Detroit, and Cleveland. The changes that impelled some Poles to take factory jobs in an attempt to hold onto, acquire, or enlarge their paltry landholdings in Poland infused other Poles with the resolve to spurn both their rural past and their possible industrial future and try to "get ahead" by striking out on their own. Though relatively few Poles pursued small-business opportunity in America—a 1920 census sample° showed only 1.7 percent of Polish-speaking immigrants and their children as "salesmen" in stores, compared to 2.7 percent of the

°The sample consisted of immigrants in selected states, Massachusetts, New York, Pennsylvania, Michigan, Minnesota, and Wisconsin, all of which had sizeable Polish populations.

Czech-speaking, 5.2 percent of the Italian-speaking, and a huge 59.7 percent of the Yiddish-speaking groups studied[2]—some did open small businesses and shops. It was these men—and sometimes women—who created Polonia's first institution and made the first effort at rendering immigrant life less fragile in America.

Some of the immigrants who owned businesses and shops were not new to business at all. In the Polish countryside, Jews had often monopolized local trade and, with their prior mercantile experience, knowledge of Polish, and familiarity with peasant culture, were well fitted to serve a Polish clientele in the United States. Despite the fact that many Polish Jewish merchants maintained good relations over many years with their working-class Roman Catholic Polish customers, their hold on the Polish trade remained tenuous. The Jews themselves were outsiders in the immigrant Poles' Catholic world. By relying on the loyalty of their immigrant coreligionists, Roman Catholic German Poles—and later ambitious Galician and Russian Poles—easily gained a foothold in the immigrant economy. Later, using such slogans as "Patronize Your Own," meaning "Buy Polish," in the 1910s and 1920s the most aggressive Poles came to dominate Polonia's economic life.

Despite a seemingly unlimited range of possibilities, Polonia's business owners tended to follow certain lines of trade. For lack of a market, they left the restaurant business to the more urbanized Greeks and Italians. Frugal working-class Poles of peasant stock might consume bar food, which came with the price of a beer, but they ate meals at home that were cooked by wives or mothers; they did not "eat out." Poles also shunned businesses that required a lot of capital to operate. Polonia's furniture and clothing stores therefore long remained in German or Jewish hands. Poles clustered in two other types of business—small artisanal or retail shops like bakeries, butchers, or saloons, or businesses that met specialized immigrant needs like printshops (Polonia's intellectual and political nerve-center), the retail of religious and patriotic goods, or Polish funeral parlors. Though all business owners ignored rural proscriptions against engaging in commerce, the somber men who ran the funeral parlors departed even more from Polish rural cultural norms. In Poland making a living out of burying the dead violated rural taboos. In America "undertaking" became entrepreneurship par excellence.

There were two types of immigrant small-business owners. Small proprietors always formed the clear majority. Usually hard-working immigrants of modest means, they retained the lifestyle, loyalties, friendships, and family ties of their working-class customers. Small proprietors were often indistinguishable from their working-class conationals. They were men and women who were not upwardly mobile; unsuccessful business owners in the process of slipping back into anonymous blue-collar jobs; or those very small or part-time business operators, often working-class wives, who ran little shops out of the front rooms of their homes just to "make ends meet." All such marginal proprietors were a permanent part of the immigrant workers' world.

The second type of Polish business operator, the successful immigrant entrepreneur, really formed the immigrant middle class. These business people exerted a real impact on Polonia's economy and society and rooted the fragile Polish communities to their location. Of the immigrant entrepreneurs, none more typified the group than John Lemke of Detroit. Lemke had been a merchant in German Poland; in America he used his skills and capital to open an eastside tailor shop in 1859. Lemke plowed his profits back into Polonia's economy; in ten years or so he had diversified his enterprise and successfully consolidated his growing wealth. As the owner of a grocery store/saloon and a mogul in neighborhood real estate, Lemke fathered a whole family of Polish success stories a hardware merchant, a bank manager cum alderman, a politician, and, for good measure, a priest. Elsewhere, the Lemke saga was repeated. Vincent Domanski, motherless at sixteen but with a rich aunt in Poznań, became an intrepid peddler in rural Wisconsin, where he sold plaster busts of Jan Sobieski° and other Polish heroes. Moving to Philadelphia in the 1870s, Domanski served as an immigrant agent, Polonia banker, and one of the founders of the Polish National Alliance (PNA). In Chicago, Anthony Smarzewski, carpenter and 1830 insurrectionist, changed his name to Schermann in order to compete better for the city's German immigrant trade and became one of Chicago Polonia's leading lights. It is claimed that he brought 100,000 of his fellow Poles to America. In Milwaukee, Joseph Rudzinski, a former innkeeper from Poznań, became a community leader, society organizer, and the first treasurer of the Polish Roman Catholic Union (PRCU). Though all began as small proprietors, by capitalizing on literacy and artisanal training, resources, and the competitive advantage of having arrived in America early in the migration years, Polonia's entrepreneurs parlayed skill and money into wealth and power in immigrant settlements.

Immigrant entrepreneurs like John Lemke became pillars of the fragile Polish immigrant enclaves because they commanded sufficient resources to help poor, jobless, lonely, and sometimes desolate peasant immigrants hang on, settle in, and perhaps even prosper. The successful business owners translated immigrants' letters, held their money, found them jobs, kept them out of jail, and generally showed them how to get by in what must have been, for men and women who

---

°John III Sobieski (1629–1696), the Polish king who raised the Turkish siege of Vienna in 1683.

spoke little or no English, extremely bewildering surroundings. Polish entrepreneurs performed these and other services in order to
curry the lucrative immigrant trade. They also did it, as one elderly
Polish lawyer in Bayonne, New Jersey, recalled, " . . . to help out the
Polish people."[3] In return, ordinary Poles accepted them as their settlement's leaders.

Over the bar-rail and at the shop counter, middle- and working-
class Poles bound themselves informally together as patrons and
clients in a relationship that resembled the mutual dependencies that
had crisscrossed Poland's manorial world. Yet because it was so much
less fixed than that between peasant and landlord—where one
worked for the other—immigrant entrepreneurs and workers had
need of more formal connections. The entrepreneurs needed a political outlet for their growing social influence and immigrant workers
needed a greater measure of social security. Their mutual needs inspired Polonia's second major institution, the network of voluntary
associations that wove the fragile strands of Polonia together during
the Polish settlement's early years.

In Poland and in America Poles were familiar with voluntary associations. In the 1840s, political émigrés in the United States chartered
various patriotic and cultural groups such as the Democratic Society
of Polish Exiles and the Polish-Slavonian Literary Association in the
State of New York. In the late nineteenth century, rural Poles, who
had routinely cooperated during planting and harvest, also organized
formally in land banks and village cooperatives. Drawing on the principles of patriotism and mutual aid that both types of groups embodied, the Poles' middle-class leaders—and later their priests—
helped found organizations with political and practical purposes.
They established a host of local fraternal benevolent associations, mutual aid societies, and building-and-loan associations—some entirely
secular, others parish-based—for their fellow Poles' "mutual moral
and material assistance."[4]

In the days before public welfare, workers' compensation, or employee health insurance programs, Poles derived a minimum of social
protection from the organizations they founded. Regularly, often on
a monthly basis, they paid dues into their mutual aid society treasuries. In return, they—or their beneficiaries—could draw out modest
accident, sickness, or death benefits. If the need arose, societies furnished mourners and pallbearers to members in good standing. Societies sometimes paid out loans to small businesses or for home
mortgages. Success went to society organizers who kept their word.
When the leaders of a young organization, the Polish National Alliance of Brooklyn, U.S.A.°, made good on their promise to compen-

°The Polish National Alliance of Brooklyn, U.S.A., is a regional fraternal headquartered in Brooklyn and is a separate organization from the large, Chicago-based national fraternal the Polish National Alliance.

sate the widow of a man who had paid dues for just a few months —in 1903, the group's first year of operation—local Poles flocked to join the organization.

By the 1910s, 800,000 Poles—approximately three-fourths of America's Polish immigrants—belonged to at least one of the approximately seven thousand immigrant societies that had sprung up. Organized Polonia was not as fragmented as it seemed. Forward-looking immigrant lay and clerical leaders had reached far beyond the narrow confines of their local neighborhoods and parishes to create national fraternal bodies such as the Polish Roman Catholic Union (1873), the Polish National Alliance (1880), the Polish Union of the United States of North America (1890), the Association of the Sons of Poland (1903), and the Polish White Eagle Association (1906). They organized nationally in order to boost membership; by 1924-1925, Polonia's largest fraternal organization, the PNA, counted 220,000 on its rolls, while the PRCU roster numbered 188,000. By pooling their resources, organizers hoped to protect individual society treasuries against heavy casualty losses. They also wanted to create a national power base for themselves.

Significantly, immigrant organizational life did not remain a male preserve. Polish women also organized, exerted political power and carved out a public role for themselves in Polonia and the larger American society. Parishes often sponsored Polish women's religious societies with mutual aid functions, while Polish fraternals usually organized separate local women's groups. In 1898, middle-class Polish women in Chicago founded their own benevolent society, which they soon renamed the Polish Women's Alliance. By 1924-1925, the group had become national. Its female organizers boasted a membership of 25,000, an Education Division, and their own monthly newspaper, *Głos Polek* (Voice of Polish Women). Espousing Polish immigrant feminism, group leaders stood up for temperance, progressive social causes, and women's political rights. "The liberated, awakened woman," one of *Głos Polek's* female writers observed, is "a person in the full meaning of that word, does not recognize the double morality, which is lenient for men and absolutely rigorous for women." The newspaper's editors also took on conservative Polish immigrant priests who might have wished to slow female progress. "In the area of rights," they told the male clerics, "everything must be taken and one must never wait to be given (them) for they will never be given. And so with Woman when she struggles for a right she must win it and take it."[5] Responding to pressure from its female members, in 1925 the clericalist PRCU established a Women's Department, headed by a female vice-president.

Had they truly become "new men" here, Polonia's rising middle-class leaders might have rested content with their organizational handiwork, which would mobilize—and later politicize—almost a million of their fellow Poles. Polonia's entrepreneurs, unlike members of many other rising middle classes in nineteenth-century Europe, were never secular, atheistic, or materialistic enough. Like their peasant conationals, they came from an unusually devout people, men and women who celebrated namedays° instead of birthdays. Poles held the record for male church attendance among Roman Catholic immigrant groups. Initially, these religious immigrants worshipped in the Germans' American churches. Polish immigrants gravitated toward the German settlements but were always considered outsiders, just as Polish Jews remained outside the Polish community. Strange customs and a language learned under duress made the Poles feel ill at ease. They also bitterly resented the fact that the Germans considered them socially and racially "inferior" and sometimes made them sit in segregated pews. When the number of Polish families in a neighborhood grew large enough—probably a hundred or two—Polonia's middle-class leaders formed parish-organizing committees, collected money, bought land, and erected Polish churches, like Chicago's St. Stanislaus Kostka, built in 1869, or Detroit's St. Albertus, dedicated in 1872. In doing so they created Polonia's most important institution. By 1900, over 517 Polish churches stood.

Some immigrant lay leaders may have had rather banal reasons for parish-organizing, like naming a church after themselves, but most truly believed themselves caretakers of their own and their fellows' immortal souls. Accordingly, parish and church occupied the center of their social world. In troubled moments they probably would have agreed with the assessment of one New York immigrant, that priests were "medicine for the people."[6] Immigrant parishes were critical both for what they did and for what they meant. Lending their names to the Polish immigrant neighborhoods—so that the area around St. Stanislaus *(Św. Stanisław)* became *Stanisławowo,* or that around St. Adalbert's *(Św. Wojciech) Wojciechowo*, as if they were Polish villages—Polonia's churches gave the immigrants a corporate identity in faceless American cities. Encompassing all baptized Poles, virtually all Polish immigrants, parishes tied Poles of disparate backgrounds, occupations, and politics tightly together: the parish became the immigrant community.

More than any other institution, Polonia's parishes linked Poles to the world they had left behind and at once set them apart from other immigrant groups in America. Unlike Irish Catholics, Poles had escaped the rationalist influence of the Protestant Reformation and, if anything, had become more traditional and devotional as a reaction to it. Theirs was an almost medieval religion that enveloped the faithful everyday and at each ritual moment of their lives. What really

°The feastdays of saints after whom they were named.

distinguished Polish religion from other western Catholic traditions, however, was the way Poles venerated the Blessed Virgin Mary, "Poland's Queen." Throughout Poland, the faithful frequented local Marian pilgrimage sites; in America, Polish immigrants eventually built one of their own in Doylestown, Pennsylvania. Each Polish church had its cadre of Mary-like nuns, its Marian altar, and its image of the sacred "Black Madonna,"° Our Lady of Częstochowa, Poland's patroness. Devout Poles immersed themselves in Marian devotions— the rosaries, the litanies, the Lenten *Gorzkie Żale* (Bitter Laments). Before banks of flickering votive candles, immigrant Poles knelt down and begged forgiveness for their sins.

After founding parishes from scratch, the Poles' middle-class leaders might have hoped they could have a say in naming their own pastors. In rural Poland one remnant of feudal tradition—the *ius patronatus*—had accorded local nobles that patronage right. Immigrant laymen did write to Poland encouraging clerical acquaintances or relatives to emigrate. They also petitioned their respective dioceses for regular pastors who, as the organizers of one Brooklyn Polish and Lithuanian parish put it, "would guide properly."[7] Poles found that clerical staffing was no easy matter. The ratio of Polish clerics to immigrant parishioners was a whopping 1:4000 at a time when it was 1:1000 for the American Church at large. With the arrival of the first Polish priests in America, lay leaders faced men with political pretensions of their own, supported by a tremendous authority —the ability to touch the Consecrated Host and sacerdotal religious tradition. To ambitious immigrant entrepreneurs, the creation of the immigrant clergy became an inadvertent throwback to a set of traditional power relations that, throughout history, rising middle classes have tried to abolish or escape. Middle-class immigrants had called the shots during Polonia's early days. After their arrival, Polish clerics wanted to have the final say over what Poles did or did not do in America.

Very quickly, Polish laymen watched their influence over parish staffing erode. Newly arrived Polish priests politicked diocesan authorities rather than settlement leaders in hopes of gaining pastoral berths. Polish missionary orders also tried to place their members in Polonia's pulpits. One such order was the Congregation of the Resurrection of our Lord Jesus Christ, a religious outgrowth of Poland's failed November Insurrection of 1830. In 1871, the order's shrewd superior-general, Rev. Jerome Kajsiewicz, struck a deal with the

°This painting of a royal-looking Mary and her tiaraed Christ Child is called the "Black Madonna" because of the complexion of the figures. Stories attribute the color to a scorching the image allegedly received in a fire it miraculously survived or, more prosaically, to a darkening caused by the smoke of votive candles. Black madonnas, however, are common iconographic figures in the Near East, from whence the picture is believed to have originated.

equally shrewd Bishop of Chicago: the Resurrectionist Fathers won
the right to administer all nondiocesan Polish parishes in the diocese
for the next ninety-nine years. With the blessings, and sometimes the
active encouragement, of American churchmen, home-grown clerics
too would soon come forward to staff Polish parish rectories. In 1886,
Bishop Caspar Borgess of Detroit allowed the Polish insurrectionary
veteran turned priest, Rev. Joseph Dąbrowski, to establish a Polish
seminary in his city. The first Polish seminary in the United States, it
was more necessary to the Poles' well-being, the austere, dedicated
Dąbrowski argued, "than the building of expensive churches." By
1888, Detroit's SS. Cyril and Methodius Seminary had enrolled sixty-
five students.[8] Soon outgrowing its Detroit quarters, it later moved to
nearby Orchard Lake.

With the re-creation of a "clerical estate" in America, the middle-
class Poles' new world began to resemble the "old country" they had
left. Throughout rural Europe the powerful upper clergy had depended upon the support of a landed aristocracy when that aristocracy was declining. Thus the clergy was forced to watch social change
and political influence pass its members by. In immigrant America an
important change occurred. Polish priests became, in a certain sense,
"modern." They cultivated immigrant middle-class allies and operated as though they were part of Polonia's rising middle class.

As a result, Polonia's "brick-and-mortar" pastors often eclipsed the
immigrant laymen who had been instrumental in bringing them to
America. The very way some of these almost regal men lived—Detroit's Rev. Dominik Kolasiński rode through the city in a carriage
driven by a liveried coachman—exuded status and authority. Polonia's priests—who sometimes administered parishes of 40,000 souls
—held enormous power not only because they lived so well, but because, like the immigrant entrepreneurs, they orchestrated immigrant secular life. In Chicago, Rev. Vincent Barzyński, C.R., founded
an immigrant bank, which held $550,000 in deposits in the 1890s. Ba-
rzyński also presided over $500,000 worth of parish real estate at a
time when the entire assets of the secular PNA added up to only
$96,529. In New Britain, Connecticut, Rev. Lucyan Bójnowski built
a complex of schools and an orphanage for his Polish parishioners.
Neither of these priests was atypical. Barzyński, Bójnowski, Buffalo's
Rev. Jan Pitass, and hundreds of less known priests organized and led
parish-based societies and fraternals, helped Poles find jobs, and often intervened in local politics. Of course, these "priest-titans,"[9] as
one historian has called them, tried to guide the morals of their flock,
intoning against occasional immigrant vices like "loafing in bars,
drinking bouts, playing cards, . . . and shooting dice."[10] Most immigrants probably agreed with this. But priests often wanted to tell immigrants not only how they should behave but what they should think

as well. That disturbed many of the members of Polonia's aspiring middle-class elite.

The stage was set for conflict in the Polish immigrant settlement. Vying for the loyalties of their immigrant conationals, ambitious, sometimes idealistic, middle-class Poles and Polish priests confronted one another again and again. Sometimes they fought for power, sometimes for profit. Ultimately, however, both knew they were engaged in philosophical battles of a fundamental sort—not just over who would rule Polonia, but over what Polonia would be.

Between the 1870s and 1890s, reports of sharp factional disputes within America's Polish settlements routinely punctuated the pages of the immigrant press. In 1870, in Poland Corner, Wisconsin, for example, local tavernkeepers tried to kill their Polish pastor, none other than Rev. Joseph Dąbrowski of Polish seminary fame, by placing hollowed-out logs filled with gunpowder in the priest's woodpile. Dąbrowski had changed the site of the parish church to a location far distant from their businesses. Between 1867 and 1869, Polish factions in Chicago clashed over where to site the new St. Stanislaus Kostka Church. Should it stand near land owned by Peter Kiołbassa, a prominent Polish layman, or near the printshop and grocery store owned by two of the city's other Polish leaders? Affairs in Detroit were even more turbulent. In 1885, lay opponents had flamboyant and immensely popular Rev. Dominik Kolasiński suspended from pastoral duties for alleged mismanagement of parish affairs, financial irregularities, and "carnal adventurism"—keeping house with a woman who was really not his sister.[11] When Rev. Joseph Dąbrowski, who had earlier escaped death at the hands of angry Wisconsin parishioners, tried to take Kolasiński's place, a fullscale riot broke out. One man hauled Dąbrowski down from the altar and an angry crowd of Kolasiński's female partisans threw the hapless priest out of the church. In 1898, Omaha parishioners ended a similar conflict with a Wild West-style gunfight.

However confusing to outsiders, Polish antagonists understood why they grappled so fiercely during Polonia's early years. Pastors and entrepreneurs were divided over who would lead their fellow immigrant newcomers. Immigrant business owners clashed over parish patronage. Popular young curates sometimes undercut established Polish pastors in hopes of winning a pulpit of their own. But why did ordinary working people throw themselves into these affrays? They stormed rectories, nailed church doors shut, and marched on Polish saloons, sometimes with guns drawn, because the fights that rocked their parishes and neighborhoods touched their lives. It was their nickels and dollars that had built Polonia's fine brick and stone churches—sometimes at a cost well in excess of $100,000 at a time when workers made $1.50 a day. Their concern went beyond the hard-earned dollars that bought the parish churches' marble, gold, and granite. They believed the churches nurtured their families and their homes. They felt this so strongly that Poles sometimes named a child after the parish patron saint (the first-born child in Brooklyn's St. Stanislaus Kostka parish, Stanislaus Garstka, himself went on to become a priest).

The churches, whose soaring Gothic spires stood as tall as the smokestacks of the factories where they worked, gave Polish immigrants dignity and self-respect. When ordinary Poles took to the streets, they were not merely being litigious peasants or fighting for parishioner democracy, as has been claimed. They had an immediate, sincere reaction against injustice—against the Brooklyn parish organizers who embezzeled parish money; against the Brooklyn pastor who padded parish gas receipts; against the New York priest who allegedly owned apartment buildings and kept race horses on Long Island, all presumably bought with parish funds; against the men who mismanaged the assets in Rev. Barzyński's parish bank to produce $400,000 in debts. Ordinary immigrants fought bitterly when they felt betrayed. One Polish rural custom—dragging Judas figures through the streets during Holy Week—did not long survive the transatlantic crossing. Poles in America had little need of it; they had their own live Judases—ambitious laymen and pastors. They often nearly revolted when these Judases sold out their own communities.

Local parish fights had wide repercussions during the mass migration years. Committees of lay trustees, used to Polish rural traditions of lay influence in local parishes, determined to hold on to the deeds to the church property they had purchased, often collided with bishops—usually Irish or German—who, following the centralizing trends of the nineteenth-century Church, were no less determined to have the deeds signed over to them. When these parish squabbles became nasty enough—when bishops handled affairs ineptly or insensitively or when local Polish priests also clashed with their dioceses—Poles sometimes broke with what they derisively called the "One, Holy, *Irish*, Apostolic Church." Rev. Anthony Klawiter in Buffalo, Rev. Francis Kolaszewski in Cleveland (actually a German named Rademacher), and Rev. Stefan Kamiński in Buffalo and Omaha all led local parish splits. More significant still, one priest in Chicago, Rev. Anthony Kozłowski, parting ways with both the powerful Resurrectionists and his diocese, became schismatic, and got himself ordained a bishop in the Old Catholic sect.° Though Kozłowski claimed 75,000 to 100,000 adherents in twenty-three breakaway parishes by 1907— probably an exaggeration—he never succeeded in elevating local

°The Old Catholic sect is a loosely grouped schismatic movement organized under the Union of Utrecht (1889) and led by Utrecht's archbishop.

discontent to the level of a cause, however deep the discontent with the American Church. In 1896, however, when a local dispute in a Scranton, Pennsylvania, Polish parish mixed with the growingly popular ideology of Polish nationalism, schism raced like a mine-fire across the anthracite fields of eastern Pennsylvania and beyond. Led by Rev. Francis Hodur of Nanticoke, Pennsylvania, Scranton insurgents pounded out a program resounding with Polish nationalism: "The Polish people [should] control . . . all churches built and maintained by them; . . . the Polish people [should] administer their own church property, through a committee chosen by their own parishioners; . . . the Polish people [should] choose their own pastors."[12] In 1904, Hodur's "independent" or "people's" church united the evergrowing numbers of breakaway Polish congregations into the Polish National Catholic Church in America. With over thirty parishes and nearly 30,000 communicants by 1916—conservative estimates—Polish National Catholicism became the only permanent major schism ever to fracture the Roman Catholic Church in the United States.

Debates on the events in Poland increasingly preoccupied Polonia's warring lay and clerical leaders. The revolution that had transformed the Polish countryside, propelled Poles toward migration, and helped create Polonia's nascent middle class, it should be recalled, was a dual revolution. It produced economic ferment but also gave rise to a great national awakening. The liberal capitalist formula of "organic work" (investment and rural self-help) had welded the peasantry to Poland more than ever before: Polish nationalist politics revived, insurrectionary solutions again became popular, and Poles —even school children—soundly rejected Germanization and Russification programs. Polonia's factional quarrels soon became overshadowed—more dangerous still, tied to—the distant Polish nationalist ferment. Though they lived in America, and though most had decided to remain permanently, immigrants did not forget that they were Poles—and that their homeland was still suffering partition. Polonia's leaders well remembered the original aims of their fraternal organizations: to aid their fellow Poles in America and abroad; and—in the emotionally charged language of the times—to work for the resurrection of their beloved, martyred Poland.

The grinding twenty-year fight, pitting middle-class secular nationalists in the PNA against the Polish clergy and the PRCU, lent real coherence to the local factional struggles and the various "independent" church movements that erupted in Polonia in the 1880s and 1890s. Poles had slugged their grubby factional squabbles out handto-hand; they fought this war with words. Immigrant editors were the main combatants and immigrant newspapers the principal battleground. Proclericalist organs like Buffalo's *Polak w Ameryce* (The Pole in America), the PRCU's *Naród Polski* (The Polish Nation) and

Dziennik Chicagoski (The Polish Daily News), and Milwaukee's *Now-iny Polskie* (The Polish News) squared off against the PNA's *Zgoda* (Harmony), Milwaukee's *Kuryer Polski* (The Polish Courier), the socialist *Dziennik Ludowy* (People's Daily), Detroit's *Dziennik Polski* (Polish Daily), and other secular nationalist journals. On their pages, Poles argued over who should lead Polonia and what Polonia's destiny should be.

To a large extent, the positions the two sides argued are familiar to anyone who has followed the course of the middle-class revolution that swept Europe during the 1830s and 1840s—the "Springtime of Nations." Like middle-class revolutionaries of all nationalities, the PNA's lay leaders wanted an ethnically and religiously pluralistic, liberal Polish State that would reunite Poland's fractured territories. That state, not the Church, would define what Poland would become: it would be secular. In America, Polonia's nondenominational, umbrella organization, the PNA, would encompass all of Polonia's factions. Until Poland's rebirth, lay leaders wanted the inclusive PNA to serve as a kind of shadow government or, in their words, Poland's "fourth partition." Like Poland's upper clergy, the priests who led the PRCU in the 1880s, on the other hand, talked far less about Polish independence than their middle-class PNA counterparts. They felt more comfortable with the social status quo, in which churchmen held traditional social authority and middle-class laymen lacked the civic or political authority that might have challenged it. Preserving Polish culture and religion in America was the immigrants' most important task, they argued, and could best be accomplished if Poles would honor Polish traditions and obey their clergy. These themes were neither new nor particular to immigrant America.

Another feature of Polonia's nationalist debate affected immigrants more than it did partisans in Poland. For all they argued about their homeland, both PNA and PRCU antagonists concentrated on a more basic question that concerned immigrant identity. The Polish nationalist debate seemed to hinge on this issue and its answer would decide who would control the Polish settlement in America. In the end, what was a *true* Pole? Was "Polishness" a matter of citizenship, allegiance, and place of birth—the secular nationalist position? Were middle-class Poles Polonia's legitimate leaders? Or was "Polishness" a matter of culture and religion—the clergy's stance? Were the priests who fostered these qualities the "natural leaders" of the Polish Nation? In short, was the immigrant a Roman Catholic *Pole* or a Polish *Roman Catholic?*

Ordinary Poles found these questions important. They cared intensely about politics and religion. What is more, whether they found the words to frame the questions, they wondered who they were in this alienating new land. Temporary immigrants especially felt far away from a Poland to which they wanted to return but could not while the partitions, as they believed, continued to make life in Poland so hard. The immigrants' own children might not know them if they returned after five, ten, or twenty years. But they could never know them unless the Polish immigrants—"Poles in America" or "American Poles"—knew themselves. This is why ordinary immigrants followed—and sometimes joined in—the fight between the PNA and the PRCU.

The fight was not between two absolutes. Neither the Polish clergy nor the immigrant middle class was monolithic in the 1880s and 1890s. Immigrants mixed and matched views on these heated subjects and opinions shaded one into the other. Some middle-class Poles, of course, always followed the mainstream clerical line. Conversely, some priests responded in a different way to the challenge of changing circumstances and controversies than the PRCU leaders and tried to fashion creative new answers to the Poles' dilemma of identity and politics. Rev. Hodur, of the Polish National Catholic Church, tried to redefine the relationship between Poles and their faith that lay beneath the question of Polish identity. Hodur blamed the Church in Rome and the pontiff for recognizing the Polish partitions, thus legitimizing the country's subjugation. Echoing the themes of 1830s Polish Messianism and the concerns of Polish rural populism, the gaunt-faced Hodur decried Roman Catholic prelates who built "magnificent basilicas"[13] but ignored "the poor, spurned, disinherited . . . masses of the [Polish] nation."[14] A Pole could be a Catholic and a Catholic a Pole interchangeably, Hodur argued, but only if there were such a thing as *Polish* Catholicism. Breaking away from Rome, Hodur wanted Polish National Catholicism to become Polonia's and Poland's identity and national religion.

Another immigrant priest, Rev. Wenceslaus Kruszka of Ripon, Wisconsin, deftly charted an alternative to Hodur's position, which kept him in the Church but nonetheless branded him a notorious renegade. In the early 1900s, Kruszka and his brother Michael, editor of Milwaukee's *Kuryer Polski*, urged Rome to change. In his famous 1901 article, "Polyglot Bishops for Polyglot Dioceses," the young Wisconsin cleric insisted that "if a diocese is polyglot, the bishop must be polyglot, too . . . ," for taking the mitre without adequate linguistic skills constituted a mortal sin. Kruszka's position, called *równouprawnienie* (equality of rights) by the Poles, asked "EQUAL treatment in the ecclesiastical hierarchy" and the appointment of Polish immigrant bishops.[15] If America's Irish Church would internationalize, become truly *catholic*, Kruszka believed, the problem of immigrant identity—religious and secular—would go away.

Because positions were so nuanced and because eventually there was a generational "changing of the guard," by the late 1890s PNA

and PRCU antagonists began to meet on common ground. Devout
middle-class Poles and priests steeped in Polish nationalism now
agreed they would share leadership and power. The immigrant community would be defined as the field in which power and leadership
would be shared. Immigrants would not have to call themselves Roman Catholic *Poles* or Polish *Roman Catholics*, but could be Poles *and*
Roman Catholics, each identity coterminous and equal. Poland's future would be as an ethnically and religiously homogeneous, liberal
capitalist, modern nation-state. "Faith and Fatherland"/"God and
Country" now became their dual slogan. With the consecration of
Rev. Paul Rhode° in 1908, before an audience of 20,000 (the steelworkers of Rhode's St. Michael's parish had gotten the afternoon off),
as America's first Polish auxiliary bishop, the PNA and PRCU found a
common leader. Rhode was a Roman Catholic priest, but also an ar-
dent Polish nationalist.

The political and ideological convergence that created, in effect, an
alliance between the middle class and the clergy happened at an auspicious moment in the history of Polonia and of European politics.
Tensions between Europe's Great Powers had heightened. The nationalist movement in Poland had finally produced formally organized political parties—openly in Galicia, clandestine or in exile
elsewhere. The political evolution of Polonia placed American Poles
at the center of action in new ways. The consensus reached by
middle-class Poles and their priests allied them with Poland's anti-
German, middle-class National Democratic—or "Endek," after its
Polish initials—Party.

Yet Poland's—and Polonia's—dual revolution had not created a
homogeneous middle-class world. The same developments that had
boosted some Poles into middle-class occupations had squeezed others off the land and forced them into the factories of Poland's infant
industrial centers and America's industrial heartland. In Poland and
Polonia, society and economy were both in flux; that turmoil continued to unsettle Polish politics both in Poland and in America. In Poland, middle-class Endek leaders faced serious challenge in the
factories, in urban neighborhoods, and on Poland's large landed estates. That opposition congealed in the Polish Socialist Party (PPS), a
coalition of radical intellectuals, industrial workers, and agricultural
wage laborers who wanted a pluralistic, reformist Polish state; who
believed in immediate armed insurrection and therefore followed the
Polish hero of the 1905–1906 insurrection against the Russian tsar,
blunt but colorful Józef Piłsudski; and who, with Piłsudski, considered the Russian Empire Poland's gravest foe. In America, during a
time when socialism and industrial unionism were both attracting fol-

°Rhode's family name in Poland had been Roda.

lowers, radicalized immigrant workers and radical publicists—
though never numerous—adulated Piłsudski, embraced the PPS, and
shattered Polonia's newfound calm. The radicals advanced a different
vision of what Poland and Polonia should be. They believed that Polish nationalism should bring economic justice, political democracy,
and basic social change that, in Poland, would topple the landed aristocracy and, in America, would undercut Polonia's arrogant pastors
and acquisitive businessmen. To them, the true Pole was both a nationalist and a political progressive.

While all were committed to the idea of "one Poland," immigrants
still asked, whither Poland, whither Polonia, and what was a Pole?
Could they ever pull together? With war clouds looming in Europe,
in 1912 leaders of the Polish Falcons, a paramilitary fraternal that espoused Polish national rejuvenation through self-discipline and physical fitness, briefly called Polonia's warring factions together in a
so-called Committee for National Defense, the *Komitet Obrony Nar-
odowej* (KON). After Piłsudski supporters took it over, KON
splintered. Priests and PRCU delegates bolted from the group, en-
listed the support of Polonia's lay middle class, and in 1913 formed
their own majority nationalist coalition, the pro-Endek Polish National Council.

When war broke out in Europe the following year, Bishop Rhode,
Chicago banker John Smulski, and other leaders of the Polish National Council held a commanding position. They lobbied Colonel
House, President Woodrow Wilson's closest adviser, on behalf of Polish independence and brought Endek leaders, like the celebrated
pianist-politician Ignatz Jan Paderewski, to argue Poland's case before the American people. They got America and its allies to endorse
the idea of a united, independent Poland and to recognize the Endek's Polish National Committee in Switzerland as its provisional
government. Polish National Council leaders recruited their countrymen for service in Endek General Joseph Haller's "Blue Army"—
named after the color of its uniforms—which had been formed to
fight in France; and, after American entry in the war, they also raised
troops for the United States army. (When the guns fell silent in November of 1918, three times more American Poles—in percentage
terms—had given their lives in the war then there were Poles in the
American population.) Polish National Council leaders soon watched
their Polish socialist opposition crumble. In May 1918, KON was
broken up by United States Military Intelligence; always most fearful
of Russia, KON had backed Austria and hence the Central Powers. In
a stroke, Polonia's "heretics" and "revolutionaries" had become "enemy aliens."

As the curtain fell on the 1910s, the thirteenth of Woodrow Wilson's famous "Fourteen Points" had finally come to pass, paid for with

emphatic words, hard-earned dollars, and young Polish immigrant
lives. Deliriously happy American Poles, without regard to political
affiliation, celebrated wildly as an independent Polish state once
again appeared on a redrawn European map. However obscure and
confusing they may seem today, Polonia's wartime efforts had clearly
riveted the attention of Polish immigrants and their leaders in much
the same way that, for example, the exploits of organizations like the
National Association for the Advancement of Colored People
(NAACP) and the Universal Negro Improvement Association (UNIA)
electrified early twentieth-century Black American history. And as
Black America's organizational debates inevitably turned to questions of color and race, as Jewish Zionist and Irish Fenian struggles
hinged on ideology and religion, Polonia's factions once again pried
open the matter of immigrant identity. This question could not be
separated from discussions of Polish nationhood. But middle-class
Poles and their priests already had answered it. They had defined
who were Poles by determining who were *not:* non-Catholics, atheists, socialists, and radicals. None of them belonged in the Polish
"community" that Polonia's conservative leaders had wrought. None
were true Poles.

According to the Bible, God, *Pan Bóg*, took six days to create the
universe. Perhaps because immigrant Poles did not read the Book—
and instead fingered their rosary beads and prayed from their missals
—it took them forty years or so to create theirs. When they had, Polonia's dual revolution was complete. Along the way, the immigrants
had made Polonia more homogeneous and, in that sense, more of a
community, with more clearly defined social boundaries, than it had
been before. Along social and economic lines, however, the immigrant community had become less of a real community because it had
become more divided. What had happened in Detroit's Polonia typified the social and economic shift that had taken place throughout Polish America during the twenty years or so that Poles had been
engrossed in political and ideological battles. Little but their industry
and perhaps their luck had differentiated America's early Polish immigrants from one another, but by 1908 one Detroit Pole owned a
brewery worth more than $200,000 and, because of his extraordinary
wealth, another immigrant had won the nickname, the "king of the
Poles." As the scale of immigrant enterprise rocketed, the sheer number of immigrant businesses in Detroit's Polonia had also swelled,
from one tailor shop in the 1860s to about 611 businesses in 1907, to
2,500 seven years later.[16] Though America's Polish leaders had united
their countrymen and countrywomen behind the slogan "one Poland," they now presided over not one, but two Polonias— their own
middle-class Polonia and the working-class Polonia of Jan, the Polish
miner. Never again would the two meet.

Indeed, if two immigrant communities now existed, was there any community at all? Apologetic accounts from the period describe faithful Catholics cheerfully following lay leaders and Roman Catholic priests, but this is not the image conveyed by the photographs contained in the Poles' own parish histories and commemorative journals. There stand dour-looking priests in rumpled cassocks and humorless laymen with handle-bar mustaches and natty dress suits, but no callused Polish workingmen nor kerchiefed immigrant women. Why are they not in these pictures? Because, in a very real sense, they had dropped out of sight. Polonia's self-made leaders, who assembled these volumes to commemorate their own achievements at parish-organizing, society-founding, and Polish nation-building, viewed themselves as the only immigrant community that really mattered. Their Polonia was a place to make money, win honor, or exercise power. It was no longer a web of cohesive face-to-face relationships among friends, neighbors, and relatives that constituted the immigrant workers' day-to-day world.

Clearly, Polonia had changed. It would change again. At one time few Polish villagers had thought of themselves as Poles but considered themselves instead "peasants" or "Catholics" or "Kaiser's people"—anything but citizens of a yet-to-be reborn Polish Nation. After years of travail, Polonia's immigrants knew who they were.[17] What they did not know, though, was how they would relate to *Polonia Restituta*, restored Poland. Should they stay in America? Could they go "home"? How had time and circumstance changed them? What had these "true Poles" become in the factory districts of industrial America? And what were their American-born children becoming there?

Most Polish immigrants came from the Polish countryside; but few lived as well as this family. In addition to the house (back, center), there are thatched livestock barns (foreground) and grain storage barns (far right). (Polesie, circa 1935.) *Obrebski Collection, Archives, University Library, University of Massachusetts/ Amherst.*

Emigration depopulated many Polish villages, leaving behind the elderly and the very young. (Polesie, circa 1935.) *Obrebski Collection, Archives, University Library, University of Massachusetts/ Amherst.*

A Polish mining family in their new home in Washington, Pennsylvania, in 1918. Bean plants climbing the porch supplement the household budget. *Courtesy of Edith Markow and the Kosciuszko Foundation Picture Archives.*

A christening portrait (Bush, Illinois, 1912). The baby wears a crucifix; the immigrant father, probably a religious medal. This immigrant wife probably made the lace trim on both her own dress and her baby's gown, but she also worked outdoors, witness her gnarled hands and deeply tanned face. Her lighter forehead and ears suggest that she normally wore a babushka (kerchief), which shielded her from the sun. *Courtesy of Irena Słosek and the Kosciuszko Foundation Picture Archives.*

Many early Polish immigrants were young single males who did not live in nuclear families but became boarders or lodgers. This slight landlady washed, cooked, and cleaned for ten strapping men. (Pennsylvania coal country, 1915.) *Courtesy of the Kosciuszko Foundation Picture Archives.*

At an Aluminum Company of America (Alcoa) factory in Niagara Falls, New York, a gang of Polish workers pose with Mr. Flay (left), their non-Polish foreman (1912). In many places, workers had to pay bribes and "tips" to keep their jobs. *Courtesy of the Kosciuszko Foundation Picture Archives.*

A Polish farming family in Thorp, Wisconsin, poses with their new steam-driven threshing machine in 1900. In contrast, in many parts of Poland, reaping and threshing were still done by hand. *Courtesy of the Kosciuszko Foundation Picture Archives.*

Middle-class Poles like this store owner, pictured beside his neatly painted, lace-curtained, clapboard house and his sporty horse and buggy, acquired wealth, power, and influence in immigrant settlements. (Milwaukee, undated.) *Roman B. J. Kwasniewski Collection, Special Collections, Golda Meir Library, University of Wisconsin-Milwaukee.*

This postcard of Polish wrestler Stanisław Cyganiewicz gives evidence of immigrant cultural nationalism and growing ethnic pride. Cyganiewicz adopted the name Zbyszko, from a medieval Polish hero. (Circa 1920.) *Roman B. J. Kwasniewski Collection, Special Collections, Golda Meir Library, University of Wisconsin-Milwaukee.*

Standing before a religious picture and an American flag, Endek leader Ignatz Jan Paderewski presents the medal of Polonia Restituta (Restored Poland) to a Milwaukee priest in 1926. Rev. Wenceslaus Kruszka (foreground, third from left), proponent of *równouprawnienie* (equality in the hierarchy of the Church), looks on. By the 1920s, the clergy and the immigrant middle class had settled their differences and together controlled Polish America's political and economic life. *Roman B. J. Kwasniewski Collection, Special Collections, Golda Meir Library, University of Wisconsin-Milwaukee.*

In the 1920s, assimilation eroded the ethnic attachments of Polish-American youth. In this Americanization pageant in Detroit, one young Polish-American is costumed as the Statue of Liberty. (Undated.) *Polish Activities League Box, Michigan Historical Collections, Bentley Historical Library, University of Michigan.*

Sit-down strikers at the Dodge Main plant in the heavily Polish city of Hamtramck, Michigan, in 1937. Immigrant workers of all nationalities were less assimilated than they were homogenized as a class—in the workplace and on the picket line. *The Archives of Labor and Urban Affairs, Wayne State University.*

Mobilization in the armed services during the Second World War Americanized young second-generation Polish-American males and hastened the demise of urban ethnic enclaves. (Milwaukee, undated.) *Roman B. J. Kwasniewski Collection, Special Collections, Golda Meir Library, University of Wisconsin-Milwaukee.*

With the outbreak of World War Two, for the first time Polish women of the second generation—even those with children—began to enter the workforce in large numbers. The three women in the center of this Office of War Information photograph are Polish-American. (Pitcairn, Pennsylvania, 1943.) *Photo by Marjorie Collins; Library of Congress, Prints and Photographs Division. Courtesy of the Kosciuszko Foundation Picture Archives.*

Women's space in the second generation: the outdoor market. Shrewd women shoppers still formed the backbone of the household economy. (Detroit, 1943.) *Courtesy of the Burton Historical Collection of the Detroit Public Library.*

Fifth- and sixth-grade pupils, separated by sex, sit in a Polish Roman Catholic parochial school classroom in Watervliet, New York, in 1958. Discipline, obedience, religious devotion, and group and family loyalty shaped the curriculum. *Courtesy of the Kosciuszko Foundation Picture Archives.*

Men's space in the second generation: the neighborhood bar. Ethnic bars, clubs, and fraternals lent critical support to 1930s and 1940s CIO union-organizing drives. (Milwaukee, 1941.) *Roman B. J. Kwasniewski Collection, Special Collections, Golda Meir Library, University of Wisconsin-Milwaukee.*

The generations of Polonia. Family ties buttress Polish-American ethnicity. Note the Felician nun in the center. (Milwaukee, 1930.) *Roman B. J. Kwasniewski Collection, Special Collections, Golda Meir Library, University of Wisconsin-Milwaukee.*

Long before the rise of Poland's Solidarity movement, Polish-American ideology was anti-Soviet and anti-Communist. In 1974, for example, the Polish American Congress of Michigan protested a celebration of the thirteenth anniversary of the Polish People's Republic. (Hamtramck, Michigan.) *Photo by M. Lewandowski. Courtesy of the Kosciuszko Foundation Picture Archives.*

Karol Cardinal Wojtyła of Cracow stopped in Detroit during his 1969 visit to the United States. A symbol of Polish-American pride and the ethnic revival, in 1978 Wojtyła became Pope John Paul II, the "Polish Pope." *Photo by M. Lewandowski. Courtesy of the Kosciuszko Foundation Picture Archives.*

Memorial Day Parade, Detroit, 1971. Ethnic pride is visible and vocal with the social, economic, and political "coming of age" of the group. *Photo by J. Berndt. Courtesy of the Kosciuszko Foundation Picture Archives.*

Once regarded as a group caricature, with the ethnic revival polka bands and polka fans—sometimes organized in clubs of "polka boosters"—play upon and amplify Polish-American pride. (Buffalo, circa 1975.) *Photo by Richard Blau. Courtesy of the Kosciuszko Foundation Picture Archives.*

What is Polish-American ethnicity today? At Buffalo's Broadway Market thousands of Polish-Americans buy meat, produce, and ethnic baked goods. Polish foodways remain one identifiable ethnic cultural carryover. (Circa 1975.) *Courtesy of the Kosciuszko Foundation Picture Archives.*

In Brooklyn's still heavily Polish Greenpoint section, children dress up in folk costume and learn to identify with their group, but probably grow up to lead daily lives not unlike those of most other Americans (1983). *Photo by Krystyna Włodarska-Baker.*

4

CONTINUITY AND CHANGE IN THE 1920S AND 1930S

From Polish to Polish-American

> Conscious attitudes toward "Americaniza-
> tion" lag behind actual practice in regard
> to the assumption of American ways. Many
> native-born Poles express attitudes in favor
> of the preservation of the Polish language,
> the maintenance of a Polish community life
> . . . , and the conservation of Polish cul-
> ture, but as a matter of fact, their behavior
> often belies their attitude. In other words,
> they refuse to admit to themselves that
> they have changed and are changing in the
> new environment.
>
> —Niles Carpenter and Daniel
> Katz, *A Study of Acculturization
> in the Polish Group of
> Buffalo, 1926–1928*

At the end of World War I, upon entering a Polish immigrant enclave in the industrial Northeast where Poles had concentrated, it would have been difficult to tell that America's Poles had traded one crisis, Poland's resurrection, for another, Polonia's survival. Though increasingly polarized along social and economic lines, by 1920 America's Polish settlements had done quite well for themselves. There were 400,000 first- and second-generation Poles (respectively, immigrants and their children) in Chicago; Pittsburgh and New York each had 200,000; Buffalo, Detroit, and Milwaukee each had 100,000; Cleveland and Philadelphia each had 50,000; and there were smaller clusters in eastern Pennsylvania, New England, New Jersey, Baltimore, and elsewhere. Some colonies had grown up as secondary settlements. In the decade following the World War, Polish birthrates

remained high and Polish church attendance was up in immigrant settlements. Polish parishes had multiplied and Polish neighborhoods
had become more heavily "Polish." In short, in America hearty immigrant survivors had held families together; had hung onto jobs,
homes, and small pieces of land; had "made it" in the New World
more or less on their own terms.

As crowds of jubilant Poles watched Polish victory parades march
down the centers of their festive neighborhoods the blaring trumpets
and rattling drums could not drown out a discordant note that
sounded in the ears of many onlookers who asked themselves, what
now? Even as the strains of "The Star Spangled Banner" mingled with
voices singing the Polish anthem, *Jeszcze Polska Nie Zgineła* (Poland is still living), some probably silently repeated the counter-
pointal lament uttered by Jan, the Polish miner, interviewed by the
magazine reporter ten years previously. "America is a wonderful
land," Jan had said, " . . . but it is a land of forgetfulness. My children
are not my children, for my children have forgotten that they are
Poles."[1] This was Polonia's "heart of darkness," its gravest crisis yet.
What could Poles do when they discovered that America was not the
promised land where, in the words of one little Polish pupil, "good
Polish boys went when they died,"[2] but a country to which, alas,
Poles went to die *as Poles*, where their culture and identity were extinguished?

Even the most sanguine of America's Polish settlers might have
gleaned an inkling of Polonia's other crisis if they had glanced at the
fuzzy newspaper photographs of the *Hallerczycy*—the veterans of
Endek General Joseph Haller's "Blue Army"—who returned from
Poland to the United States in 1920, who did not stay in the country
they had helped liberate. In ironic contrast to the antique images of
the Polish immigrants who appeared restless and anxious, but clearly
full of hope at arriving in America, the stubbled veterans of the Polish
army, standing in clots at the deck-rail of their oceanliner smoking
cigarettes and trying to keep warm, looked only haggard, beaten,
worn, and forlorn. They were leaving their homeland *again.* Strangers in America, they found themselves strangers in postwar Poland. It
was no longer the country they had left. Did they have a home? Perhaps not. Perhaps the photographs aptly showed them aboard ships
on the ocean, caught between two worlds.

Poland's sudden independence confronted all immigrant Poles, not
just the Hallerczycy, with an unavoidable choice, which most would
have preferred not to make. Having fought so hard to achieve Poland's freedom and to define Polish identity in America, could they in
good conscience opt to remain exiled overseas? Should they hurry
back to rebuild the land of their birth? As the shards of partitioned
Poland shattered to the earth, some Polish immigrants—fortune-

hunters as well as patriots—did go home. But most, like the Haller-czycy, felt they had no place there. Poles who had never left their country felt considerable resentment toward these "Americans"—America's Polish immigrants—who had "fled" and now returned. American Poles thus received an icy welcome from their erstwhile countrymen and countrywomen who needed neither their bad-intentioned meddling nor well-meaning, ill-informed advice. Most Polish immigrants spared themselves the disillusionment and abuse of going "home." In the aftermath of the World War, they came upon a sobering realization: no longer temporary sojourners, they found themselves too at home to leave America. They had settled in. Polonia's social composition was thus fixed for the next two decades. Political developments in Poland strengthened immigrant resolve to rest content with their new lives in the United States. As Polish politics veered left in the early 1920s and Józef Piłsudski eclipsed the Endek leader Ignatz Jan Paderewski, America's middle-class and clerical Polish immigrant leaders realized they had won the battle but lost the war: Poland was free but not the Poland of which they had dreamed. Disillusioned with this turn of political events, disappointed with the endemic chaos of the postwar Polish economy, and upset by what they perceived to be their fellow Poles' rank ingratitude for the help they had so generously given through the years, immigrant Poles underscored their decision to stay put, turn inward, and tend their own American garden.In the 1920s, the immigrants' leaders coined an almost smug slogan, which plainly expressed their intention: *"Wychodźtwo dla Wychodźtwa,"* The Emigrants *for Themselves.*

Immigrant leaders such as banker John Smulski and Bishop Paul Rhode found much to favor in this insular reorientation because they saw that American Polonia was not an island. If it were, it was an island under attack. The outbreak of war in 1914 signalled an opportunity for Polish freedom, and heralded a constriction of the immigrants' situation in America. Heightening already strong currents of American nativism, the war produced a dark suspicion of all things foreign and inflamed native-born Americans' xenophobic tendencies. On the intellectual front, men like the patriotically named author Madison Grant hawked pseudoscientific race theories that warned Americans of Nordic stock that prolific "new" immigrants like the Poles, Italians, and Jews—"the weak, the broken and the mentally crippled of all races"—threatened to out-reproduce them.[3] American sociologist Edward A. Ross, meanwhile, called Poles and other East Europeans "noisome and repulsive," "the beaten members of beaten breeds."[4] Race theories, however, acquired a broader impact on public policy after the forty-one-volume Senate Immigration Commission Report of 1911 rested arguments in favor of immigration restriction on race stereotypes. When the rising tide of industrial strikes in the 1910s linked immigrants with radicalism, when foreignness and subversion became wartime synonyms, something had to give.

Because they were officially considered "enemy aliens," all German and Austrian Poles should have quaked before the rising nativist tremors. Yet, except for vocal supporters of the pro-Austrian Committee for National Defense (KON), Polish immigrants—unlike America's German nationals—usually escaped harsh repressive measures because they were considered "obedient" and "docile" Roman Catholics who detested both the Kaiser and the Bolsheviks.

Despite their benign reputation, Poles could not elude the broader train of events the war set in motion. When Congress finally acted to create a general immigration restriction policy between 1921 and 1924, "racially inferior" Poles were subsumed under the quota legislation as much as any other "new" immigrant minority. In 1921, census figures report that over 95,000 Poles had entered the United States; in 1925, the number dropped to a mere 5,341. This "unfair" system of restriction, one Polish newspaper bitterly observed, "favors the recent enemies of the United States (Germans), and discriminates against such patriotic U.S. minority groups as, for example, the Poles. . . ."[5]

Yet even as Liberty's lamp dimmed and the Golden Door was locked, American policymakers faced a problem of stupendous proportions: what to do with the vast numbers of immigrants already here? Some progressive social workers believed that immigrants like the Poles had "the sterling qualities of character needed to make them the right kind of American citizens" and would absorb civic virtue in the American environment if only given half a chance.[6] Proponents of race theory often grudgingly supported this notion as the only practical alternative to an otherwise bleak situation. If "inferior" races could never become Nordics or Anglo-Saxons, at least they could be made to behave like them or rather as they wanted immigrants to behave. Beginning during the war, civic authorities and industrialists launched a determined campaign to "Americanize" immigrants and make them conform to the middle-class Anglo-Saxon Protestant vision of civic propriety. Through industrial classes, citizens committees, the Young Men's Christian Association (YMCA), local chambers of commerce, public schools, and patriotic fetes, the Americanization campaign tried to reach immigrants in order to obliterate disruptive or offensive vestiges of their cultural past and, of course, to naturalize them.

During the "tribal twenties," it was not nativism alone that set native-born, white Anglo-Saxon Protestant middle-class Americans to take action against the "foreign menace." Rather, in the shadow of

Russia's Bolshevik Revolution, defenders of "civilization"—private property, middle-class rule, and the bourgeois state—saw working-class immigrants, their ingrown communities, and their divided loyalties as a conduit for the cancer of revolution to spread in America. Nativism, immigration restriction, and Americanization therefore were aimed principally at immigrant working people. They might also presume that middle-class immigrants carried the alien subversive virus because, after all, they too suffered from "foreignism." The onslaught against immigrant Poles clearly threatened to undermine ethnic patronage and clientage networks and the economic gains that Polish entrepreneurs and proprietors had won. This external threat caused Poles of all social and economic positions to pull together behind the leadership of their clergy, their businessmen, and their professionals. Socially they may no longer have been cohesive but in time of need they could act politically as if they were, a pattern evident to the present day.

Immigrant priests focused their attentions on combatting nativism, which continued in the Church. Rev. Paul Rhode was consecrated as Chicago's, and America's, first Polish bishop in 1908; and Church officials appointed Rev. Edward Kozłowski as Milwaukee's ordinary in 1914. Kozłowski died a year later and another Pole did not receive the mitre until 1926, after which time Polish appointments remained rare. Nativism also crept into general Church policy in the 1920s. In 1923, Church officials in the heavily Polish Buffalo diocese ordered that only English be used in the parochial schools there. In 1929, George Cardinal Mundelein of Chicago, long exasperated at what he called "the exaggerated spirit of nationalism . . . rampant today among these various Slav races, amounting almost to a mania,"[7] converted the Polish parish of St. Thecla's from a nationality (ethnic) into a territorial parish. This threatened all ethnic parishes with the possibility of juridical extinction. Against this steady assault, Polish priests and their parishioners hotly protested. At a Polish Roman Catholic Union convention, Bishop Rhode had remarked, "If we forget our Polish heritage we become nothing but ships in the wind without anchors."[8] He demonstrated that Poles must not only remember their heritage but also defend it. In the 1920s, Rhode himself emerged as a proponent of *równouprawnienie*, Polish equality in the hierarchy of the Church.

In the secular sphere Poles opposed nativism through the vehicle of electoral politics. In the 1880s and 1890s, Polish alignments in the American political arena had generally mirrored Polonia's factional divisions—the PRCU and the Polish clergy customarily backing the Democrats, and the Polish National Alliance and its middle-class leaders typically endorsing the Republicans. By the early twentieth century Polish political loyalties lurched radically as Poles used their votes to underscore ethnic pride and resist nativism. In 1912, for example, many Poles punished Democratic presidential candidate Woodrow Wilson for nativist statements he had written in the 1890s while still a Princeton professor. Wilson, one group of angry Polish voters charged, was "an enemy of European immigration in general, an enemy of the Poles, an enemy of the Roman Catholic Church, an enemy of the workers and the workers' unions, an enemy of the noble aspirations of each nation, striving to regain its independence; in short,. . . an enemy of progress and . . . a backward looking person."[9] Chastened, by 1916 Wilson had come around, backed Polish independence, and won the "Polish vote."

Despite their efforts, however, nativism and Americanization fever grew to epidemic proportions by the early 1920s. Polish immigrant leaders desperately sought a means to check this dual assault on their group's survival. Paradoxically, they concluded that they could only preserve their communities, their culture, and their Polish identity in America by modifying them. To defend themselves against charges of disloyalty and foreignism, middle-class Polish leaders embraced Americanism, founded civic and political clubs, and plunged into naturalization work. America's Polish immigrants already had become *Polish-Americans*, they insisted, American enough not to be perennially suspect. In a pluralistic "nation of immigrants," hyphens could connect as well as divide.

In "Polish-Americanism," Polonia's elite found a new avenue of career mobility via government service and American party politics. They also crafted a thoroughly secular identity for their Polish immigrant community, one that finally gave them the upper hand in their on-going rivalry with Polonia's priests. All Poles reaped huge, intangible benefits from calling themselves Polish-Americans and therefore campaigned hard for Polish monuments and street names during the 1920s and organized Pulaski Day parades. Through these activities, they stood up and shouted, we helped build America! We have a right to live here! In 1930, Polish-American delegates to the Warsaw congress of the World Union of Poles from Abroad, an organization established by the Polish government to tie dispersed members of the "Polish nation" to one another and their Polish homeland, emphasized this position. Defining Polish-American participation in the congress, Prof. Francis X. Świetlik, the PNA representative to Warsaw, wrote, "Polonia in America is neither a Polish colony nor a national minority, but a component part of the great American nation. . . . [10]

To America's Polish immigrants, becoming "Polish-American" represented a personal and collective breakthrough and a symbolic break with their Polish past. The step they took was shorter than it seemed. Świetlik, for example, was quick to add that Polish America was also "proud . . . of its Polish origin and careful to implant in the hearts of the younger generation a love for all that is Polish."[11] In effect, becoming "Polish-American" was mostly a matter of political loyalty to their adoptive country and the intention to remain in it, nothing more. Immigrant Poles wanted to have their cake and eat it too: they wanted to be American on the outside but culturally Polish within. Here was the Polish-Americans' greatest problem of all in the 1920s. Immigrant Poles could repel Americanization because it attacked Polonia in the open and by storm. But, with the influx of Poles sharply curtailed and Polonia lacking "fresh troops," could they resist assimilation, the silent enemy that was undermining their churches, families, and homes? Jan, the Polish miner, knew that he would always be "from the old country," *z kraju*, but not so his children. Polish names like *Stanisław* and *Stanisława* soon became Stanley and Stella, and other things changed besides what they called themselves. They had become true ethnic Americans whose culture was more new than it was old.

By the late 1920s typical young second-generation Polish-Americans in their late teens or early twenties might still speak Polish at home, might want to maintain Polish community life, and would not marry outside their group. But most differed from their immigrant parents in many other ways. The majority did not object to the idea of ethnic intermarriage; and most, while retaining Polish customs, had absorbed a great deal of American culture. Among second-generation Poles surveyed in Buffalo between 1926 and 1928, for example, over 67 percent had at least a "fair" knowledge of the origins of the legend of George Washington and the cherry tree; 62 percent, the origins of Thanksgiving; and 88 percent, the origins of the Fourth of July. Clearly, it was more in their cultural orientation than in their social life that these young Poles were changing most. Would social patterns soon follow suit given how much their culture already had changed? Most of these young Poles had heard of Polish figures like Sienkiewicz, Paderewski, and Kościuszko, but only half could identify Piłsudski, despite his recent exploits. Yet all knew Lincoln, Washington, and a quintessentially American cultural hero, Babe Ruth. When young female workers at a heavily Polish Brooklyn sugar refinery went on strike in 1921, they did not walk out singing the Polish national anthem or peasant folk songs, but rather popular jazz numbers.[12] Without a doubt, Polonia's youth stood astride a dual cultural world whose Polish part seemed steadily shrinking and American part steadily growing.

What did the young Poles consider themselves? Of the Buffalo Poles studied, more considered themselves full-fledged Americans (53.6%) than either "Polish-Americans" (11.8%), "American Poles" (26.8%), or just plain "Poles" (7.8%). Some of these young Poles felt "angry" at their parents' "stubborn Polishness," their refusing to "Americanize."[13] In conflict with their children over how much the latter should contribute to the household economy, over whom they would marry, and over what kind of work they would do, many older Polish immigrants in turn believed that in this "crazy America" they were "losing" their young.[14]

While ordinary immigrant Poles may only have fretted and complained, America's Polish leaders tried to dam the assimilationist currents that threatened to sweep off Polonia's youth. In the 1920s, under Bishop Rhode's lead, Polish Roman Catholic priests doggedly defended the use of Polish in their parochial schools, tried to foster the "Polish spirit" among immigrant youth, and urged them to enroll in Polish-American organizations. Later, Rev. Justyn Figas of Buffalo took to the airwaves to keep Poles within the ethnic, Roman Catholic fold. Begun in 1931, "Father Justyn's Rosary Hour" eventually was syndicated nationally and heard on over fifty radio stations. Yet the most important Church-related barrier to the "loss" of immigrant youth was not nearly so "modern." It was the parochial school system.

Begun in the late 1860s, the Polish immigrant parochial education system at first consisted of a motley group of instructors—church organists, lay teachers, and occasionally priests—a handful of pupils, and rude little schoolrooms that sometimes doubled as churches. Soon enterprising pastors invited Polish female religious congregations, newly formed in Poland, to furnish teaching nuns for their parish schools. Between the late 1860s and early 1900s, the Sisters of St. Felix (or Felicians), the Sisters of the Holy Family of Nazareth, and almost a dozen other groups of Polish nuns established convent houses in America. While the sisterhoods gave young working-class Polish immigrant women an avenue to professional advancement unavailable to them in secular life, they had an even more profound impact on generations of Polonia's impressionable youth. Nuns inculcated in their students virtues prized by Church leaders and immigrant parents—loyalty to family and community, obedience to authority, Marian devotion, prayer, humility, and respect.

The sweep of the Polish parochial education system was impressive. In 1921, 511 schools operating in Polish America's 762 parishes taught 219,711, roughly two-thirds, of Polonia's youth. These high attendance figures—70 percent in Chicago, 65 percent in Detroit, 60 percent in Milwaukee, and 40 percent in Philadelphia— understate the extent of the schools' reach, for most immigrant children attended parochial school classes for at least a few years while preparing for their first Holy Communion. Despite the undeniable fact that the school system formed a veritable bulwark against assimilation, some immigrant parents wondered which master, Church or Nation, parochial education ultimately served. Could it succeed in staying the erosion of Polish culture and loyalties if that were not its principal aim? One critic, cited in a 1924 study of Poles in Greater New York, accused parochial schools of "teaching children in a way that does not help them to become Americans but yet causes them to forget that they are Poles."[15] Another writer, describing the work of the Felicians, echoed this complaint. The nuns "desperately try to make the students forget their history, to be ashamed of being Polish, and of speaking Polish," this group historian charged. "And they succeed in making them feel empty, and angry, inside."[16] Secular Polish nationalists apparently believed that the real goal of parochial education was to promote Catholic loyalty rather than Polish identity, a familiar theme. Poles themselves admitted—and regretted—the general overcrowding that characterized the "cramped, poorly ventilated classrooms" where Polish children were "packed like herrings in a barrel. . . ."[17] American educators levelled other charges. Citing the chronic shortage of teachers in parochial schools, the poor training of their faculties, and the heavy religious content in their curriculum, critics suggested that parochial education left immigrant youth relatively ill equipped to meet the competitive challenges of the highly individualistic American environment precisely because it fostered community loyalty and family ties.

Dissatisfied with efforts of Polish priests and nuns to retain the cultural loyalties of Polish youth, middle-class lay leaders—and the occasional Polish socialist—tried to preserve a secular *Polskość*—the elusive, ephemeral "Polishness" of language, values, loyalties, and culture—which little by little was slipping away. Cleveland's left-wing *Wiadomości Codzienne* (Daily News) believed that only the boldest measures closing the physical gulf separating young American Poles from their ancestral homeland could arrest Polonia's cultural erosion. "We must retain our identity as Poles," the newspaper urged its readers, "by sending our children to Poland to study and to marry. . . ."[18] Most Polish-American leaders reckoned this proposed solution either inconvenient, impractical, or, after Piłsudski's rise to power, ideologically unpalatable and tried for less heroic measures nearer to home. To complement—and sometimes replace—Polish parochial schools, laymen established Saturday "Polish schools" that reinforced secular Polish culture and Polish nationalist ideology among the immigrant young. The middle-class leaders of the Polish Women's Alliance directed their energies to the education of Polish women and children. Immigrant leaders also encouraged youth-oriented recreational activities like Polish youth associations, Polish libraries, and Polish drama circles; and the editors of Polish-language newspapers began publishing columns in English in order to interest young Americanized Poles in the affairs of their own communities. Some Polish leaders seemed to feel that Polonia's youth was slipping away in large measure because Polonia's parents had grown too casual about adhering to and passing on Polish customs. If this were true, efforts at cultural preservation needed to be spread farther afield.

Groups like Chicago's Polish-American Tatra Society (later the Polish Highlanders Alliance in America) attempted to revive a piece of southern Poland's highlander (*góral*) cultural past. Such attempts at resuscitating Polish popular culture were not as common as efforts to promote Polish high culture. Two important national cultural bodies arose. In 1925, the Kosciuszko Foundation was founded in New York City by Stephen Mizwa, an "immigrant Horatio Alger" who had arrived in the United States in 1910. Mizwa had first worked peeling potatoes, washing dishes, and beating rugs; later took a bachelor of arts degree at Amherst College and a master's degree at Harvard; and by 1924 had won a teaching position at Drake University in Des Moines, Iowa. Under the stewardship of Miecislaus Haiman, the don of Polish-American historians, other Poles formed the PRCU's Polish Museum and Archive in Chicago in 1935. Trying to enhance the position of Polish-Americans in the United States, both organizations supported scholarship in Polish studies and publicized Polish achievements. The Kosciuszko Foundation also tried to foster better cultural relations between the United States and Poland. Institutions like the PNA-sponsored Alliance College, founded in 1912 in Cambridge Springs, Pennsylvania, organizations like the Polish Medical and Dental Association (1928), and the myriad local Polish bakers' associations, grocers' associations, business groups, and Polish chambers of commerce that cropped up in the 1920s helped make it easier to be both upwardly mobile and still a Pole. Through self-help activities and political lobbying, business associations especially bolstered Polonia's general economic and political interests in America.

Middle-class and second-generation Polonians, groping after social status by trying to redefine what it meant to be a Pole in America, formed groups like the Polish Arts Club of Chicago (1926), the Milwaukee Polish Fine Arts Club (1930), and similar societies in Buffalo; Cleveland; Detroit; Minneapolis; Newark, New Jersey; Scranton, Pennsylvania; South Bend, Indiana; Youngstown, Ohio; and elsewhere. These clubs and societies scorned peasant folk culture and its working-class Polish-American variants. Instead they extolled the cultural accomplishments of Poland's intellectuals, clergy, and gentry. In the style of the Daughters of the American Revolution they commemorated immigrant achievements of antiquarian and patriotic interest. Not surprisingly, the Poles who organized all of these groups did not halt the erosion of Polonia's living cultural legacy of language, values, and customs—they never tried. Instead, by associating themselves with Poland's upper-class past, they merely underscored the division between working-class Poles and the immigrant elite that had become pronounced during the preceding decade.

Even if Polonia's middle-class and clerical leaders had pumped their energies into preserving immigrant popular culture they could not have succeeded because the cause of Polonia's cultural erosion lay beyond their control. Cultural contact with native-born American society per se was not endangering Polonia's cultural survival. Rather, developments in the American economy were integrating Poles into the larger American society and breaking down their own insular walls. In the 1920s, upward occupational mobility pulled only a few Poles out of their working-class enclaves. Middle-class nativists typically tore up applications of job-seekers whose last names ended in "ski." Some young Poles probably resigned themselves to having no chance of professional employment because they had a "funny name."[19] But if Poles did not—or could not—leave their communities to lose themselves in the American economy, that economy steadily seeped in on them. In the late 1920s, for example, 26 percent of the American-born Poles surveyed in a Buffalo study owned automobiles. In 1930, 26 percent of the families in the heavily Polish town of Hamtramck, Michigan, already owned radios; ten years later, fully 90 percent did. Poles succumbed to the advertisements and consumed many of the products that the ingenuity and productivity of American capitalism incessantly churned out—as did other immigrant groups and native-born Americans. This occurred no matter where they lived. In 1930, fully 6.5 percent of America's foreign-born population of Polish mother-tongue still practiced farm occupations, while another 10.5 percent lived in rural areas working in nonfarm callings. These Poles experienced the pull of assimilation, but at a somewhat slower pace than the urban rate.

To survive as a distinct cultural community Polonia had to remain socially and economically isolated during America's prosperous 1920s—an impossibility. If not, all the efforts that middle-class Poles and their priests would make to preserve immigrant culture, even those that aimed at a working-class audience, inevitably would falter. Events accomplished what Polonia's leaders had failed to do since the end of the World War. After the stockmarket crash of 1929 touched off America's Great Depression, Polish-American working people came face-to-face with America's crisis: factories closed, wages were slashed, hours were cut back, and there were—in their own words— the "big layoffs of 1931, 1932, and 1933," "long lines," and "no work."[20] Cut off from the homogenizing influences of a consumption society, Poles once again clung to their cultural forms. Blocked from occupational mobility, an entire generation of Polonia remained within the immigrant enclave for lack of anyplace else to go. Beseiged by economic crisis, average Polish working people defended a way of

life that prosperity and prosperity-induced assimilation had threatened, that economic collapse seemed about to overwhelm.

Like the other 13 to 16 million Americans (25 to 30 percent of the
workforce) who found themselves jobless in 1933, the trough of the
Depression, Poles showed all the signs of dire social distress—
mortgage foreclosures, a revival of the institution of boarding, increasing incidence of divorce and desertion, a rising rate of
alcoholism, the occasional suicide. Even before their arrival in America Polish-Americans had not been strangers to recurrent economic
hardship. They may, therefore, have been better equipped to handle
it than other, longer established ethnic groups. In order to blunt the
effects of the sudden economic crisis, Polish-American families once
again became more a unit of production and less one of consumption.
Their members—like most American citizens—cut corners, stretched
pennies, and tried to get by as they had done in previous slack times.
Seeking scapegoats for the inexplicable plight in which they found
themselves, some embittered native-born Americans believed that
"nogood" foreigners, like the Poles, lived off relief and government
handouts while hanging on to scarce jobs in the depressed economy,
jobs that could otherwise have gone to *real* American working people.[21] In short, they blamed their fellow victims. Some Poles did accept relief—over half of the Polish families in Hamtramck, Michigan,
received public welfare in 1932. But, as they tell it in the 1980s, most
Polish-Americans tried their hardest to stay off the relief rolls. True
to their peasant heritage, Polish-Americans prized self-reliance, independence, and hard work. They found it difficult to take "something for nothing" and were suspicious of the invisible strings that
might be attached to the "free lunch." Yet it was because of their habits of frugality and thrift, also peasant traits, that Polish-Americans
may have had a cushion of savings that allowed them to escape reliance on the public dole. The Poles' persistent pattern of family and
community cohesiveness, recreated by the needs of working-class
life, allowed them to get by—at least at first—by relying upon themselves.

Polish-Americans turned to their own institutions to try to break
their sudden economic fall. The most destitute Polish-American families got help from organizations like the parish-based St. Vincent de
Paul Society, which paid out small sums in the 1930s in order to help
the very poor. Average Polish-American families swallowed their
pride and looked to their neighborhood Polish grocer, haberdasher,
and butcher for long-term credit—again and again. But as the Depression deepened, sometimes this source of assistance simply dried
up. At one New York gas station, for example, the list of unpaid accounts could grow only so long before the good-hearted Polish small-
businessman—beset by his own debts—had to shut off the credit

spigot and himself give up the ghost.[22] Like this one New York Pole, many marginal, chronically under-capitalized small proprietors were forced back into the working-class world.

Because of the tenuous state of institutional sources of assistance, most Polish-American families had to rely upon the resourcefulness of their members to pull them through. As Polish husbands lost their jobs, for example, married Polish women with children went out to work for the first time—perhaps cleaning offices—in order to pick up the slack. At home, after improvising their livelihood, Polish women and their families pieced together the bare necessities. They made their own clothes and raised some of their own food—vegetables, a few chickens, maybe some ducks or rabbits. They sometimes tried more precarious ways of shoring up the families' finances. "We even tried to make moonshine," one Polish woman from Pennsylvania reminisced nearly fifty years later. "We sold a couple of quarts and got a little money that way."[23] Immigrant sons and daughters contributed their share. In one New Jersey factory town, for example, streetwise Polish youths stole loose coal from railroad flatcars and dragged home railroad ties for their families' heating fuel.[24]

The Depression was perhaps toughest on these young Polish-Americans. Whether they harbored dreams of "improving themselves" or whether they had just wanted to consolidate the economic foothold that their immigrant parents' hard work and sacrifice had won for them in America, all saw opportunity shrink and horizons narrow as the economy rolled back. One young Connecticut Pole, while still in high school, realized that the local brass mill would be his "college" and in 1936 took a job as a typist in the superintendent's office.[25] Others fared less well than he. A Polish-American woman in New Jersey lacked enough money for a high school graduation dress,[26] while a Pittsburgh youth had to borrow a pair of pants and a graduation coat. They were among the lucky ones; they finished school. Others had to drop out. In the words of one Nanticoke, Pennsylvania, Polish woman, "If you didn't have the money, you just didn't go to school." Another Philadelphia woman left school in 1936 and went to work because "things were rough at home." As she recalled, "I had no choice."[27] Economic catastrophe nipped the possibility of upward mobility in the bud for these young Poles and forced them back into the ethnic enclave, the familiar workers' world. Yet in reinforcing the bonds of mutual dependence and a reliance upon family and community ties, the Depression also strangely served to buttress and strengthen America's Polonia. Paradoxically, it gave back their young.

In honoring the duties of family and the ties of neighborhood and community, young Polish-Americans showed that, despite all appearances, they were their parents' children. They were still very much

Poles. It was often their willing sacrifices that pulled immigrant families through hard times, perhaps allowed them to stave off mortgage
foreclosure and hang onto the symbol of quiet, modest success for
which they had worked so hard—their own little house and its small
city lot. Yet these Polish immigrants and their children found that,
however heroic, their individual efforts to counteract the effects of
general economic collapse were not enough to turn the situation
around. As they had done during the Polish nationalist movement,
Poles looked to organized activity as a more effective response to the
Depression than individual heroism ever could be. They mobilized
familiar loyalties—organizational, ethnic, and community—and
sometimes joined with neighbors, friends, and fellow workers from
outside the ethnic fold.

As they had done in times past, for example, Polonia's better educated, small-propertied elite stepped to the fore and organized an assortment of ethnic self-help activities to buttress their own economic
position and brace the interests of the Polish settlements in which
they lived. On the northwest side of Chicago, Polish-American homeowners, threatened with the loss of their property, joined with
Polish-American businessowners to form the United Home Owners of
Illinois in 1933. Basically a taxpayers' lobby, the United Home Owners fought against foreclosures and campaigned for mortgage aid.
Polish-Americans also organized by profession and trade. In 1931,
Polish-American lawyers, a profession hit especially hard by the Depression, formed the Polish Lawyers' Association. Similarly, Polish-
American businessowners joined forces against adversity—the
economic downturn combined with the problems of trying to keep a
small business afloat in the face of murderous department and chain-
store competition. In 1936, they organized the Federated Merchants'
Organization of America, which disseminated business advice and
published *Przewodnik Kupiecki* (The Merchants' Guide), its monthly
journal. Some Polish-Americans directed their energies toward more
altruistic ends. In 1937, Detroit social worker Clara Swieczkowska
chartered the Polish League of Social Activities in the USA and won
election as its first president.

The efforts of Polish-American small-property holders were aimed
at conserving the stake they had won in American society. Polish
working people—especially second-generation Poles—mounted
their own campaigns, often fundamentally conservative, during the
turbulent Depression decade. In trying to protect their families and
their community, for the first time working-class Poles took the lead
in fighting to preserve Polonia's cultural world. Yet because the values they defended flew in the face of existing power arrangements in
the American economy and society, in the 1930s these Polish-
Americans—and other native-born and immigrant working people—

were promoting social change whether they realized it or not. Ironically, they too were being transformed—transforming themselves—in terms of their identity and in terms of how they lived their lives.

The Depression continued to wreak havoc on ethnic working-class households. In July 1935, Mary Zuk, the 31-year-old daughter of a Polish-American coalminer, led a group of outraged Hamtramck, Michigan, women in picketing the meat markets of the heavily Polish city. Their aim: a 20 percent roll-back in extortionate meat prices. Middle-class Poles criticized Zuk and local officials branded her a "Communist,"[28] a charge she vehemently denied. In the 1930s, Polish-Americans like Mary Zuk were not afraid to say that traditional values like economic justice, human dignity, and the notion of a "just price" were better than the American way of avarice and greed, which had aggravated their families' plight. Promising, in the words of Mrs. Zuk, "to win the fight on meat and go on to the other necessities of life,"[29] these Polish-Americans became "radical" because they wanted to humanize the American capitalist economy in which they found themselves.

Try as they might, irate Polish-American consumers and homeowners did not remake their world; their protests were simply too spontaneous, too small, and too short-lived. When Polish-American working people—with the other American workers who had kept their jobs—shifted their efforts away from the neighborhood and began to fight for rights in the workplace, however, they did alter American society profoundly. Immigrants had waged industrial protests before, between the 1880s and the 1910s, but things were different in the 1930s. Second-generation Poles had a greater stake than their parents in America's factories. They had the self-confidence of full-fledged Americans, and the savvy of second-generation industrial workers. They also finally acquired the legal right to organize, guaranteed them by the National Labor Relations Act of 1935. Thus armed, by 1937 the sons and daughters of immigrants had created modern American industrial unionism.

It is no exaggeration to claim that Poles in Detroit, Chicago, eastern Pennsylvania, and elsewhere played a central role in sparking the wave of union-organizing activity that virtually remade industrial America between the early 1930s and the early 1940s. Of course, there is the gripping, though caricatured, image in *Black Fury*, the 1935 Paul Muni film portrayal of Joe Radek, Polish coalminer, sputtering and stammering in broken, drunken English as he became a strike hero after barricading himself in and threatening to blow up the company mine. Real Polish-American working people in the 1930s were not as crude, innocent, or inarticulate as this movie parody. Poles figured prominently among the men and women who sweated blood to organize the "unorganizable." Leo Krzycki, Milwaukee socialist, "torrential orator," and clothing worker organizer, branded America's sweatshops "social cesspools" and threw himself into organizing their hapless victims, many of whom were young Polish women and girls.[30] Through his efforts, and the efforts of others like him, in 1933 the Amalgamated Clothing Workers of America gained 50,000 new members. In Detroit, organizer Stanley Nowak broke his ankle after jumping out of the second-storey window of a cigar factory he was helping to organize, steps ahead of invading police. A member of Detroit's Polish Auto Workers Organizing Committee, Nowak later won election to the Michigan state senate and supported the 1941 drive to unionize the Ford Rouge plant, where a young Pole named Joe York (Jurkiewicz) had been killed nine years earlier during the famed Ford Hunger March. Al Malicki and Stella Nowicki in the meat packing industry, BolesJaw (Bill) Gebert in the Pennsylvania steel mills, Valeria Wojcik in the Detroit cigar industry, and probably a dozen other Polish organizers helped launch local or regional union drives. Yet is was the thousands of anonymous Polish working people—like those among the 10,000 Hamtramck, Michigan, sit-down strikers whose victory at Dodge Main helped cement the fortunes of the United Automobile Workers Union—who deserve the most credit for making places like Pittsburgh and Chicago, South Bend and Detroit into solid union towns. Because of their sacrifices, automobile, coal, rubber, steel, and electrical industry unions were organized and, in 1938, federated into the powerful Congress of Industrial Organizations—the CIO. By the end of the Second World War, the CIO boasted over 6 million members, about 600,000 of whom were Poles. Of those who joined during the heroic 1935–1937 period, however, fully 25 percent were Poles or other Slavs.

Ethnic workers turned to industrial unionism to protect their imperiled communities and used ethnic institutions to get their union-organizing drives off the ground. Fraternal members by night, workers by day, Polish strikers often met at ethnic fraternal lodges and drew upon their societies' moral and material aid. During the bitter Ford strike in 1941, for example, presidents of the Polish Women's Alliance of Michigan, a Polish Roman Catholic Union chapter, and several Polish National Alliance groups lent moral support to their striking fellow Poles by signing a fiery manifesto that pointed to the well-known links between Adolf Hitler and Henry Ford. While ethnicity tended to reinforce unionism in the 1930s and vice versa, the union message itself urged Polish-Americans and other ethnic working people to transcend parochial ethnic loyalties for the common good. There was no such thing as Irish coal or Polish coal or Negro coal—just coal, United Mine Workers president John Mitchell once remarked. And, as the CIO showed, there were no such people as Irish workers or Polish workers or Black workers. Ethnic Americans concurred: they were all just plain workers. Regardless of the color of their skin or the accent of their speech, they were all human beings, fighting for basic human rights.

The fight that Polish consumers, homeowners, workers, and small-business people waged in their neighborhoods was carried to America's polling booths. Fast becoming naturalized citizens with American-born children approaching voting age, by 1928 Polish-Americans had already shifted toward the Democratic party and Governor Al Smith of New York's Tammany machine, an anti-Prohibition Democrat, a Roman Catholic, and the party's presidential standard-bearer. In Chicago, for example, Smith carried 80 percent of the Polish vote. When the Democratic party nominated Franklin D. Roosevelt for president in 1932 as the champion of the "forgotten man," Polish Americans remembered to vote their conscience and made what was not to them merely a pragmatic political choice on cultural issues but also a moral endorsement of economic reform. Rejecting the dour Republican engineer, Herbert Hoover, they gave their hearts to the patrician New Yorker with the warm, winning grin who promised them compassion and a future. They became part of the liberal New Deal coalition of urban machine voters, organized labor, Southern Democrats, other "new" immigrants, and (after 1936) Black Americans that catapulted the Democratic Roosevelt into the White House, captured Congress, and marked 1932 as a year of a major realigning election, a political watershed.

For their support as a group, Polish-Americans received political rewards through the Democratic party. These reinforced intraethnic ties. In 1933, for example, Democratic Polish-Americans in Chicago formed the Polish American Democratic Organization (PADO), which campaigned for FDR and pushed for local party favors. In return for delivering Chicago's Polish-American ballots to Roosevelt, Matt Szymczak, city controller in the administration of Chicago Mayor Anton Cermak and PADO's founder, won appointment to the Federal Reserve Board of Governors in 1933. Elsewhere Poles replayed the political bargain struck in Chicago. In Detroit, Polish-American Democrats received congressional nominations from their party in recognition of the whopping 90 to 94 percent majorities that Polish areas forked over to Roosevelt there. In Milwaukee, too, Polish-Americans traded support for political preferment. Even where immediate rewards were not forthcoming, group ties often held. When, for example, Manhattan Polish Democrats withheld their electoral support from Democratic Governor Lehman in 1938 because "too few Americans of Polish extraction received State or Federal jobs," Brooklyn Poles remained faithful. The Brooklyn Polish

Democrats' reasoning was simple: "Just because we get only a little piece of the pie, that doesn't mean that we ought to stab mamma in the back."[31]

Coming from tightly-knit working-class communities criss-crossed by mutual dependencies of kinship, friendship, and clientage, ethnic voters implicitly understood the principles of political loyalty, obligation, and patronage that underpinned the Democratic party. These new rank-and-file ethnic voters remained true to FDR's party because it gave them something historically more significant—and perhaps more gratifying—than a few political pay-offs. Poles—and other ethnic Americans—won recognition as a group from the Democratic party, which, for the first time in modern American history, made being ethnic a respectable thing in the eyes of their fellow Americans. At their prodding, the Democratic party thus institutionalized ethnicity in American politics and gave ethnic communities like Polonia a powerful new rationale for sticking together.

Industrial America's sudden economic collapse ended prosperity and derailed the assimilation—the economic integration—process. It also forced working-class Polish-Americans, through time-honored family survival strategies, protest, organizing, and politics, to defend their communities and their culture. What they preserved, though, was different from that with which they had started. However much they still looked like the immigrant families of the preceding generation, the Polish-American families of the 1930s—and the men, women, and children who made them up—were no longer *Polish* or *peasant* families as the immigrant families of a decade ago had been. What were they?

Polonia's leaders had claimed that immigrant Poles and their children were "Polish-American" while at the same time fearing that their "Polish half" was on the wane. The real Polish-American working people who survived the Great Depression demonstrated that something had happened to them, but not what their leaders had alternately praised and criticized. They showed that assimilation no longer meant mixing of two inert substances; adding a little "American culture," removing a little "Polish culture," laying on a "Polish-American" veneer of loyalty, citizenship, and identity. As the Depression pressurized their settlements, forcing them to hold closely together once again, assimilation proved to be a kind of crucible in which the elements—American, Polish, Polish-American—fused together or reacted dynamically with each other, with their surroundings, and with the events of a difficult decade. It was like a chemical reaction out of whose smoke, flash, and heat a new alloy was born.

Out of the flesh-and-blood lives that they had made for themselves in America, the aging immigrants and their growing sons and daugh-

ters were forging a new cultural synthesis. They fused cultural practices and forms brought over from the "old country" with a raft of
Americanisms that had come into their daily lives, like Democratic
voting patterns or American recreations such as baseball and pool.
The Polish-Americans added to these other values and attitudes,
practices and beliefs that they had improvised in America. Some of
these inventions and adaptations were entirely their own and all
new—like Polonized English words or the trade union solidarity that
grew out of their ethnic fraternals. Others looked like Polish peasant
virtues—thrift, hard work, and family cohesiveness—but had been
refreshed and renewed by the obstacles and challenges of American
working-class life: they had recreated these in America. They added
to this the assorted values and loyalties that had come out of the past
as well as the present—love for God and *two* countries; for neighborhood, parish, and family; clubs, fraternals, and CIO union locals; for
the Democratic party and FDR. By the 1930s, "Polish-American" was
no longer just a hyphenate identity, a makeshift ideology, or a set of
dual loyalties, as it had been in the early 1920s, but an ethnic way of
life.

While their way of life was particular to Polish-Americans, in another sense it was far from unique. Polish-Americans were neither
alone in the way they had fashioned their social and cultural world in
the 1930s nor in the way that the wider world affected them. The
Polish-Americans' *ethnic* way of life was also a *class* way of life, one
shared in large measure by people who performed the same kinds of
jobs and belonged to the same economic stratum, regardless of their
ethnic background. In their day-to-day existence, ethnic working-
class people—whether of Polish or Italian or Hungarian or Ukrainian
extraction—had come to have more in common with one another
than with ethnic professionals and entrepreneurs who often spoke for
their fellow ethnics but lived differently from them. Though they
may have eaten different foods and said different prayers, though
their associational patterns and their family structures may have varied, working-class Americans of all ethnic groups had come to share
the cultural values and practices that comprised the wider, blue-
collar world.

The "assimilation" of working-class Polish-Americans in the 1930s,
if it should be called that, was an ethnic variation of a larger working-
class social and cultural pattern born of shared union struggles, political fights, and living and working conditions. More self-assured and
assertive, less tradition-bound, their ethnic variation had virtually
nothing to do with Poland any more. The Polish-Americans' way of
life was "made in America," just as the coal that they mined or the
steel ingots that they rolled.

In the next two decades, Polish-Americans, as they married one another and stayed in their urban working-class communities, would perpetuate this ethnic working-class way of life, complete in its broad outlines, by passing it on to their youngsters. As it passed on, their way of life took on a kind of life of its own. As fixed and complete as it may have seemed by the late 1930s, events were still molding the Polish-Americans' way of life just as Polish-Americans were still shaping and bending themselves. As the picture of the forlorn Hallerczycy adrift between two worlds had faded into photographs of grim-faced, sit-down strikers who were making—and making peace with—an American blue-collar world of their own, yet-to-be-taken portraits in Polish-American family albums would soon show how they continued to change. The snap-shot images of three or four generations posed together were sharp and crisp. But they hid the fact that the Polish-American "community," identity, and "traditional" ethnicity had all started to fade measurably. No-longer-young second-generation Polish-Americans, who once had wanted so much to "fit in," would soon mourn what fitting in had meant in modern America. They knew the gains they had made were great. So were the costs.

5

THE DECLINE OF THE URBAN ETHNIC ENCLAVE

Polish America Transformed, WW II–Present

> The inhabitants of these [Polish] areas real-
> ize that even with financial considerations
> aside, they can never recreate their "vil-
> lage" in the sterile suburbs. . . . It is one of
> the reasons why resistance to the Blacks
> has been so strong and angry. They repre-
> sent the spearhead of the outside world
> which threatens to destroy the community.
>
> —Thaddeus Radzialowski, "The
> View From a Polish Ghetto:
> Some Observations on the
> First One Hundred Years
> in Detroit" (1974)

Just as immigrants in America's Polish enclaves had found that they could not turn the clock back to a faraway village world, the working-class Polish-Americans, who had forged their own ethnic blue-collar way of life, discovered they could not make time stand still. On September 1, 1939, America's Poles heard news on their radios that ended Polonia's brief respite of stability and insularity: Nazi armies had invaded Poland from the west. Two weeks later, Soviet forces would overrun its eastern borders. The reports that followed in the next three weeks left Polish-Americans little hope. The Luftwaffe easily dominated Poland's skies. The German Panzer divisions' 2,600 tanks faced only 150 Polish tanks and, in many places, only lightly armed infantry and cavalry. On September 27, a bombed-out Warsaw

Map 3. Partition of Poland, 1939.

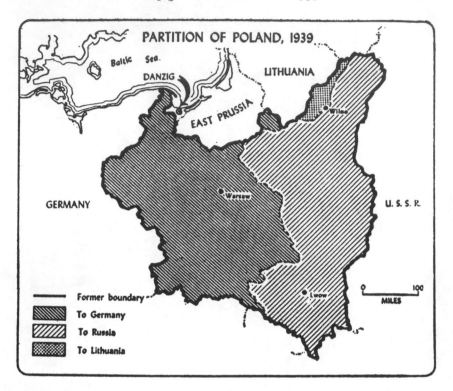

Source: J. A. Wytrwal, *America's Polish Heritage: A Social History of the Poles in America* (Detroit: Endurance Press, 1961), p. 264.

fell. The next day, Poland's conquerers chopped the defeated country into two parts. Thus began the Second World War. (See Map 3.)

For twenty years, Polish-American leaders may have wondered whether the rebirth of Poland had begun Polonia's demise. As they looked at America's Jews and Ukrainians—and Black Americans too —they could see how much strength and vitality ethnic communities could draw from political causes like Zionism, nationalism, or civil rights that had yet to reach their aim. If Polish-Americans needed the cause of Polish freedom to keep their own communities and identity alive in America, they now had that cause back again. While the war briefly revived Polish identity and gave the Polish-Americans a rallying point, it also touched off a chain of events that resumed the process of economic integration and assimilation that had been interrupted during the depressed 1930s. In the end, many Polish-Americans probably felt that the wartime and postwar developments had made many of Polonia's urban neighborhoods similar to Poland's devastated towns and cities—depopulated and sometimes destroyed. With the dispersal of residents and the physical decline of Polish areas, Polish-Americans had to ask themselves, could their culture and identity long survive?

Questions about Poland's survival preoccupied Polish-Americans in late 1939 in a way they had not since the Treaty of Versailles restored Poland to the map of Europe. They turned out again in public displays, made speeches, and marched in parades, all reminiscent of the immigrant generation's Polish nationalist ferment, but not as intense. Even though most second-generation Polish-Americans had never been to Poland, the 1939 Pulaski Day parade in New York City gave vivid proof that the umbilical cord tying Polish-Americans to *Matka Polska,* their motherland, though frayed, was not cut. As 100,000 tearful marchers clogged the Fifth Avenue parade route, 15,000 parade goers listened as former President Herbert Hoover told them something they already knew. "The spirit of a great race does not die from oppression," Hoover told the crowd. "Poland is not dead. Poland will rise again."[1]

Organized Polonia rose up in response to Poland's crisis. The Polish-American press—consisting of ten dailies, forty-eight weeklies, and forty-five other newspapers that had survived the Depression—deplored the dismemberment of Poland, requested relief contributions, and called for the country's rescue in editorials and editorial cartoons. Roman Catholic and secular newspapers alike appealed through a religious idiom—a characteristically Polish Marianism—to mobilize Polish-American sentiment. In a cartoon that appeared in a Brooklyn Polish-language newspaper in November 1939, for example, a thorn-crowned, shackled woman, dressed in royal robes that bore the Polish coat of arms, grieved beside a thorn-framed visionary panorama of a war-devastated Polish countryside.[2] Another political cartoon of the period showed a blood-stained sword plunged into the smoking ruins of a Polish city. A peasant woman, labeled "Poland," hung from the hilt of the sword: the woman had been crucified.[3] Polonia's moribund societies, associations, and insurance fraternals also came to Poland's aid and, in the process, gained new life. In 1939, Polish-Americans formed the Polish American Council to coordinate their war relief efforts and lend support to Poland's government-in-exile organized in Paris, then London, by General Władysław Sikorski. When the Japanese surprise attack on Pearl Harbor brought the United States into the war in December 1941, the Polish-Americans' cause received official sanction as well. In 1943, the Catholic League for Religious Assistance to Poland was formed and soon became a major relief organization. Meanwhile, through

their parishes and organizations Polish-Americans gave money, do-
nated blood, bought war bonds, rolled bandages, knitted sweaters,
collected newspapers and scrap iron, and marched in patriotic rallies
—all for the war effort.

Though this upsurge of interest in Poland would do little to make
the Polish-Americans' synthetic culture more Polish, it did revive
their Polish identity and political connections, which had lapsed in
the past two decades. Men and women, who a short time earlier were
referring to themselves as "Americans," now began to call themselves
"Americans *of Polish descent.*" America's Poles received an unex-
pected benefit from their assistance to Poland that, for a short time,
made owning up to their ethnic heritage easier than it had been in the
1920s. Polish valor in the face of the Nazi onslaught won America's
Poles new recognition and respect from their native-born fellow
Americans. For the time being, Poles were no longer the butt of cruel
slurs and rude nativist stereotypes. All of a sudden native-born Americans could find nothing funny to say about descendants of a people
who had sacrificed over 60,000 lives to stay the brutal Nazi menace,
even if only for twenty-seven bloody days. A 1942 Jack Benny movie,
a comedy/propaganda feature called *To Be or Not to Be,* showed ex-
actly what kind of American cultural ripples had been produced
when the martyred Poland went down to defeat. The tale of a comedy
troupe in occupied Warsaw, the film was replete with black humor,
but it was decidedly not anti-Polish. Contrary to existing stereotypes
of the "dumb and brutish Polack," the film showed sophisticated Polish
thespians outsmarting their clever Nazi overlords and, what is more,
living to boast about it. Nazis were not funny in this film, but Poles
could laugh at them nonetheless. What might this motion picture
have signified to Polish-American audiences? When put to the test, it
seemed to say, they could best the "Aryan supermen" in distant Poland—perhaps also in American neighborhoods.

The rise of Polish America's stock in America and the reinvigora-
tion of the Poles' communities did not win the group the kind of
dignified voice in American policy circles that its leaders felt they had
earned. Neither did it cement the ideological fractures that had divided Polonia since the rise of the leftwing Committee for National
Defense (KON) during the period of World War I.

As they mobilized Polish-Americans might have noticed that Poland's position deteriorated the more "allies" it acquired. In 1939, attacked from two sides, Poles at least knew who their enemies were. In
June 1941, however, after Hitler launched a surprise attack against his
erstwhile partner, the Soviet Union, the Great Russian bear pulled on
an Allied uniform—as the Poles had done two years earlier—and
joined the Allied camp. This caused pro-Soviet Polish-Americans to

worry more about the Nazi threat to the USSR than any threat the USSR may have posed toward Poland. To give voice to their concerns, Leo Krzycki, the Milwaukee socialist and labor organizer, in 1942 founded the pro-Soviet American Slav Congress. The following year, Krzycki joined with Rev. Stanislaus Orlemanski of Springfield, Massachusetts, and University of Chicago economist Oscar Lange to form the Kosciuszko Patriotic League in Detroit, another pro-Soviet body. Most Polish-Americans who remembered Soviet complicity in the Nazi attack on Poland in 1939, however, believed that the Russian bear was a wolf in disguise and that its new Allied combat dress was merely ill-fitting sheep's clothing.

At the instigation of New York *Nowy Świat* (New World) publisher Maximilian Węgrzynek, Polish-American leaders of a Polish nationalist bent resolved to counter Krzycki's pro-Soviet activities. They organized their own body, the National Committee of Americans of Polish Descent (KNAPP, after its Polish initials). KNAPP had one main intent: to oppose American cooperation with the Soviets vis-á-vis Poland.

Had KNAPP's concerns merely been a bout of ideologically motivated paranoia, Polish-Americans might have ignored what group leaders had to say. The bombshell dropped in April 1943, however, when Nazi propagandists revealed a shocking and sensational discovery in Poland's occupied eastern territory. Apparently, when the Russian army controlled the area in 1940, Soviet troops had executed several thousand captured Polish military officers and buried their bodies in a mass grave in the Katyn Forest. Though most Americans at the time were probably inclined to dismiss news of the discovery as "Nazi propaganda," word of the Katyn Massacre—which proved to be true—did not augur well for Poland. Poland's future, in fact, looked quite grim. Prime Minister Sikorski of the exiled London government had been killed in a plane crash off Gibraltar. With Soviet troops on the counterattack, Soviet leader Joseph Stalin had a free hand to install the pro-Soviet Lublin government in "liberated" eastern Poland. A short time later, Soviet armies halted their advance on the east bank of the Vistula, allowing the Nazis time to crush the uprising of the Polish underground in Warsaw and at once wipe out a potential source of postwar opposition to Soviet influence there. Significantly, Soviet authorities denied the United States permission to use Soviet airfields to rush aid to the insurgents. "When the Soviet Army finally advanced into the ruins on 17 January 1945," historian Norman Davies wrote, "a city which six years before had housed 1,289,000 inhabitants" had 93 percent of its dwellings destroyed or damaged beyond repair and "did not contain a living soul."[4] Soviet control was ratified in 1945 at the Yalta Conference. Sanctioning ter-

Map 4. Poland: Territorial Changes, 1939–1952.

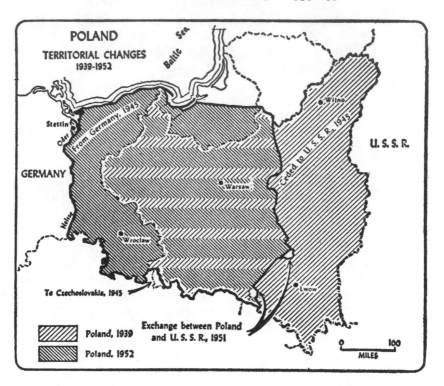

Source: J. A. Wytrwal, *America's Polish Heritage: A Social History of the Poles in North America* (Detroit: Endurance Press, 1961), p. 264.

ritorial spoils bitterly condemned only six year earlier, Roosevelt, Prime Minister Winston Churchill of Great Britain, and Stalin agreed to four points:

1. the USSR would retain the territory it had gained—about 70,000 square miles—as a result of its September 1939 invasion of Poland;

2. in compensation, Poland would receive about 40,000 square miles of land in the west from Germany (see Map 4);

3. the pro-Soviet Lublin government, once reorganized, would govern the liberated country during a postwar transition period; and

4. thereupon "free and open elections"[5] would take place in order

to establish postwar Poland's permanent government—a promise on which Stalin later reneged.

Ironically, Poland's new boundaries roughly overlapped those ethno-
graphically Polish lands that, before the First World War, the Polish
National Democratic (Endek) party had considered the logical basis
for a resurrected Polish state. In the west, however, the boundaries
did enclose territory that had been mostly German.

As more questions about Soviet intentions toward Poland arose,
and as the position of Polonia's pro-Soviet faction became less and less
tenable, in 1944 leaders of KNAPP, the American Slav Congress, Polonia's fraternals, and Polish-American political and civic associations
convened in Buffalo and, in a remarkable display of unity, established
the Polish American Congress (out of concern that their loyalty to
America would be impugned, they did not hyphenate the name). This
group, henceforth the "voice" of organized Polish America, lobbied
diligently against Allied cooperation with Stalin, obviously to little
effect. The Yalta agreement was signed by FDR's shaky hand just two
months before he died. Polish-Americans roundly condemned it as a
"betrayal," a "double-cross," and a "sell-out." Polish American Congress leaders bitterly denounced the pact—and would continue to do
so to the present day. Lawyer and Polish National Alliance head
Charles Rozmarek, in his capacity as president of the Congress, vocif-
erously blamed FDR, the State Department, and the Democratic
party for what he called "their tragic historic blunder." The "short-
sighted policy of appeasement," Rozmarek said, "is only paving the
way for world chaos." To a Wilkes-Barre, Pennsylvania, audience in
April 1948, Rozmarek went further still. There he urged "the threat
of the atomic bomb" as a means "to force Russia to remove her armies, puppet government and fifth column" from Poland.[6] One Hamtramck, Michigan, woman had a name for Polish-Americans who
could find something good to say about Yalta. She branded one such
man a Communist and a "traitor" to his Polish name.[7]

President Roosevelt may have worried about how his accommodation with the Russians would be seen by the 6 million Polish-
American voters in the United States. Yet Roosevelt also thought that
his political problems were being made thornier because Poles were
generically a "quarrelsome people . . . not only at home but also
abroad . . . ," "at home" meaning in the ethnic wards of places like
Detroit, Chicago, Buffalo, and Brooklyn.[8] With no Polish-Americans
holding seats in the Senate or prominent State Department posts
from which they could have influenced policy, Roosevelt therefore
bowed to what he considered larger and more basic concerns. The
president decided to trust Stalin and attempted to coax the Soviet
Union into what still promised to be a protracted, costly fight to sub-

due the Japanese. Clearly, the Yalta agreement responded to political and military exigencies. The principal difficulty thus was not with the agreement, but—to quote historian Henry Steele Commager—with its "flagrant violation" after the war.[9] The United States was neither in a military position in 1945 to determine what happened east of the Curzon Line—in the Polish lands that the Yalta agreement transferred to the USSR—nor in a political position to enforce democratic practices in Soviet-occupied postwar Poland. By 1945, the American people—Polish-Americans included—had had their fill of war.

As Polish-Americans continued to support Poland's exiled London government in the years after the war, they grew more stridently anti-Russian and anti-Soviet. Their homeland a Soviet "satellite," ideologically they came to resemble the descendants of Eastern Europe's other "captive nations"—the Latvians, Estonians, Lithuanians, and Ukrainians. Unlike these countries, Poland remained at least nominally free. A growing anti-communist sentiment caused Polish-Americans to recoil from the intermittent radicalism of the Depression years and reach a political turning point that would have important repercussions for the Democratic party, which so many of them had joined. Though still wedded to New Deal liberalism on economic and social issues, Polish-Americans had become—in the words of the Polish American Congress—"shock troops of democracy" in the incipient Cold War.[10]

The outbreak of World War II in 1939 recast Polish-American ideology and identity—at least for a time—changed the social composition of its only recently self-contained enclaves, and revised its organizational life. A generation of Polish intellectuals—many of them Jewish—sought refuge in the United States, for example, and imposed upon Polonia an internationally renowned, Polish-born intelligentsia not steeped in Polish-American political battles nor in Polish-American social and cultural life. Oscar Halecki and other exiled members of the Polish Academy of Sciences in 1941 organized the Polish Institute of Arts and Sciences in America, in New York City. It aimed "to assemble, preserve, and harness for posterity the values of the [Polish] nation" and, with Poland overrun by the Nazis, "to represent Polish thought in the world."[11] Resembling the Kosciuszko Foundation, but for its émigré and more scholarly cast, the Polish Institute almost immediately organized a Commission for Research on Polish Immigration in 1942. Led in its early years by Miecislaus Haiman of the Polish Museum in Chicago and Rev. Joseph Swastek, after 1944 the Commission published its own journal, the then rather filiopietistic *Polish American Studies*, and eventually evolved into an independent body, the Polish American Historical Association, headquartered at the Polish Seminary in Orchard Lake, Michigan. Another result of Polish flight from the Nazis was the Józef Piłsudski

Institute of America for Research in the Modern History of Poland, established in New York City in 1943 by Polish émigrés and Polish-American sympathizers. Poland's exiled minister of education, Wacław Jędrzejewicz, served as its executive director.

The war did not exile only this handful of scholars, artists, and scientists. It uprooted thousands of other Polish refugees—some fled Nazi oppression; others, the Soviet "iron curtain" (Churchill's chilling phrase) that fell over postwar Eastern Europe. Poland's—and Europe's—"displaced persons" ran into the strict quotas on American immigration set in the 1920s. The Polish American Congress and KNAPP lobbied that they be eased and 151,978 persons born in Poland did enter the United States under assorted refugee legislative acts and presidential directives implemented between 1945 and 1953. This influx was relatively insignificant in numerical terms, amounting to only about 5 percent of the total Polish-American population or less.° These Polish newcomers did nonetheless exert a profound influence on Polish America's leadership, ideology, and social composition.

Because over a quarter of a million Poles had served in the wartime military (after the Americans and the British, the third largest contingent under Supreme Allied Command), at war's end many displaced persons were Polish veterans who had been released from Nazi concentration camps or Soviet prisons, denied permission to return to Poland by Stalinist authorities, or were simply in flight from Poland's new government. Between the end of the Second World War and 1968, about 40,000 Polish ex-servicemen and underground insurgents came to the United States. Some entered the existing Polish Army Veterans Association of America (*Stowarzyszenie Weteranów Armji Polskiej*, SWAP), which veterans of Haller's "Blue Army" had formed in 1921, or they joined older fraternals where some rose to positions of leadership. Others followed a pattern set by earlier waves of Polish immigrants and established their own organizations like the Polish Veterans of World War Two (*Stowarzyszenie Polskich Kombatantów*, SPK), formally organized in 1953 by Polish armed forces veterans, and the small but influential Polish Home Army Veterans Association (*Armia Krajowa*), composed of veterans of the Polish Underground Army. The refugee Poles in these groups, with members of the Polish Legion of American Veterans, USA, a body formed by Polish-American U.S. military veterans after the First World War, sharpened ideological lines in American Polonia. Still bitter about their experiences during the war—"deported to a Russian concentra-

°This figure, of course, does not include Polish Jews who survived the war and made it to the United States. With few exceptions, they did not become part of Polish America, but rather Jewish America—an obvious example of the ethnoreligious nature of group life here.

tion camp," "no food and very little water," "16 sleepless nights and days of interrogations," "hard labor . . . in all weather . . . -60 degrees centigrade," "Poland . . . sold out,"[12]—they deepened Polish-American anti-communism and became an important wing of the "Poland lobby."

Most Polish displaced persons, whether they were veterans or not, did not come to America to carry on political or ideological battles but to rebuild their own disrupted lives. Like most of America's political refugees, they migrated as families and intended to stay here; they had no place else to go. They consisted of adults in early middle age and occasional oldsters; about a third were infants, children, and teenagers, some of whom were orphans. Whether child or adult, all were settled with sponsor families—many of them not Polish—throughout America. As might be expected, they were concentrated most heavily in industrial states with large Polish-American populations: New York, New Jersey, Illinois, Connecticut, and Michigan.

Displaced children who came to America from Poland adjusted fairly well to their new life, although traumatized orphans were described by social caseworkers as "undisciplined, unstable, primitive, even bestial but longing for affection . . . precocious and hardened."[13] In many cases, adult refugees faced larger problems of transition and adjustment. Wrenching wartime experiences in prison camps, as forced laborers, and later in refugee centers had made them, according to one report, "*sensitive,* suspicious, and generally alert against real or imaginary threats to their dignity, security and welfare."[14] Despite the hardships and losses they had suffered, many also carried with them a painful sense of guilt. As one Polish refugee said, " . . . you shouldn't leave your native country in the moment of crisis."[15]

With scant information about the United States—and that gleaned from books, magazines, movies, letters, and American GIs—refugee Poles did not fit easily into American society. Because refugee immigration policy favored persons with agricultural backgrounds, many displaced Poles—most with urban backgrounds—lied in order to get into the United States. They soon found themselves placed in unsatisfying farm occupations for which they had no skills. On sugar plantations in southern Louisiana, some landowners preferred Polish displaced persons to Black workers because they needed "less supervision." The Poles, however, wanted their wages in cash and did not wish to work under exploitative sharecropping arrangements. As a result, employers criticized them for "expecting too much."[16] "Stirred up" by stories of wages elsewhere that were higher than the $3 to $4 they could earn a day, many left rural areas as soon as they were able.[17] About 40 percent of the displaced persons who had arrived in a Louisiana study area in the spring and summer of 1949 had left by about a year later. Heavily middle-class in background those refugee Poles who did make their way into better paying factory jobs, the only employment for which many were suited because they lacked English-language skills, now felt déclassé. Many of the displaced persons, according to one report, "came into this country with the idea that everybody is rich and that they could also become rich in a short time."[18] Some were probably trying to repair their sense of self-worth by giving voice to such ambitions. But it is little wonder that some Polish refugees acquired a distorted picture of life in the United States. The standard orientation program, through which all refugees passed, featured lectures that aimed to teach the newcomers that "no stigma attached to any form of honest physical labor here" by showing that "a modest start as a day laborer, clerk, farmhand, or factory worker" could bring "fortune and perhaps fame."[19]

Polish displaced persons with working-class, artisanal, and farming backgrounds integrated easily into blue-collar Polish America. Most refugees—largely middle-class in composition—fitted no better in Polonia than they did in mainstream American society. Many shunned the older Polish-American working-class urban enclaves and gravitated to the suburbs. The intelligentsia among them, though often forced into factory jobs, "did not know how to act like workers and did not want to learn," which is to say, they rejected working-class Polish-Americans' way of life. Older Polish-Americans—immigrants and their children—came to resent these Polish displaced persons, whom they derisively called "DPs." They felt jealous of the latter's superior education, higher social status, and greater chances for upward mobility and tried, through threats and ridicule, to "teach them how to work." They mockingly called them "princes," "barons," or "masters" for their middle-class dress, their educated speech, and their predilection for Polish military titles, a pretense reminiscent of a Polish aristocratic past that peasant immigrants had tried to escape. When the refugees attempted to speak for Polish America, older Polonians took offense because they expected to be followed, not led by the newcomers. When the refugees emphasized their "European superiority," older Polish-Americans called them "show-offs" or "ingrates."[20]

On their part, displaced Poles were not happy with what they found in Polonia or with the way the older Polish-Americans treated them. They resented being condescendingly called *"Biedaki,"* "poor souls," by people they thought worked "like peasants," were "completely uneducated," and "completely divorced from Polish culture." They expected to assume the traditional class roles that persons of their position had held in prewar Poland and were dismayed to find a "lack of respect for educated people" among Polish-Americans.[21] Like one former Polish officer, many well-educated Polish refugees

felt "shock" at the "poor" Polish spoken by Polish-Americans who retained peasant linguistic characteristics and made patois-like use of
American forms and words. Others were horrified that they did not
find what they expected in the United States. "[T]hese people are already *Americans*," one Polish actress who had settled in Chicago said.
[Italics added.][22]

The most significant effect of the 1940s was how the war touched
the lives of first- and second-generation Polish-Americans. The war
would begin the population dispersal and neighborhood decline that
would go on for the next forty years in Polish enclaves throughout
America. The Depression had extinguished the opportunities for mobility of young working-class, second-generation Polish-Americans
and stuffed them back into their ethnic enclaves. The mass mobilization associated with the Second World War had quite the opposite
effect. In all, fully 900,000 Polish-Americans served in the United
States armed forces during the war; never before had an entire generation of Polonia's youth been so wrenched up and spread about.
When they returned, they were not the same people who had left; it
was as though they were seeing their changing ethnic
neighborhoods—and the lives they had led there—through different
eyes.

The home of a typical second-generation Polish-American family
after the war would be unmistakably different from a Polish immigrant household of the mass migration years. The position that
women occupied in the household had changed dramatically in forty
years. Whereas an immigrant bride may have worked outside the
home for a time, after her first child she would have become a full-
time housewife, tending to household chores, taking care of the family's boarders, and managing the household accounts. The married
second-generation Polish-American woman may have entered the
workforce when her husband lost his job in the 1930s. She was even
more likely to have done so during the wartime mobilization, when
the conscription of male workers caused an acute wartime labor
shortage, which caused sex barriers in hiring to fall. Polish-American
women joined others to become like Rosie the Riveter of defense
plant fame. Significantly, they would hold onto these jobs after the
war whenever they could. When they could not, they would get
other jobs. By 1969, according to data assembled by economist
Thomas Sowell, working Polish-American women of all generations
clustered, by descending order of concentration, in clerical occupations (35.6%), operative jobs (19.2%), service work (15.5%), and professional and technical positions (13.1%).° Ten years later, according

°The remaining 16.6 percent fell into assorted categories: sales (8.5%), managers, officers, and proprietors (3.4%), private household workers (2.1%), farm foreman and
larborers (1.3%), craftsmen, foreman, and kindred workers (1.1%), laborers, except
mine and farm (.3%).

to a Census Bureau special study, *Ancestry and Language in the United States*, 49 percent of Polish-American women sixteen years of age or older were in the labor force, three percentage points below the national average but virtually identical to the figures for women in the Irish-American and Italian-American groups. The role of the traditional Polish-American woman had changed a lot.

Typical second-generation Polish-American males came home from the war to a world that differed from that of their immigrant forebears. Unlike their older brothers, who had found economic opportunity stunted during the Depression years, many young Polish-American men came into unprecedented chances for jobs and career mobility in the burgeoning postwar economy. Unlike upwardly mobile members of their parents' generation, however, they did not become small-scale proprietors whose economic options remained confined to serving an ever dwindling ethnic clientele—the classic "mobility trap." As a result of the general economic upswing—augmented by the GI Bill, which subsidized those who wished to continue their education—second-generation Polish-American males moved into white-collar occupations in greater numbers than ever before. Judging by the postwar employment experience of Pittsburgh's Poles, most of these jobs were low-level managerial positions in the industries that still employed large numbers of blue-collar Poles. Some men moved into mainstream nonmanual jobs that drew them outside the ethnic fold. By 1969, 24.4 percent of employed Polish-American males (of all generations) were craftsmen or foremen; 19.6 percent were operatives; 15.2 percent were managers, officers, or proprietors; and 14.5 percent were professional or technical workers.[23]

Having moved "up," many young, second-generation Polish-American men and women wanted to move "out." Learning how native-born Americans defined success and happiness, they grew displeased with the cramped, smoky city blocks where their immigrant parents lived in small, often decaying, old houses. Desiring a newer, cleaner, greener space in which to live and bring up children the war had postponed, they looked to the modern suburbs for a slice of the promised "good life" and, frankly, a chance to leave their sometimes embarrassing hyphenate ethnic past far behind.

In practical terms, those who moved out of the cities had a relatively easy time of it because the postwar period brought a suburban housing boom. The availability of federally financed home mortgages—a legacy of the New Deal—enabled average ethnic working-class families to afford the new suburban colonial, ranch, duplex, and split-level style homes that popped up like mushrooms after rain outside most American cities in the two decades following the war. Other second-generation Polish-Americans relocated for a more basic reason. Not only were working-class people leaving older cities in the postwar period; so were factories and their jobs. Corporate managers found their multistorey urban factories fast becoming obsolete. They sought suburban locations where rents were low or where land was cheap and they could build large, single-floor structures that would accommodate continuous-flow, assembly-line production. Industrialists—and atomic age strategic planners—may also have begun to see the wisdom of scattering industrial facilities outside of cities when they reviewed the damage that places like Dresden, Tokyo, and the Ruhr had suffered from conventional aerial bombing during the Second World War. Meanwhile, federal transportation policy under the Eisenhower administration used a new gasoline tax not to improve the passenger railroad system, which had served the central city, but to build a network of federal "defense" highways. The interstates would surpass the effectiveness of Germany's vaunted Autobahn and, incidentally, give urban working people the means to follow their relocated jobs.

As young Polish-Americans began to leave their older, urban neighborhoods, a fresh wave of urban newcomers began to take their places in the industrial Northeast. Some were Hispanics who, between the 1930s and 1960s, escaped the grinding poverty of places like Puerto Rico by flocking to the "land of opportunity" in the North. Most, however, were refugees from the Black South, whose migration had begun in the 1890s, Dixie's Jim Crow years; rose after World War I, after the coming of the boll weevil and a series of disastrous floods devastated Southern cotton culture; and snowballed during and after the Second World War, when mechanization of Southern farming pushed many off the land and labor-hungry defense plants pulled jobless Black Southerners to the North. Their rather sudden arrival—in Detroit, for example, the Black population grew from 149,119 in 1919 to 1,623,452 in 1940—presented first- and second-generation Polish-Americans who had remained in their aging, urban ethnic enclaves with a fresh set of challenges to their way of life.

Long before the Second World War, Poles had lived near Black Americans and had acquired a reputation for treating their Black neighbors—with whom they shared an agricultural past, strong family ties, deep religiosity, and recent unfreedom as serf or slave—more cordially than native-born whites treated either of them. In Chicago, for example, Poles reportedly had been "entirely friendly toward negroes" as late as 1914.[24] Because both were seeking a better life, they soon found themselves locked in a desperate struggle for jobs and housing in America's crowded industrial cities that set the tone for relations between the two groups until the present day. In 1919, Chicago employers used Black "scabs"—as they once had used the Poles—to break a strike by Polish and Lithuanian packinghouse workers, a common practice throughout American industry during the period. During the same "Red Summer" of anti-Black rioting in Chicago, anti-Black diatribes began to appear for the first time in newspapers like Chicago's *Naród Polski* (The Polish Nation). In the 1920s, second-generation Polish-Americans surveyed in Buffalo demonstrated that learning such racism went with "acculturization." Though Poles as a whole "did not share the American prejudice toward the Negro . . . ," the study concluded, native-born Poles who responded to the question of whether "the Negro should be permitted all the privileges and rights accorded to the whites . . . " showed that they had "begun to acquire a prejudice which their parents evidently did not possess."[25]

Not surprisingly, Blacks responded in kind to the competitive animosity they felt growing among Poles and other white immigrants. Blacks like those interviewed in St. Clair Drake's and Horace R. Cayton's classic 1945 study of Chicago, *Black Metropolis*, would observe that, among the city's various ethnic groups, Poles were "rather prejudiced." One of their respondents summarized her attitudes about integration with Poles and other white ethnics: "I didn't come this far to live among the Polacks, Dagoes, and other low class white trash. I prefer living among my own group."[26] Because many Blacks held the immigrants in contempt, "Hunky"—the epithet for Central European immigrant workers—became "Honkie," the generic term for whites in the Black urban argot. This hostility was grounded in the Black Americans' longstanding and fairly accurate appraisal of the relationship between immigrants and themselves in American society. As Booker T. Washington, the Southern Black educator, had observed in 1895 in his celebrated Atlanta Exposition Address, Hungarians, Italians, Poles, and other immigrants were stealing the livelihood away from the Negro native-born.

Probably as long as Blacks acted deferentially toward the older ethnic residents, however, the two groups coexisted fairly well. Polish-Americans and Blacks belonged to the same CIO union locals and got along together as work-mates, neighbors, and even friends. In Detroit, there are the reports of a Black dentist with mostly Polish patients, of Polish families adopting racially mixed children, of an interracial parish, and of Polish contributions to African missions.[27] In Buffalo, Black school children reportedly identified with images of Our Lady of Częstochowa, Poland's "Black Madonna."[28] With Black aspirations and population both rising, relations between the two groups grew visibly strained. Because so many Poles had not followed the "ethnic succession" model, but instead clung to their old urban parishes and neighborhoods, they formed an obstacle to Black mobility. Because their own achievements were still all too fragile, Polish-

Americans feared and distrusted the group immediately below them
in social rank that threatened to push them from their neighborhoods
and take their jobs.

In Detroit's tight wartime labor and housing market, for example,
white ethnics like the Poles did take the offensive against Black
"invaders"—one Polish pastor referred to them as "primitive Southern Niggers"[29]—in such celebrated episodes as the Sojourner Truth
housing controversy, opposition to an integrated public housing project, of 1941–42 and the 1943 race riot; but in twenty years the tables
turned. America's urban minority populations asserted themselves in
a series of riots that swept many heavily Polish cities between 1965
and 1968, including Newark and Jersey City in the state of New Jersey and Detroit. In 1966, civil rights leader Rev. Martin Luther King,
Jr., brought peaceful protest for nondiscriminatory "open housing"
to some of Chicago's Polish suburbs. On their part, Poles fought back.
In 1968, the president of a Chicago Polish Homeowners Association
was arrested while raising a flag that had been flying at half-mast in
honor of the slain Dr. King. In 1971, a Michigan federal court ruled
that, via its urban renewal program, the heavily Polish city of Hamtramck was practicing "Negro removal," which had caused its Black
population to decline during the preceding decade.[30] Polish-
Americans began to trickle out of the urban neighborhoods in which
they had been born. Others with a strong rootedness to their homes,
neighborhoods, and parishes—a cultural carryover from their peasant past—bought bars for their windows and strong locks for their
doors and resolved to tough it out. No one would drive them away; no
mere newcomer could make them that afraid.

Because they resented America's Black urban newcomers and because they participated—though in small numbers—in "white
flight," Poles were called "racists" by white liberals who had themselves fled to prosperous suburbs long ago. Many working-class
Polish-American men and women, embittered or frustrated with
their own lives, did express racist hostility toward "the Blacks." They
made a convenient scapegoat for a raft of ills. Most, however, were
not as much racists as victims, in the same way that Black Americans
were victims. Poles resented "blockbusting," integration practiced
by unscrupulous real estate operators, because they really did fear
that the value of their homes, their only major economic asset, would
go down. They also resisted "affirmative action" hiring policies that
attacked seniority rights because they undercut the job security for
which they had fought so long and hard. In a racist modern America,
they also knew, introducing Black workers into "white men's jobs"
eroded the tenuous social status that white ethnic working people
like themselves held. Yet it was neither they nor their Black counterparts who had created the labor and housing markets in which the

groups were at each other's throats. Nor was it they, Polish-Americans pointed out, who had invented slavery, racism, or the urban public policy that had framed Black America's plight. In fact, because they had stayed in their urban neighborhoods long after many other whites had fled, Polish-Americans—and other working-class white ethnics—represented the country's last best hope for a viable, if not painless, racial integration. Perhaps their concerns should have been answered and their culture better understood by public policymakers. When they were, instead, scoffed at, many of America's political and social options went up in smoke.

Polish-American city dwellers were not mean-spirited by nature; they just wanted to be left alone. Vastly more sophisticated—more discriminating than discriminatory—than their undeserved image, they drew a sharp distinction between those they considered "good," working- and middle-class Blacks, and the "bad" ones, the "young toughs into the drug scene" and the "men who don't work," who, they felt, were ruining their once quiet, safe neighborhoods.[31] Here was a clash of class and culture, not one principally of race. In terms of class and culture, however, Polish-Americans sometimes felt a bittersweet affinity with the strangers at their gates. What one second-generation Polish-American woman in New Jersey said about her Hispanic neighbors could have been said as easily about their Black counterparts. "I don't dislike Puerto Ricans," she said. "I see in them me when I was young. . . . I don't dislike Puerto Ricans"; in crowded houses, with a lot of kids, they are just like we once were.[32] Still, the arrival of Puerto Ricans, Blacks, Albanians, Yugoslavs, or other groups was changing the Polish-American character of neighborhoods and costing Poles the only world they knew.

Between 1940 and 1960, the urban neighborhoods of Polish America held their own. In the Polish Hill and Southside neighborhoods of Pittsburgh, more Poles had moved into white-collar and skilled occupations (from 22.1 percent to 27.6 percent of the workforce in Polish Hill, 13.4 percent to 24.8 percent in Southside) and more Poles owned their homes (from 33 percent in Polish Hill and 42.5 percent in Southside in 1930 to nearly 75 percent by 1960). Economic and population decline, however, had begun and both picked up momentum in the next twenty-five years. In some places, "slum clearance"—later euphemistically renamed "urban renewal"—destroyed local housing and, in forcing area residents to move out, robbed Polish parishes and small businesses of the critical population mass necessary for survival. Ethnic small businesses were particularly imperiled. Chain-stores and shopping malls undersold them and post-New Deal public welfare programs undercut many of the functions their owners had once served. On the northside area of Brooklyn's Williamsburg district, factory expansion tore into Polish neighborhoods. Highway and road

construction cut broad swaths through older neighborhoods and displaced those who lived there: Interstate 94 bisected Detroit's eastside Polish corridor; the approaches to New York's Long Island
Expressway doomed a large tract of Polish-American homes in the
Greenpoint section of Brooklyn along a street ironically leading to
the Kosciuszko Bridge.

After older ethnic neighborhoods began to show signs of demographic and economic decline, urban neglect usually piled on top of
other ills. After the 1960s urban upheaval, banks often "red-lined"
entire "high-risk" neighborhoods. They refused to make mortgage,
home-improvement, or small-business loans to anyone, however
credit worthy, who lived there. Red-lined areas subsequently faced
greater physical deterioration, population loss, and a kind of civic
abandonment as cities wrote them off as unsalvagable and reduced
sanitation, fire protection, and police services. Roman Catholic diocesan authorities also practiced their own kind of ecclesiastical "red-
lining," closing parochial schools with declining enrollments,
shutting churches or removing their national (ethnic) designation, refusing to train and assign them Polish-speaking clerics. The decisions
made good economic and administrative sense, but also made it
harder for Polish-Americans to sustain their urban way of life. Economic change showed many Polish-Americans that they were not
wrong if they had kept attitudes resembling "peasant fatalism;" the
gray clouds that had descended over Polonia's urban neighborhoods
had gray linings. In the 1970s and 1980s, northern factories that, in the
words of John Mankowski, a Connecticut brassworker, "had such obsolete equipment that they probably didn't want to do anything to get
up-to-date or improved . . . "[33] began to close, sounding the death
knell of many local Polonias. But the reindustrialization of some urban areas—like Detroit, where the Dodge Main plant in neighboring
Hamtramck, Michigan, had recently shut down—sometimes proved
more fatal still. There, construction of a new General Motors factory
in the early 1980s required the leveling of a 465.5–acre residential
area still inhabited by 500 to 700 Polish households.

Rural Polish America followed a path similar in many ways to that
taken by the urban neighborhoods. In Southampton, Long Island,
one Polish-American son usually took over his aging father's farm. As
a result, the total number of Polish-American farms did not immediately decline. Landless siblings probably did leave the land for urban
jobs. In Harrah, Oklahoma, second-generation Poles turned their
backs on farming and took up work at one of the town's two cotton
gins, the local cannery, or a nearby gas and electric company generat-
ing station. After the 1960s, those who continued to farm had to mod-
ernize and sometimes could not do so fast enough, faced with rising

costs and growth of agribusiness. Others found they could make more money selling their land for suburban development than farming it. As a result, 11 percent of second-generation Poles followed farm occupations; among their children a mere 1 percent would do so.

Economic and demographic change had remade Polish America during the postwar years. The typical Polish-American family in 1910 had immigrated from Poland, resided in the factory district of an industrial city, had about five children, and lived on wages derived from blue-collar work done by the "man of the house." By the 1960s and 1970s, it had grown difficult to say what was "typical." There were Polish displaced persons and their offspring who differed from old Polonia, the descendants of the immigration "for bread." This book really is not about them. There were second-generation Polish-American suburbanites, lower middle-class blue- or white-collar families with two or three children and possibly two wage-earners, living, frankly, as many other Americans lived. There were second-generation, mostly working-class Polish Americans who did not quit their city homes for the suburbs. As their suburbanized brothers and sisters mowed lawns, paneled basements, and polished the chrome on fancy cars, immobile—or rather, stable[34]—second-generation Polish-Americans in Polonia's aging urban neighborhoods did things much as they always had. At least they tried to. Their world was slipping away from them as the postwar world wore on. When they went out of doors on the weekends to paint the trim on houses, pick up leaves, or fix their cars, they cast suspicious glances at the unfamiliar brown or tan faces of "intruders" in their neighborhoods. As they sat at their kitchen tables or in front of their TVs, they began each evening by checking the newspaper obituary columns to see which of their friends, neighbors, or distant relatives had passed away the night before.

In addition to these second-generation men and women, however, there were still a handful of the immigrant generation's survivors, the "last of the first." The old Polish men were visible when they sat on park benches, porches, sidewalks, and stoops with their cats, dogs, and a few old friends. Forgotten by their upwardly mobile, suburbanized offspring, some lived out lonely lives, waiting to die. One Baltimore Pole, with three children, described what his life was like. "They come much like they would visit a sick man in the hospital," he said. "They say, 'How are you, pa? Here are some oranges.' They talk a little, then go home."[35] Others had made great gains, which the wistful narrator of a 1972 documentary summed up: " . . . I got my house, my garden, pension, social security. I'm retired. I said to my wife, who would have guessed you would have all this? My son is a salesman, makes good money. The family's together. My grandson, he goes to college. . . . " But there were costs. "I think about the old days a lot, " he continued. "You know, in the end I got to be a real American, but it was long, long journey. It took a lifetime."[36]

As these old men, who so symbolized a rootedness in times past, died off, old Polish neighborhoods acquired a deserted look. The withered Polish grandmothers still inside were unseen. Because many lived longer lives these women outlived their husbands and so peeked out at a confusing, lonely world through drawn fiberglass curtains and closed venetian blinds. They were more vulnerable than their departed spouses. Most had never ventured far into American society and therefore perhaps never learned English very well. They clung to their independence and continued to live by themselves, deriving social support from at least one offspring—usually a daughter—and, as one old woman said, from "my prayers." Some kept up an active, involved community life, frequenting masses, society meetings, funerals, "senior citizens'" bus trips, the hairdresser's, and church bingo for as long as their health permitted. Others led lonely lives, like one Polish woman who said, "I live here fifteen years and I never went to nobody's house."[37] What did such women conclude? "I should have stayed in Poland," one said, whether she meant it or not.[38]

Finally, there were the young Polish-Americans of the third generation, grandchildren with an assortment of last names—Italian, Irish, English, as well as Polish—and first names that sounded indistinguishably "American" and "modern"—Eric, Michele, Roy, Gary, Sandra, Dennis, Robin, Brian. Just how "typical" and how "Polish" were they?

These typical Polish-Americans of all generations shared two characteristics. First, all were more observers than actors in the social and economic revolution that had remade Polish America since the Second World War. Second, as they watched the old, urban ethnic enclaves decline and looked at Polonia's population statistics—Polish foreign-born had fallen from 1,268,583 in 1930 to 747,000 in 1960, more precipitously still if the 150,000 refugees and displaced persons who arrived after the war were excluded—all might have wondered whether ethnicity as they had known it was fading away. They may have wondered, in short, what is a Polish-American now, today?

6

WHAT IS A POLISH-AMERICAN?

The Revival of Ethnic Identity

> But what about the second, third and
> fourth generations? What of the children
> born of German, Irish, or American moth-
> ers? Sooner or later they will forget. They
> will change everything, even their names,
> which English teeth find too difficult to
> chew and which interfere with business.
> How long this will take is difficult to say.
> But just as Poland disappeared, so will this
> same sad fate inevitably befall her children
> who, today, are scattered throughout the
> world.
>
> —Henryk Sienkiewicz, *Portrait*
> *of America: Letters of*
> *Henry Sienkiewicz* [1876–1878]

American social scientists in the postwar period did not share the
concerns of Polish-Americans who feared themselves an endangered
species. While the total number of foreign-born Poles in the United
States had fallen sharply since the mass migration years, the 1960 census still identified 2,780,026 first- and second-generation Poles in the
American population, fully a million more than appeared in the 1910
enumeration. What is more, the 1960 figures probably represent a
low estimate of persons descended from Polish immigrants. Following trends in the general population, Polish-Americans were gradually moving out of the industrial Northeast and North Central states,
filtering into the South and West. In 1930, 93 percent of the foreign-
born Poles lived in old areas of settlement; by 1960, only 86 percent
of first- and second-generation Poles did. California, in particular, became home to many Polish-Americans. While the percentage of first-
and second-generation Poles in the American population went up 63
percent between 1910 and 1960, in that state their numbers rose over

fifteenfold, an amazing 1,523 percent! Clearly, the Polish presence in the United States had gone from regional to national over a brief number of years.

It was not from these statistics, but from the place that Polish-Americans and other ethnic groups occupied in postwar American society that convinced social scientists that ethnicity was not disappearing from the American social landscape. Still structurally separate from mainstream America, Polish-Americans and other ethnics were living evidence that America was a culturally pluralistic place and would probably stay that way.

In the postwar period, cultural pluralism became the dominant view of American society, underscoring the enduring importance of groups like the Poles in national life. After the revelation that the Nazi Holocaust had consumed 6 million European Jews and some 7 million others—including 2.5 million Poles, whom the Nazis also considered racially inferior—many Americans recoiled from racism and nativism, European variants of which had brought the world to such a terrible pass, and embraced cultural pluralism instead. As the Cold War chill settled more deeply over the land and a consensus view of American society swept American social science, cultural pluralism also appealed as an ideology to those who sought a politically palatable alternative to radical social analyses based upon the concept of class. The institutionalization of ethnic political power in the Democratic party, the rise in disposable income of ethnic American consumers, who now formed a formidable and identifiable segment of the market, and the training of a generation of social scientists who themselves had ethnic roots—Nathan Glazer, Oscar Handlin, Daniel Patrick Moynihan, and others—helped establish cultural pluralism in the American political arena, the American society and economy, and American social thought.

Some Polish-Americans, however, worried about the place their group occupied in America, wondered whether it would survive, and asked themselves questions about the meaning of their ethnicity. Their concerns were not without reason. During the post-war years, countervailing developments continued to erode traditional ethnicity and to change what ethnicity would mean for the third- and fourth-generation descendants of America's Polish immigrants.

Polish-Americans did not need a battery of esteemed social scientists to tell them that their position in postwar America remained structurally separate from the mainstream. Thirty-thousand young Polish-Americans gave their lives during the Second World War. Yet returning servicemen, like one second-generation New Jersey Pole, recalled being passed over for promotion because of their "unpronounceable" surnames.[1] A Brooklyn Pole was told to change his—from Poskropski to Poster, a nickname—when applying for a job as a sports writer because his editor said, "No Polaks read English, so we can't have a Polish by-line."[2] In addition to such external obstacles to Polish occupational mobility and economic integration, conditions within the group dampened young Poles' chances to better themselves economically. Because they gave heavily to their parishes, Polish-Americans had less money to spend on housing or education or to invest in small businesses. Because they learned deference to authority at home, in church, and in their parochial schools, they were less well suited to the rigors of the highly individualistic, competitive marketplace. It probably could be shown that working-class ethnics like the Poles tended to think in the passive voice: the world acted *upon them.* Because their parents often tried to keep them "Polish," those young Polish-Americans who ventured into the nativist larger society always carried a cultural handicap. Many others simply did not make the attempt. Socialized to an ethnic, working-class way of life, they prized security, stability, and community over more individualistic goals like money, power, and status. "I have no need to be better than my father," the young Pole in a documentary film on Polish immigration thus was made to say.[3]

Polish-Americans compiled a disturbing statistical profile that showed the group had not done badly in the postwar period; neither had it done particularly well. While there were more college educated third-generation Polish-Americans than Irish-Americans or Italian-Americans, by the 1970s, for example, only 872 "Polish-sounding surnames" appeared among the 35,000 students in the University of Michigan, an elite institution in a state with large Polish representation, or about 13 percent of the total white population there. Similarly, while 34 percent of third-generation Polish-American males had attained white-collar positions by the early 1960s, compared to 12 percent for second-generation Poles, both generations remained heavily blue-collar—65 and 77 percent respectively. These blue-collar Poles often held well-paying factory jobs, causing median family income for Polish-Americans in 1970 ($11,619), while vastly below that of Jewish-Americans ($19,259), to compare favorably with that of several other ethnic groups: Italian-Americans ($11,089), Irish-Americans ($9,964), and German-Americans ($10,402).* By 1979, the rankings had changed: Polish-American ($16,977) cf., Italian-Americans ($16,993), Irish-Americans ($16,092), and German-Americans ($17,531). Yet these well-paid second- and third-generation blue-collar Polish-Americans, like the immigrant shopkeepers before them, had fallen into their own kind of mobility trap. They had done so well in industrial occupations that their children chose to hang onto them instead of grabbing the often low-paid

*These figures do not control for age.

bottom rungs of occupational mobility ladders. The chronic disadvantages of class—combined with anti-Polish discrimination—reduced Polish-American representation in the upper reaches of the occupational hierarchy and American class structure. In 1968 Poles represented about one out of six Roman Catholics in the United States. At the same time, according to the *Catholic Directory*, they formed less than 3 percent of the Church's cardinals, archbishops, and bishops in America—8 of 267. Similarly, a 1984 draft report prepared by Chicago's Institute of Urban Life for the National Center for Urban Ethnic Affairs demonstrated that, relative to their percentage of the metropolitan-area population of a city like Chicago, Poles were still "grossly underrepresented" on the boards or as officers in ninety-two of the city's largest corporations and had made only minute numerical gains since an earlier, 1973 study. The study revealed a similarly dismal record for Italians, Hispanics, and Blacks.[4]

Polish-Americans had been integrated into the society and economy far enough that the cultural erosion that had begun to undermine their communities in the 1920s proceeded more quickly and more noticeably in the postwar years. Between 1940 and 1960, only 20 percent of the children of Polish-American ethnic leaders spoke Polish regularly, compared to 50 percent for the Ukrainian group; 1969 figures showed that 92.6 percent of Polish-Americans usually spoke English. Preparing their children to be successful in American society, second-generation Polish-Americans did not teach their offspring the language, or even use it much themselves at home, because, as one Polish-American anthropologist remembered of his own 1950s upbringing, "they were perceptive enough to know that learning Polish was more of a liability than an asset."[5] This also effectively cut their children off from Polish-speaking grandparents, the carriers of traditional ethnic culture. Others apparently felt the same about carrying Polish names. In Chicago, one young third-generation Pole said he would change his name to something more "American-sounding" if it promised to help his acting career, and he was not alone.[6] In the early 1960s, 3,000 of the Detroit area's 300,000 Polish-Americans changed their names each year.

Assimilation, however, was not changing Polish-Americans and other ethnics as profoundly as a process they encountered as they entered the larger American society: homogenization. Mobilized during the war, Polish-Americans were more thoroughly Americanized than had ever seemed possible. The war also mixed them together with members of other groups in American defense plants and military units. While such mixing probably brought individual Polish-Americans social and cultural benefits, it proved detrimental to group survival. Not surprisingly, postwar intermarriage rates soared (Polish-American women were more likely than Polish-American men to marry outside their group). Whereas 89 percent of the parents of the Polish-American respondents to a National Opinion Research Center (NORC) study in 1963–1964 were endogamous (had married other Poles), only 50 percent of the children married within the group. Curiously, endogamy was somewhat more common among urban Poles (53 percent) than rural Poles (50 percent) in the NORC sample. The larger size of Polish communities in cities, and more organized intragroup social life, probably account for the disparity in figures. Those who chose non-Polish partners married persons of German (17%), Italian (10%), East European (8%), Irish (5%), French-Canadian (4%), Spanish-speaking (2%), Lithuanian (2%), and English (1%) backgrounds. They tended to remain religiously endogamous and some married "up." Still, judging by the percentage of group members reporting only a single ancestry in a recent special census report on *Language and Ancestry*, in 1979 the 8 million Polish-Americans had intermarried more often than members of several other ethnic groups. While 57.3 percent of the Greeks, 52 percent of the Italians and Sicilians, and 44 percent of the Ukrainians reported single-ancestry, the figure for the Poles was only 41.5 percent.

Intermarriage, however important as a homogenizing force, only touched half the Polish-Americans. Upwardly mobile, and with higher household incomes—thanks to better jobs, working wives, and high postwar wages—all Polish-Americans were drawn into the 1950s mass consumption economy, the real homogenizing agent in the postwar period. Breaking with the immigrant generation's pattern of frugality and underconsumption, Polish-Americans, and all Americans of a minimum income level, filled their homes with mass consumption goods—refrigerators, ranges, washing machines, toasters, recreation equipment, cars—that revolutionized and flattened out the differences in their everyday lives. As a homogenizing force, mass consumption was accompanied by mass marketing and mass culture. The most important single moment in the cultural lives of Polish-Americans—of all Americans—in the postwar years was the day they purchased their first black-and-white television set. It brought the advertising slogans and jingles; the jokes, songs, and images; the faces and symbols that supplanted local, regional, class, or ethnic customs, traditions, and folkways with a national culture for the first time in American history. This represented a different kind of assimilation than Polish-Americans had undergone in the 1930s, when working people of all ethnic backgrounds, though they may have seen the same motion pictures, still partook of broad blue-collar patterns grounded in the neighborhood, the workplace, the parish, the community, and the home. Americanized by Madison Avenue and Hollywood, Poles assimilated by becoming mass consumers.

Surveying their group's cultural landscape in the postwar period,

and not the separate position it occupied in the American social structure, Polish-Americans had ample cause to wonder whether their
ethnicity would long survive. First, cultural assimilation, more pronounced among the better educated and upwardly mobile, was more
evident in the suburbs and in newer and more heavily middle-class
and professional Polish-American communities, if they could still be
called that, like San Jose and Los Angeles-Long Beach in California
and Washington, D.C. Second, the homogenization of mass culture
seemed to affect middle- and working-class Polish-Americans without
distinction. In 1977, one second-generation Polish-American at his
family's Polish Christmas Eve supper in Chicago remarked, "young
people are not going to follow these kinds of traditions"; his son
wanted to become a rock guitarist and not, as his mother wanted, the
next "polka king."7 Finally, Polish America faced more cultural frag-
mentation than ever before. Culturally, how much did middle-class
third- and fourth-generation Polish-Americans have in common with
their working-class contemporaries? How much did either have in
common with the post–WW II displaced persons who had such different memories of Poland and such a different past? And what about
the Polish political émigrés of more recent vintage? As the postwar
period wore on, it had grown more difficult to find a common cultural
core of values, customs, traditions, and associations—ethnicity as it
was lived—that tied all Polish-Americans together. Here, then, was
the heart of Polonia's crisis: in any meaningful sense, did a common
"Polishness" still exist for all members of the group?

What did still tie all group members together, regardless of generation, class, religion, or politics, was their common ethnic identity—
what others called them, what they called themselves. In the 1920s,
group leaders had already recognized the importance of ethnic identity to group survival. They could also urge immigrants and their children to identify themselves and be identified as Polish-Americans for
a practical reason, too. Though they had not, did not want to, and
probably could not fully assimilate, by calling themselves Polish-
Americans group members nonetheless could claim a place in American society with its privileges and rights. In the postwar years, many
group members had assimilated or wanted to; unlike Black Americans, who because they could not change the color of their skin could
never fully "blend in," most Polish-Americans finally now could. The
real problem in relying upon a shared Polish-American identity to tie
group members together was that most Americans regarded "Polish"
and "Polish-American" as negative labels. As labels, they were too
easy to shed—by changing one's name.

In surveying postwar American culture, Polish-Americans may
have felt dismay, but not surprise, that some of the negative attitudes

that Americans held toward them only carried on the anti-Polish bias of the mass migration years. Postwar social scientists like August B. Hollingshead could still write in 1949 that in "Elmtown," a typical small town, "The Poles are believed to be scabs, filthy, ignorant, law breakers, 'damn fond of their women and whiskey,' 'dumb,' unable to learn American ways, pretty good citizens, a problem in the school."[8] Assimilation, upward mobility, and even intermarriage would not wipe out these kinds of stereotypes. In 1985, one young university student in the still heavily Polish city of Detroit reported that, in anger, her Irish-American mother would sometimes call her Polish-American father a "dumb Polack."[9]

A relatively new twist, however, also made some Polish-Americans uncomfortable with their ethnic identity and with being members of their ethnic group in the postwar period. At a time when the Holocaust and the civil rights movement seemed to have discredited bigotry once and for all, they were accused of being racists and anti-Semites. White liberals blamed groups like the Polish-Americans for the race tensions that plagued America's changing cities. Relations between Polish-Americans and Jewish-Americans, whose economic symbiosis in rural Poland and urban America was sometimes punctuated by conflict, became an even thornier issue as Jews recalled instances of Polish anti-Semitism; as sporadic Polish complicity in the terrible Nazi Holocaust came to light; and, after 1968, as reports of anti-Semitic governmental policies poured out of People's Poland. In their own defense, Polish-Americans pointed out that many Polish Jews had been saved by Polish heroism and self-sacrifice, and that the Nazis also slaughtered many Polish Catholics. But counter examples seem to have satisfied few of the Poles' or the Polish-Americans' detractors. As late as 1979, novelist William Styron's best-selling novel, *Sophie's Choice*, would absurdly suggest that Poland had invented anti-Semitism! By extension, Polish-Americans continued to be excoriated as anti-Semites and thus lumped together with the hated Nazis. Some Polish-Americans likened this to victim blaming victim. Others, while perhaps not contesting the findings of Chicago's NORC that Polish-Americans "score high on anti-Semitism,"[10] noted prominent Jewish-Americans, particularly Jewish entertainers, who themselves expressed prejudice against Polish-Americans and Poles. In the 1960s, in one exaggerated example, Polish-Jewish relations in Chicago grew strained after a local newspaper published an account of a party:

> To celebrate Mr. H——'s birthday at their "Spectacular Northbrook summer house" they gave a "Polish Picnic" to which guests arrived in a U-Haul truck, dressed in overalls, undershirts, and tennis shoes. "Polish presents" were distributed from a garbage can.[11]

Such gaucherie hardly made for mutual understanding. More to the point, it helped spread negative feelings about the Polish-American group and showed that anti-Polish bigotry had become socially acceptable in middle-class America.

The purveyors of American mass culture also treated Polish-Americans with disdain. Postwar mass culture absorbed none of the positive elements of Polish-American culture as it had adopted and accepted Jewish, Yiddish, and Black forms. Absent in the media were both positive depictions of Polish-American characters and characters to whom blue-collar ethnic viewers and their children could relate. Instead, they regularly encountered anti-Polish bias and stereotypes that undercut group identity. In the 1951 film version of Tennessee Williams's play *A Streetcar Named Desire*, for example, Marlon Brando played Stanley Kowalski, Hollywood's and America's archetypal "Polak": crude, physical, violent, hard-drinking, and boorish.[12] (Using anti-ethnic and sexist elements, Polish-American women also were negatively stereotyped as crude, obese or muscle-bound, homely, and dirty.) Other postwar films that stigmatized the Poles included *Call Northside 777* (1948), *Anna Lucasta* (1949), *Saturday's Hero* (1951), and *The Man with the Golden Arm* (1956). Amazingly, while anti-Black portrayals became less common by the 1970s, anti-ethnic movies continued to appear, including *Rabbit Test, The End, Blue Collar*, and *The Deer Hunter*, all released in 1978. The last named award-winning motion picture was perhaps the most vicious of the anti-ethnic genre, grotesquely implying that the allegedly macho Slavic-American culture bore some responsibility for American involvement in the Vietnam War.

The most pervasive attack against Polish-Americans, and the one that perhaps most undermined their ethnic identity, was the notorious "Polish joke." Anti-Polish gags, routines, and skits by Rowen and Martin, Frank Sinatra, Phyllis Diller, Morey Amsterdam, Dean Martin, Joan Rivers, Johnny Carson, Steve Allen, Don Rickles, and Carol Burnett littered the television airwaves in the 1960s and early 1970s, while several popular television series, like "Laverne and Shirley" and Archie Bunker's "All in the Family," portrayed stereotyped Polish characters and used anti-Polish humor. The popular press of the period got into the anti-Polish act, publishing such titles as the *It's Fun to Be a Polak* "jokebook." Mainstream politicians, including Ronald Reagan, have gotten laughs at the Poles' expense. As late as 1980, while running for president of the United States, Reagan quipped to reporters, "How do you know who the Polish guy is at a cockfight?" Answer: "He's the one with the duck."[13] Curiously, sensitivity to racism in the 1980s did not cause Americans to reject anti-Polish bigotry. When questioned about a joke she told at a party—Q.: "How can you tell the difference between a dog and a Polack who have been run over by a car?" A.: "For the Polack, there won't be any skid marks," (the driver wouldn't bother to stop)—one suburban Detroit college student replied that it had been an anti-Black joke, but she changed "Nigger" to "Polack" because she was not "prejudiced"![14]

Though many Polish-Americans—conductors Stanislaw Skrowa-czewski and Leopold Stokowski (himself half-Polish, half-Irish), sculptors Richard Stankiewicz and Janusz Korczak-Ziolkowski, artists Richard Anuszkiewicz and Karol Kozlowski, inventor Tadeusz Sen-dzimir, and biochemist Hilary Koprowski—have made substantial achievements in postwar America, their success has gone largely un-noticed and has done little to neutralize the anti-Polish stereotypes so prevalent in American mass culture. Typically, college educated Polish-American professionals have not trumpeted their own success, nor has it been trumpeted for them. In fact, many probably learned early in life that "getting ahead" could be helped along by playing down their Polish roots. Many "Polish-American" television and motion-picture celebrities changed their names—Charles Bronson (Buchinski), Stephanie Powers (Stefania Federkiewicz), partly-Polish Jack Palance (Walter Palaniuk), and Michael Landon (Orowicz)—or others changed their names for them. Their prominence was a kind of public insult to the Polish-American group. There were scores of Polish-Americans who had made their mark in professional sports—boxing champion Stanley Ketchel (Kiecal), wrestler Stanisław ("Zbyszko") Cyganiewicz, football player Bronisław ("Bronco") Na-gurski, and baseball stars Carl Yastrzemski, Stan Musial, and Joe and Phil Niekro, to name a few. However educated and articulate these athletes may have been—Cyganiewicz, for example, held a doctorate from the University of Vienna and spoke eleven languages—their ex-ploits often may have served to reinforce anti-Polish stereotypes. Americans knew these Polish athletes not for intellectual or artistic achievement, but for raw physical prowess. Many Americans prob-ably thought they were just more "strong, dumb Polacks."

It is not immediately clear why such mild-mannered, inoffensive people as the Polish-Americans should have become the butt of American commercial and folk humor. Perhaps their difficult-to-pronounce surnames made them seem to typify the unassimilable greenhorn. Perhaps their recent upward mobility called forth sym-bolic aggression from native-born Americans and other ethnics who felt politically, economically, socially, and psychologically threat-ened by them. But the themes and elements contained in some of the stereotypical portrayals of Polish-Americans in ethnic (antiethnic) humor were even more complicated. In one popular 1980s afternoon television soap opera, "Guiding Light," the serial's young "tough" was a man raised by a Polish foster-family named Lujack. Young "Lu-jack" is not bad, only rough. He began to straighten out when taken

under the patronage of the local white, Anglo-Saxon, Protestant, rich
lady. Marking "Lujack's" transit from ethnicity to respectability, his
benefactor discards his adoptive Polish name and begins to call him
Brandon. The point in introducing this vignette is to suggest a second
—and more serious—function of anti-Polish stereotypes and "humor": they also express a deep anti-working class bias in American
middle-class culture.

We can only guess the effect that this pattern of abuse has had upon
the average Polish-American, for while American liberals have moni-
tored instances of anti-Semitism and anti-Black prejudice closely,
they have largely ignored—and often participated in—attacks on the
Poles. Larry Wilde, himself of Polish Jewish extraction, justified his
own authorship of a succession of anti-Polish and other anti-ethnic
jokebooks by saying only "older people, who are less secure in their
roots," objected to them. Aloysius Mazewski, president of the Polish
American Congress, disagreed that Poles were simply being "touchy"
and "thin-skinned." "The purpose of the jokes is to subject people to
ridicule," Mazewski said. "They may not be harmful to adults, but
I've seen children coming home crying, 'Are we really that dumb?'
These jokes create an inferiority complex, even among children who
laugh at them because they think it's sophisticated."[15] Anti-Polish
jokes and stereotypes probably have damaged Polish-Americans'
self-image and psyche, judging by the question another youngster of
mixed Polish and Italian ancestry asked a Detroit Polish-American
mother: "Mom, is there something wrong with being Polish?"[16] More
tangibly, they probably have helped depress the achievement and
mobility potential of the group's young. While this sometimes may
have happened through outright discrimination in hiring decisions, it
came about through subtler means as well. How did it bias the employment interview, for example, when in the late 1970s one young
Polish-American academic was met at Iowa's Cedar Rapids airport by
a member of the faculty search committee at "liberal" Grinnell College who broke the ice by expressing surprise at the job candidate's
appearance: he had expected a "football player type"?[17]

Because Polish-American group survival depended so much upon
the maintenance of an ethnic identity that was a liability in the larger
American society, Polish America found itself impaled upon the
horns of a painful dilemma in the postwar period. Polish-Americans
were shedding the Polish rural and Polish-American working-class
cultural forms and practices that had knitted their communities together; that, of itself, was not a bad thing. Upwardly mobile, many
adopted the culture of the American middle class: this was progress.
But would they also have to deny—to betray—their families' immigrant pasts, their ethnic identity, and their people's history in order
to "get ahead"? Did achievement have to mean rootlessness, self-

hate, anger, anomie? Clearly, some Polish-Americans thought it should not. After the election of Mazewski to the presidency of the Polish American Congress in 1968, for example, its focus shifted from Cold War foreign policy concerns to such domestic issues. Individually and through their organizations they tried to defend the honor of their group.

In the 1960s and into the early 1970s, the defensive efforts of Polish-Americans grouped around three themes. First, they tried to tackle the worrisome problem of intergroup relations. In 1970, the Polish American Congress and the Anti-Defamation League of B'Nai B'rith institutionalized Polish-Jewish dialogue by forming the Permanent Committee on Polish-Jewish Relations in the United States. Apparently this and prior efforts did help. The National Conference of Christians and Jews bestowed its 1968 Human Relations Award on a Polish-American, John Joseph Cardinal Krol, and that year B'Nai B'rith and Polish-American leaders cooperated in condemning anti-Polish defamation on the airwaves. Still, all tensions between the two groups did not disappear. In 1977, the Literary Sub-Committee of the Sentinel Committee of the Michigan Division of the Polish American Congress criticized "anti-Polish pronouncements" of several Jewish authors;[18] while as recently as 1985 New York metropolitan area Polish-Americans called for the resignation of the head of the New Jersey Advisory Council on Holocaust Education—a Jewish-American—for alleged insensitivity and arrogance toward Poles. Charges of Polish and Polish-American anti-Semitism also still occasionally surface.

The second theme in the Polish-Americans' campaign to defend themselves featured assorted attempts to build a more positive self-image in Polish-Americans. Recalling the status-seeking of America's middle-class Poles in the 1920s, which separated them from the blue-collar immigrant majority, middle-class Polish-Americans once again selectively "forgot" the peasant and working-class roots of Polonia, which in distorted form had provided the content for the anti-Polish stereotypes, and instead identified with Polish high culture, however much it departed from their own personal experience. This spirit of status-seeking—boasting about Polish-American "firsts" and "bests" —even infected some Polish-Americans of modest background. As if to keep up with native-born, blue-blooded DAR° Joneses, for example, a 1961 article by one young Polish-American discussed how to create a family coat of arms![19]

The third prong of the Polish-Americans' defensive campaign was an attempt to wipe out anti-Polish defamation. Much of their energies went into combatting that particular irritant—what one Polish-

°Daughters of the American Revolution.

American letter-to-the-editor writer called the "monotonously hateful" Polish "joke"[20] and another, "cultural genocide."[21] In 1966, Polish-American protest persuaded the distributor of the *It's Fun to Be a Polak* "jokebook" to withdraw remaining copies from dealerships. The following year, Polish-Americans protested a skit on the Columbia Broadcasting System's (CBS) "Carol Burnett Show," which portrayed a flight on a "Slavic" airline replete with idiotic pilot named Kowalski; dirty, disordered stewardess; and Polish national anthem playing as background music.[22] Burnett apologized two days later. In response to bags of mail protesting several of its programs, the National Broadcasting Company (NBC) did introduce a Polish "hero" in one of its series, "Banacek," but clumsily gave a Czech spelling to his surname.[23] In 1968, Polish-Americans condemned anti-Polish defamation at the University of Notre Dame, while the following year the Polish American Congress inaugurated a major drive against anti-Polish defamation, to date still one of its major programs. Yet these efforts alone did not score great successes. Most were timid, poorly supported, and underfunded. A year after its inception, for example, the Polish American Congress' anti-defamation fund-raising drive had netted a mere 10 percent of its $500,000 goal, testimony to enduring Polish-American passivity or priorities, or perhaps to a lack of confidence in the ability of this traditional Polish-American organization to get the job done.

More significant were Polish-American initiatives that went beyond reactive, defensive apologetics to encompass the positive promotion of Polish identity and Polish culture as virtuous in their own right. In 1948, sixteen Polish-American cultural clubs formed the influential American Council of Polish Cultural Clubs, while in 1956 the Polish Institute of Arts and Sciences began publication of *The Polish Review*, a scholarly journal that would help legitimize the Polish studies field and, incidentally, give Polish-American scholars their own organ. In the following decade, Polish-Americans intermittently sponsored other similar cultural activities—cultural exchanges with Poland, Polish culture and folklore exhibits, the celebration of the Millennium of Christianity in Poland, the endowment by the Jurzykowski Foundation of a chair in Polish Language and Literature at Harvard University, and the inauguration of the $500,000 "Project Pole" campaign, under the joint sponsorship of the Orchard Lake Schools and Polish-American businessman Edward Piszek, president of Mrs. Paul's Kitchens, a Philadelphia food-processing concern. Through newspaper advertisements—for example: "One of the greatest storytellers in the English language was a Pole;" and, beneath a picture of Joseph Conrad né Korzeniowski, the addendum: "He changed his name, his language and the course of English literature"—"Project Pole" attempted to build public awareness of Polish culture and to revive the image and self-image of Polish-Americans.[24]

Perhaps these halting efforts showed that as Polish-Americans became better educated and more upwardly mobile in American society they wanted a just measure of recognition and respect not unlike that claimed by Jewish-Americans, who vocally condemned anti-Semitism, or Black Americans, who protested against racist stereotyping. Probably the most graphic example of the headway they were making came in 1958 when Random House issued *A Glass Rose* by Richard Bankowsky, one of the first major novels by a Polish-American that used Polish-American material. The vigorous promotion of Polish culture that characterized the 1960s, however, probably did little to raise the ethnic pride and consciousness of many Polish-Americans during the period because it remained external to their day-to-day lives. Most blue-collar second-generation Polish-Americans had never been to Warsaw or Cracow and perhaps never wanted to go. What they knew of Poland came from their parents' stories of "struggling for survival on a meager plot of land."[25] What did Chopin or Sienkiewicz mean to them? Artificial attempts at puffing up the group's past seem to have held little charm for third- and fourth-generation Polish-Americans—the grandchildren and great-grandchildren of the immigrants. What did any of this have to do with them during the strife-torn 1960s?

Perhaps it comes as some surprise that by the early 1970s a genuine, broad-based ethnic revival was sweeping Polish America and other ethnic enclaves as well. In sharp contrast to the postwar flight from ethnicity, U.S. Census Bureau interviewers now found that 1.1 million more persons identified themselves as Polish-Americans in 1972 than had done so a mere three years earlier. The period also witnessed a surge of interest in Polish history, folklore, and culture; a scattering of name-changes in reverse such as the Warren, Michigan, politician named Jacob returning to Jakubowski or the Detroit television news reporter bravely changing his name, Conrad, back to Korzeniowski; and the restoration of the spelling of Polish surnames that, in the words of one third-generation Connecticut Polish-American who did not restore his, had been "wrecked" at Ellis Island.[26] Of course, such a profound cultural and social movement would have political ramifications. In *The Rise of the Unmeltable Ethnics: Politics and Culture in the Seventies*, a provocative popular work published in 1971, author Michael Novak examined these at length. Novak and others also gave this phenomenon a name: the "new ethnicity." Who participated in it? Where did it come from? What did it mean?

The new ethnicity became a powerful mass movement precisely because it encompassed different segments of ethnic groups like the Polish-Americans. Blue-collar second-generation Polish-Americans, on the one hand, realized that despite the fact that they had left their

old, urban ethnic neighborhoods or had watched those neighborhoods collapse around them, assimilation into the proverbial American melting pot had not been fully realized. They suffered from
anonymity, anomie, and alienation in a changing world and felt themselves pelted by a hail of confusing contradictions. Victimized by
prejudice, Polish-Americans and others now found themselves accused of racism by white liberals and Black Americans alike. Polish-
Americans had learned that Americanism was good and had loyally
contributed their sons as cannon fodder for America's wars. In the
1970s they often heard those protesting the war in Vietnam—sometimes their own children!—call patriotism stupid and suspect. It was
not long before ethnic Americans reached the flashpoint of frustration. If Black Americans could call for Black Power and trumpet Black
Pride, so could they insist on Polish Power and Polish Pride. Insisting
that their lives and sacrifices had not been in vain, they reasserted the
traditional verities of neighborhood, church, family, flag, work,
hearth, and home—all of which had come under attack by the sweeping cultural and social changes of the 1960s and 1970s. In short, these
working people challenged both the anti-ethnic and the anti-working
class picture that American elite and mass culture had painted of
them.

Thus mobilized, Polish-Americans were participating in a grassroots cultural movement between the late 1960s and early 1980s. In
the suburb of St. Clair Shores, Michigan, for example, one heavily
Polish-American parish broke with Rome after the reforms of Vatican
II eliminated many traditional Roman Catholic liturgical forms,
which had long helped define Polish-American religion and culture.°
Another Detroit parish—and others throughout the country—took
the opportunity that the loosened liturgy offered to introduce the
controversial "polka mass." In many places Polish-Americans organized clubs of "polka boosters." However disparate these episodes
and events, all featured group members struggling to define and express a shared group identity.

Because Polish-Americans never paired this cultural impulse with a
critical political analysis of the place that ethnic working people like
themselves occupied in the American economy and society, in the
end their new ethnicity remained an odd mélange, a heterogenous
mixture of incongruous elements without lasting import. More to the
point, as second-generation Polish-Americans bought "Polish and
Proud" bumper stickers, red and white T-shirts, and "Kiss Me I'm Polish" buttons and as they catapulted Bobby Vinton, a singer with a Polish ancestry and an Americanized surname, to super-stardom during

---

°By introducing vernacular languages into the Roman Catholic mass, Vatican II reforms also undercut one raison d'être for the schismatic Polish National Catholic
Church. How that Church will ultimately adapt remains to be seen.

the years of ethnic revival, they revealed how the new ethnicity had become a purchasable and profitable commodity. The "odd" spectacles that sometimes resulted from this commercialization—like Black Americans eating *kieĮbasa* or *pierogi* (Polish sausage or filled dumplings) or dancing the polka at Polish ethnic festivals—were really no more odd than Polish-Americans listening to rhythm-and-blues, using Yiddish and Black expressions, or eating tacos, spaghetti, or egg rolls. All bore witness to the real meaning of cultural pluralism in late twentieth-century America: ethnicity had been coopted by the mass culture industry. It too could be bought and sold.

Whereas blue-collar second-generation Polish-Americans who imbibed the new ethnicity were resuscitating a submerged part of themselves, almost wholly assimilated third- and fourth-generation Poles who embraced the ethnic revival were becoming something they were not. Though the ethnic identity they shared with members of the second generation and more recent Polish émigrés was revived, they nonetheless were experiencing a very different process in America, and perhaps one with greater significance. Why did they become more consciously Polish-American again?

According to Hansen's Law, a theory propounded by historian Marcus Lee Hansen in the 1930s, "what the son wishes to forget, the grandson wishes to remember."[27] While second-generation Polish-Americans may have fled from their backgrounds, in the 1970s third- and fourth-generation Poles rediscovered theirs. They sought to recover the usable past and charted a return to the ethnicity of their grandmothers and grandfathers of the immigrant generation. In part, this movement reflected an intellectual and socio-economic "coming of age." Well educated, prosperous, upwardly mobile, ethnic Americans felt sure enough of themselves to accept a safely distant past and, in accepting it, found a powerful antidote to feelings of marginality that often came when they crossed class and ethnic lines. Yet third- and fourth-generation Polish-Americans also found the new ethnicity appealing because it touched a sensitive psychological chord, which had little to do with ethnic background per se, but had a lot to do with the more general need for roots. Mass society in the 1970s was a rather faceless place, conducive to an assortment of psychological and personality disorders: rootlessness, alienation, anomie. Not just ethnics, but all Americans experienced these feelings in a world in which the individual increasingly became a multidigit number. Some found solace by joining new and ofttimes bizarre religious cults, while others turned to history. After author Alex Haley published his 1976 bestseller *Roots*, which pieced together the history of an Afro-American family and thus conquered slavery's legacy of anonymity, Polish-Americans and other ethnics hastened to reconstruct their own pasts and make themselves whole men and women. In

1976–1977, for example, researchers from Chicago's Polish-American community created the Oral History Archives of Chicago Polonia, 350 hours of taped interviews with 140 elderly Polish Chicagoans. In the 1970s, a similar Polish Archives Project at the University of Wisconsin–Milwaukee began to collect records and papers "which tell the story of the Milwaukee Poles,"[28] while the University of Minnesota's Immigration History Research Center launched a Polish Microfilm Project that filmed and made available to researchers Polish immigrant newspapers. Significantly, these and many other similar efforts enjoyed federal, state, or foundation funding, a further indication of the rising legitimacy of ethnicity in mainstream American society.

The return of third- and fourth-generation Polish-Americans to the ethnic fold produced many curiosities. First, theirs was a selective return to roots: they chose what of their past to accept, what to recover, what to use, and what to discard. Second, many became part-time ethnics. At the ethnic festival, the Polish bar or restaurant, the Polish film or cultural event—at play—the third and fourth generation were Poles; at work, they were indistinguishable from other Americans. Ethnicity thus slipped on and off, like Galician dancing boots. Others became professional ethnics. They might earn their livelihoods in jobs related to their own ethnicity—as linguists, translators, librarians, politicians, or professional historians—while having little else about them that was particularly ethnic. Finally, these grandchildren and great-grandchildren, by now often of ethnically mixed ancestry, created multiple ethnicities. They might choose the ethnic affiliation of one of their parents—mother or father—or borrow them both alternately. A young Polish/Italian-American, for example, might be Polish on Pulaski Day and Italian at the San Gennaro Festival, changing identity according to events and circumstances.

We could fairly conclude that the new ethnicity was a superficial and artificial phenomenon, but to do so would be to miss a critical point. For assimilated, upwardly mobile, third- and fourth-generation Polish-Americans, the new ethnicity paradoxically also helped promote career advancement. As ethnic leaders once had cultivated ethnic cohesion for their own self-serving political and economic ends, many young Polish-Americans and other ethnics found that suddenly they could turn a liability into an asset. The Polish Genealogical Society of Michigan, founded in 1978, saw its membership climb from 60 in 1982, to 210 in 1984. Newspapers, like Buffalo's *Polish American Journal*, ran stories about successful Polish-Americans as if to show their Polish-American readers that they were as able as the members of any other group. Insofar as it helped young Polish-Americans improve the image they had of themselves and their group, the new ethnicity was therefore nothing new. Two things, however, were. First, the arbiters of American culture and the practitioners of social science had begun to appreciate ethnic workers, their communities, and their cultures as a vital force in American life: in short, being "ethnic" had become "in." Second, Polish-Americans of the third and fourth generation, however nostalgically, also embraced the new ethnicity in a way that let them come to terms with, and not be ashamed of, their peasant and working-class origins.

The younger Polish-Americans' revision of, and rapprochement with, their own history is perhaps best typified by the publication of Paul Wrobel's *Our Way: Family, Parish, and Neighborhood in a Polish-American Community*, a 1979 study set in a Detroit parish. Though Wrobel faced a barrage of criticism for his work from some older middle-class Polonians because the book was, in the words of one Polish-American academician who reviewed it, an anti-elitist "apologia for the world of the Polish American working class,"[29] people of whom they had always been slightly ashamed, it offered educated young Polish-Americans many reasons for taking pride in the lives their hardworking forebears had led. Similarly, while many second-generation Polish-Americans, even those who still lived there, may have regarded their group's old urban neighborhoods with a measure of embarrassment, the new ethnicity caused many third- and fourth-generation Poles to look at them not only with curiosity but also with pride and respect. Bumper stickers like the early 1980s one that read: "Hamtramck, Michigan: An Ethnic Touch in America" mirrored this sea change.

Since the 1970s, Polish-Americans have made great strides in the social status they enjoy as a group located in the larger American society. Those gains have had less to do with the new ethnicity than might appear at first glance. Polish-Americans gained a national prominence they had never known before, and this helped elevate the reputation of the entire group. Political figures like Edmund Muskie, Barbara Mikulski, Zbigniew Brzezinski, Dan Rostenkowski, and Leon Jaworski all strode into the national limelight in the sixties and seventies. Another Polish-American, John Joseph Krol, climbed up the ranks of the Roman Catholic ecclesiastical hierarchy and in 1967 became a cardinal. In America, however, ethnic and clerical politicians have always seemed slightly suspect. It therefore remained for Polish advances in the realm of high culture to raise the value of Polish-American stock. Here the 1970s and 1980s proved luminous decades, as directors Roman Polanski and Andrzej Wajda ignited the world of film; Leszek Kolakowski challenged philosophers, political theorists, and historians with his theoretical writings; Jerzy Kosinski entranced the literary scene; and poet Czesław Miłosz won a 1980 Nobel Prize. These achievements certainly sufficed for most Americans, raising their estimation of the Polish group. But many Polish-

Americans themselves might have felt ill at ease with "their" recent successes. After all, who was it that excelled in this select group? Miłosz was a Lithuanian Pole; Kolakowski a former Marxist; and Polanski, Kosinski, and Wajda all Polish Jews. For Polish-American leaders who had wedded Polish-American identity to ethnic Polish ancestry, the Roman Catholic religion, and anti-communist politics, this must have been a disquieting discovery.

A more genuine breakthrough for Polish-American recognition came in the international arena, but it was not without its problems. The election of Karol Cardinal Wojtyła of Cracow as Pope John Paul II in 1978 sent shockwaves throughout the world. This was doubly so in America, where Wojtyła had visited and from whence Polish-American Cardinal Krol had played the role of kingmaker at the Vatican election. A forceful and charismatic leader, the Polish pope swelled the ethnic pride of his American cousins, who organized pilgrimages to Poland and Rome. But the pope endorsed a socially—and sexually—conservative theology that included opposition to artificial birth control and abortion, the ordination of women, female equality, and female roles outside the family. How would the conservative ethnic culture the popular pope espoused mesh with the more liberal, modern values of the third and fourth generation? In particular, how could young Polish-American women embrace the pope's brand of ethnicity and maintain their own feminist principles, which had grown influential in the 1970s and 1980s and perhaps addressed more of their day-to-day problems than the new ethnicity ever could?

More surprising but no less problematical was the impact that Poland's Solidarity (Solidarność) trade union movement had in the United States and in Polish America in the early 1980s. Modern-day Polish nationalist sympathizers mounted a huge relief effort for their oppressed European brethren after the declaration of martial law in Poland in December 1981; and a new wave of Solidarity refugees brought Polish America an infusion of fresh blood. Through the nightly news the name of Solidarity leader Lech Wałęsa became a household word and newscasters finally learned how to pronounce Polish consonants. With the election of a Polish Pope and the daring exploits of the courageous Solidarity movement, Polish-American pride and recognition soared. It was at this time, too, that the "Polish joke" finally lost some of its currency and its nasty sting. A political cartoon by Larry Wright, published in a 1980 issue of the *Detroit News*, perfectly illustrated the change. "How Many Polish Labor Union Members Does It Take to Change a Light Bulb?" the caption asked. Answer: "35 million—One to Screw in the Bulb and 34,999,999 to watch out for the Russian Army." The "Polish joke" had become anti-Russian or anti-Soviet political satire, just as it was in Poland. Interestingly, Bantam Books delayed publication of its latest Polish "jokebook," which had been scheduled to come out at the height of the Solidarity crisis. It did bring the book out the following year.

While the Solidarity refugees brought a fresh Polish presence to the United States, they fit into Polish America no better than had the post–WW II displaced persons, perhaps even worse. Though one recent émigré to Brooklyn vowed, "I will never give up being a Pole," he and others like him, ambitious and well educated, stood a good chance of assimilating quickly into American society once they had mastered English, leaving the older Polonians behind.[30] In the meantime, as one Detroit Polish émigré observed, they faced a "quiet resentment" from the "old-line Polish community" because "their ambitions and life-styles are different"—European and more middleclass. On their part, some Solidarity era Polish émigrés criticized Americans—presumably Polish-Americans as well— for their "shallow" view of freedom.[31] Other exiled Solidarity activists grew dismayed at the priorities of Polish America's ethnic leaders and the level of support they lent to the new Polish cause. "There are more important things to fight against than the Polish joke," one recent Polish émigré said in apparent disgust.[32]

Polish-Americans might also have wondered about the nature of the honor and recognition they suddenly had won. It smacked of Cold War cynicism for Americans to condemn military dictatorship in Poland but support it in Chile, Central America, or South Korea. How transitory was American admiration for the Poles? In the shadow of the Iranian hostage crisis and Soviet intervention in Afghanistan, were Poles—and Polish-Americans, too—simply being used as pawns in the national political arena, in the renewed Cold War? Was it not also odd that Polish-Americans should suddenly have inherited esteem not for anything they themselves had built, accomplished, or done, but for the faraway exploits of Lech Wałęsa and Karol Wojtyła? Polish-Americans had won acclaim by proxy because they too were Poles: they were of the same race and shared the same blood as Poland's new heroes. What did this mean? Polish-Americans and America's other ethnic and racial minorities may have rested more easily in the aftermath of the Nazi Holocaust thinking that race theory had gone up in the smoke of the horrific gas ovens. That Polish-Americans could benefit from Poland's present glory solely because of their common ethnic link suggests, alas, that race theory was alive and well in the American popular mind of the 1980s—a rather sinister thought.

Group members might have asked themselves how long Americans —and they themselves—would remain interested in Poland, how long their revived ethnic identity, the new ethnicity, would last. Despite their recent ethnic revival, some statistics remained fairly bleak. In 1971, one survey of Polish parochial schools found that only 20.4 percent still taught Polish history or culture, 13.5 percent taught Po-

lish reading, and a mere 4.1 percent provided religious instruction using Polish. Other measures reflected this steady erosion of ethnic
culture. In 1979, for example, while 2,452,000 Polish-Americans fourteen years of age or older still claimed Polish as their mother tongue,
fewer than one-third spoke it in their own homes. Not surprisingly,
another study reported third-generation exogamy running at 80 percent, a logical corollary to the linguistic shift. A 1982 publication
cited a disheartening fact about Polish-American organizational life:
only 7 percent of the estimated 8 to 15 million Polish-Americans belonged to a Polish-American organization. As for Polish-American
identity—the group's last, best hope—so many second- and third-
generation Poles had "drifted away from the cultural heritage . . . of
their parents and grandparents" and become "oriented toward American civilization and culture," the president of the Kosciuszko Foundation admitted in 1985, that the Foundation had decided to target
fund-raising efforts at the "American public at large" as the "best way
of reaching the largest segment of the Polish-American population."[33]

Ordinary Polish-Americans, however, gained a great deal from the
1970s ethnic revival. What they gained can be seen by reviewing two
rather bizarre outcroppings of the new ethnicity in practice. First,
the proprietor of a Scranton, Pennsylvania, auto parts store during
the late 1970s issued a call for members for an organization he had
founded, the Polish Racing Drivers of America (PRDA)—part satiri-
cal, part promoting a line of PRDA products. Second, in Detroit a
self-styled "punk rock" party band called "The Polish Muslims" in the
early 1980s released their difficult-to-characterize single. On one side
of the record was "Love Polka #9," a Polonized version of the old
rock-and-roll song, "Love Potion #9"; on the other side, "Bowling
U.S.A.," a take-off on the "Beach Boys'" hit, "Surfin' U.S.A." Perhaps
these ethnic cultural blips were insensitive and in poor taste. After
all, except for comedians Eddie Murphy, Dick Gregory, and Whoopi
Goldberg, most Black Americans by contrast have assiduously
avoided such flights of satire aimed at themselves. Alternatively,
however, in these genuinely clever group and self parodies, perhaps
young working-class and middle-class Polish-Americans alike were
showing that—uptown white, Anglo-Saxon, Protestant society be
damned—they had become comfortable with themselves. Ultimately, however, Polish-Americans' new ethnicity—their revived
ethnic identity—would survive as long as it was useful to members of
the group. Did the new ethnicity hold political saliency for Polish-
Americans in the 1970s and 1980s or promise to influence Polish-
American political behavior beyond?

7

VANGUARD OR REARGUARD?

Ethnic Politics in Mass Society

> Government is further polarizing peo-
> ple. . . . [T]he ethnic worker is fooled into
> thinking that the blacks are getting every-
> thing.
> Old prejudices and new fears are ig-
> nited. The two groups end up fighting each
> other. . . . What results is angry confronta-
> tion for tokens, when there should be an
> alliance for a whole new Agenda for Amer-
> ica.
>
> —Rep. Barbara Mikulski
> [28 September 1970]

In American pluralist politics, groups have only mattered insofar as they have wielded political clout. Author Michael Novak, patron of the so-called ethnic revival, knew that well when he proposed—and predicted—that America's white ethnics would mobilize politically in the 1970s. Novak argued, first, that they had lain silent too long and had been taken for granted; second, that, organized, they finally could claim their political due. Proponents of ethnic power like Novak hoped that America's forgotten ethnic minorities might remake America for the better in the bargain, " . . . help build a just and equitable society, free of isolation, segregation, and racism."[1]

Along with Italians, Greeks, and Slavs, Polish-Americans were to have joined this political groundswell. They, too, had ample complaints about their position in America's economic structure and their chronic lack of political power and social respect. What role had they played in American politics? Were they taking part in a great ethnic political upsurge? And, if so, to what end?

It was not clear whether the 1970s were producing an ethnic political upsurge. The same cannot be said about the 1930s, when the

Great Depression gave rise to the Democratic party's Roosevelt Coalition. Young Polish-Americans, like one New Jersey woman, remember casting their first vote for FDR and thereafter making Democratic voting a matter of course for the next twenty or thirty years. Only about 48 percent of Chicago's Polish-American voters went Democratic in 1924; four years later nearly 80 percent did so. Nationally, between 1932 and 1948, 75 to 90 percent of the Polish-American vote went to Democratic presidential candidates. One expert on Polish-American politics noted: "In many working-class city wards, the Polish Democratic vote surpassed 95 percent."[2]

In the Democratic party, Polish-Americans helped shape an entire era in American politics. Domestically, in their ethnic clubs, fraternals, and CIO union halls, they supported liberal New Deal economic policies during the Roosevelt, Truman, and Kennedy administrations. In the area of foreign policy, they injected moral righteousness and an outraged immediacy into the developing anti-communist ideology of both the Democratic and Republican parties. When Poland's pianist-statesman Ignatz Jan Paderewski died in 1941, he ordered in his will that his heart be removed from his body and turned over to one of Brooklyn's Polish Democratic leaders for safekeeping until Poland was freed from totalitarian control—heady stuff, indeed. Yoked to burdens of conscience and honor, Polish-Americans would keep the memory of the Katyn Massacre and Yalta Agreement and bolster the Democratic party's Cold War wing.

In 1944, Polish America's leaders put together the Polish American Congress in order to use growing Polish-American electoral power to lobby for United States support of a "free Poland." Drawing together some 2,500 persons from twenty-six states, the Polish American Congress was called a "most colossal piece of organizational work" by one Roosevelt administration adviser. But the Polish American Congress failed either to move American policy or to accomplish its political objectives. On the one hand, its tactics were too "moderate and restrained" and its resources too small: for 1976—1978, when records were kept, its annual expenditure was a mere $62,000, minuscule when compared to the budgets of comparable Black and Jewish-American groups.[3] On the other hand, its political influence within Polish America was decidedly limited. When Charles Rozmarek, president of the Polish American Congress, endorsed the Republican party during the 1946 and 1948 elections to protest Democratic handling of the "Polish question" at Yalta, he could not deliver the vote of his putative constituents, who still voted overwhelmingly in favor of the Democratic party. Despite a protest vote in 1952 when a majority of Polish-Americans voted for Republican presidential candidate Dwight D. Eisenhower and, in Buffalo, elected Polish Republicans running against non-Polish candidates, Polish-American voters —still heavily blue-collar in composition—found foreign policy and ethnic concerns per se less salient than domestic social and economic issues. Trying to explain persistent Democratic loyalty among Polish-Americans who declined to follow the leaders of the Polish American Congress, one Congress vice-president said, "Poland is very dear" to the majority of Polish voters, "but [the] United States is much dearer."[4] Choosing to back the party of the "forgotten man," blue-collar Polish-Americans consistently voted along class lines.

While some Polish-Americans parlayed ethnic connections and Polish-American votes into political advancement—like Detroit's mayor Roman Gribbs (Grzyb)—others with non-Polish constituencies succeeded inspite of their Polish-American backgrounds—Edmund Muskie (Marciszewski) in Maine and Leon Jaworski in Texas. On the whole, Polish-Americans did not receive political patronage commensurate with their loyalty and their "enthusiastic" political participation.[5] In congressional districts with large Polish-American populations, the group did hold proportionally no fewer seats in 1981 than, for example, Italian-Americans in districts where they were concentrated—11.3 percent of 80 districts, compared to 11.1 percent of 153 districts, respectively. But one 1971 tabulation found only 82 Polish surnames among the 12,500 entries in *Who's Who in American Politics.* Similarly, though President John F. Kennedy, with the appointment of John Gronouski as postmaster general, gave Polish-Americans cabinet-level recognition, considering their numbers and voting record Polish-Americans received surprisingly little federal patronage. Though Democratic party leaders were disaffected with the Polish American Congress for its criticism of Roosevelt's and Truman's foreign policy and its subsequent flirtations with the Republicans, this alone does not account for Polish-Americans not receiving their fair share of the political spoils they helped win. Often, Poles lacked the raw numbers to call local political shots. Sometimes they were not cohesive enough to use their potential political muscle to bargain for patronage for members of their group. To this day, for example, there is no Polish-American congressional caucus comparable to the Congressional Black Caucus, even though, as of 1980, nine Polish-Americans held House seats. Meanwhile, Polish-Americans always faced certain tactical disadvantages in a political marketplace wherein "unpronounceable" surnames were a disadvantage; changing or anglicizing one's name could cost a Polish candidate Polish votes and thus erode that candidate's natural base of support. In the long run, however, Polish-Americans gradually saw their voting strength ebb as their neighborhoods changed. Gradually power bypassed them and fell instead to more recent urban migrant groups.

While Polish-Americans may have felt cheated of their just due by the Democratic party's "ungrateful" leaders, rank-and-file Polish-

American voters—still heavily working class in composition through the 1960s—continued to vote Democratic in national elections and often even more consistently so in local contests. By the late 1960s, however, three developments began to dislodge Polish-Americans from their traditional Democratic voting patterns. First, the migration of Black Americans to the North and their political mobilization via the civil rights struggle and later the Black Power movement placed two traditionally Democratic groups in direct competition for jobs, housing, and political power within the same political party. Many Polish-Americans perceived that Democratic party leaders were being more responsive to the demands of the larger and more vocal Black American group than to their own interests and concerns. Second, as a result of postwar prosperity, Polish-Americans were earning higher incomes, becoming more middle class in composition, and as they moved out of their changing urban neighborhoods— either in flight from the Black influx or in search of the "good life"— also becoming more suburban. Historically, Democratic loyalties have declined with the kind of upward mobility Polish-Americans were now experiencing. Finally, many blue-collar Polish-Americans with New Deal Democratic loyalties felt that the party was changing in bad ways. It had veered away from traditional bread-and-butter economic positions to embrace what they believed to be, alternately, the middle- or lower-class cultural, social, and ideological concerns of antiwar activists, civil libertarians, women's and gay rights advocates, counter-cultural youth, and Black Americans. They believed the party was turning its back on its own traditions; it was deserting them.

Disenchanted white ethnic working people were disparagingly called "hard-hats," "the Silent Majority," and "Middle Americans" by people they considered "phoney white liberals."[6] One fourth-generation Polish-American interviewed in the early 1970s, however, called himself "an American workingman and a family man." Perhaps his views were a "backlash"; perhaps a distorted class consciousness or an updated version of American republicanism. Most likely, they blended all three. "Hell," he said, "I've nothing against them, Negro people . . . the ordinary colored man, just trying to get by, like you and me and the next guy." But, "they should stick to their own like we do." Who were the real trouble-makers upsetting the life of this self-styled man "in the middle"? The "loud-mouthed . . . snob-students from the snob-colleges," the "professors . . . big-brain types who look down on the rest of us," "the militants, the colored ones and the white ones, and the big business people . . . ," and "the demonstrators" were wrecking the country.[7] " . . . [H]e turns his anger to race," Maryland neighborhood activist and Congresswoman Barbara Mikulski said of men and women like this Polish-American interviewee, "—when he himself is the victim of class prejudice. He has worked hard all of his life to become a 'good American'; he and his sons have fought in every battlefield—then he is made fun of because he likes the flag."[8] But whether they blamed "the Blacks" or "the politicians" for their troubles, ethnic voters had become a restive political force, loose from their moorings, up for grabs.

Would ethnic voters like the Poles translate these feelings into their own political protest? Some liberal Polish-American—and Black—political leaders tried to head off the Polish-Black political confrontation toward which both groups were careening in the late 1960s. " . . . [B]ecause of old prejudices and new fears," Mikulski continued, "anger is generated against other minority groups rather than those who have power. What is needed is an alliance of white and black; white collar, blue collar, and no collar based upon mutual need, interdependence and respect, an alliance to develop the strategy for a new kind of community organization and political participation."[9] Looking to defuse the racial powderkeg, stabilize conditions in interracial urban neighborhoods, and possibly even work out a political alliance, in Chicago Rep. Roman Pucinski and Southern Christian Leadership Conference activist Rev. Jesse Jackson explored chances for Polish-Black cooperation. In Cleveland Poles and Blacks tried to work together through an effort they named Project Bridge. In 1972 in Buffalo, twenty prominent Blacks and Polish-Americans joined together to seek "some common ground" and "ways and means of working together for the common good of Buffalo."[10] Better known, however, was Detroit's Black-Polish Conference, a valiant effort at interracial cooperation in one of America's most racially troubled cities.

As Detroit's ashes smouldered after the city's 1967 race riot, city residents wondered how they could get themselves out of the crisis into which they had plunged. Responding to charges of Polish-American racism levelled by Rev. Andrew Greeley, the Chicago sociologist, in 1968 the Detroit Archdiocesan Priests Conference for Polish Affairs, the area association of Polish Roman Catholic clergy, issued a resolution in support of equal rights that drew upon the principles affirmed in the Polish nation's historic struggle against "persecution, suppression, and prejudice" in order to acknowledge every person's rights to "freedom of opportunity . . . in housing, education, employment, use of public facilities . . . and a decent standard of living" irrespective of "color, race, or national origin."[11] While clergy leaders Rev. Daniel Bogus and Rev. Fabian Słominski were in Washington, D.C., at the behest of Detroit Black Congressman John Conyers, the idea surfaced to institutionalize the sentiments of the Polish-American priests' resolution. Soon Detroit, where Poles (with 20 percent) and Blacks (with 44 percent) made up two-thirds of the population, had its own Black-Polish Conference. During its brief existence, the Black-Polish Conference promoted neighborhood peace, lobbied for common community issues like health facilities and better sanitation, and perhaps can be credited with helping diffuse the racial issue in the following Detroit mayoral election when a Pole, Roman Gribbs, defeated a Black opponent in a campaign notable for its lack of racial rancor.

Though proponents of the new ethnicity advocated white ethnic and Black cooperation in organizations like Detroit's Black-Polish Conference, and though such efforts at cooperation often did produce considerable good, there were limits to what they could do. They could not undo the causes of white ethnic political ferment and often could not even channel it. Some white ethnics thought attempts at interracial "cooperation" usually sold them out. Polish-American critics of the Black-Polish Conference in Detroit charged, for example, that the group advanced Black political ends at the expense of Polish-American interests. In a bitter letter to the editor, "A Disturbed Polish-American" called it and other such attempts at interracial cooperation "bogus° alliances . . . contrived by people seeking their own self-gain."[12] It is indeed true that, small and largely middle class in composition, the Detroit group never really touched Black or Polish-American working people who made up a majority of its putative constituents. Nor did it necessarily address their concerns and interests. More to the point, however, if the conference aimed at stabilizing Detroit's neighborhoods, it failed miserably. In increasing numbers, Polish-Americans and other white ethnics were moving out of the city. All this, of course, did not augur well for Democratic party unity. Poles and other white ethnics seemed ready to bolt their political home of thirty years.

Because the political allegiance of Poles and other white ethnics was in flux, the 1968 presidential election held out the promise of a political volatility that Americans had not seen since the 1932 Democratic landslide carried both houses of Congress and swept Roosevelt into the chief executive's mansion. George Wallace, the former governor of Alabama who ran for president on the American Independent party ticket, grudgingly tried to pry away disaffected ethnic voters who seemed ready for a change. Wallace, the era's symbol of race hatred and political reaction, playing on fear, prejudice, and frustration, appealed to racism and the so-called white "backlash" vote. Wallace probably drew more heavily away from the Republican than from the Democratic column in many areas, but in many wards and precincts the American Independent party doubtless attracted angry, frustrated white ethnics who formerly had voted Democratic. According to Institute of American Research and NBC News data, Wal-

---

°The choice of words was probably no accident; one of the founders of the organization was Rev. Daniel Bogus.

lace voters included up to 15 percent of the Poles and other Slavs. Meanwhile, Republican candidate Richard Nixon euphemistically called forth the same genie as the Wallace campaign and made distinct gains among working- and lower-middle-class Catholic—and often ethnic—voters. But his efforts bore decidedly less fruit in Polish-American precincts. In an analysis of voting trends in New York, New Jersey, and Connecticut, one analyst found that, "the only major Catholic group . . . *not* to show a 1960–1968 shift to Nixon was the Polish contingent. . . ."[13] Many reasons may help account for the Poles' persistent loyalty to the Democrats in 1968, but one stands out most of all: the Democratic party used ethnicity to keep them in. Whatever Polish-American voters felt about Minnesota New Dealer and civil rights warrior Hubert Humphrey, the Democratic standard-bearer, they applauded his choice of a running mate. The vice-presidential nominee was Senator Edmund Muskie who, despite his changed name, was still a fellow Pole.

Though 1968 failed to produce the expected political fall-out, conservative political analyst Kevin Phillips nonetheless contended that it marked the beginning of a fundamental political swing. In *The Emerging Republican Majority*, published in 1969, Phillips predicted that, in voting for the Alabama governor, Wallace supporters, among them numerous white ethnics, had only made a brief political sojourn en route to the Republican party (GOP). Presumably, with Muskie out of the way, Polish-American voters would now tag along. Democratic professionals may have scoffed at Phillips's far-fetched scenario and have attributed Humphrey's electoral failure more simply to the candidate's civil rights record, his association with the Johnson administration and its unpopular Vietnam War, or to some other cause. What made Phillips's political prophecy rather more plausible, however, was the antecedent socioeconomic shift that second- and third-generation ethnics had experienced in the previous twenty years. Their incomes rising and their homes increasingly suburban, these Polish-Americans and other white ethnics increasingly fitted the profile of the Republican-tending "swing" voter.

During the following twenty years, how white ethnic voters like the Poles would vote was the big question that hung in the balance in every election. As 1972 approached, the GOP finally seemed about to gain ground. An antiwar, reformist faction was taking over the national Democratic party from its "old guard," which had been discredited at the raucous 1968 Chicago convention. The now "reformed" party was about to nominate South Dakota Senator George McGovern, a reformer's reformer, for president in 1972. At the same time, Polish American Congress president Aloysius Mazewski, reviving the organization's GOP connections, in 1970 announced his support of Nixon's controversial invasion of Cambodia. "We may have differences of opinion as to the justification of our initial involvement in Vietnam . . . ," Mazewski said. "However, the time for debate has ended with the entry of our gallant fighting men into Cambodia, to deny the enemy privileged sanctuaries. . . . We do not subscribe to the cries for bug-out raised by far-out dissenters, but . . . strongly subscribe to Stephen Decatur's injunction: 'Our country, right or wrong!' " To win over Polish-American support, Nixon appointed Mazewski as an alternative United States delgate to the 25th United Nations General Assembly (some Democratic Polish-Americans believed that he "was bought cheaply"). Nixon sent prominent Republican speakers to Polish-American events and ceremonies who typically endorsed the goal of a "free Poland" and praised the Poles' "spirit of liberty," and in 1970 designated October 11 as General Pulaski Memorial Day.[14] In addition to these symbolic gestures that appealed to Polish-American ethnicity, in 1972 Nixon's "law-and-order" campaign aimed at their class, economic, and race interests, ultimately all probably more important to them than any ethnic issues per se. When the ballots were finally counted in 1972, Nixon polled roughly 53 percent of the Polish vote.

For the time being, however, the Republicans were robbed of their long predicted political realignment because Polish-American and other white ethnic voters, who had swung to the GOP in 1972, in 1976 swung back to the Democrats. The Watergate scandal (featuring the delectable sight of a Polish-American, Special Prosecutor Leon Jaworski, demanding the incriminating Watergate tapes from the president); Nixon's forced resignation, which carried Vice-President Gerald Ford into the White House; and Ford's subsequent pardon of Nixon for possible misdeeds angered Polish-American voters who, it was said, had carried traditional values into the voting booth. If this were not enough to turn them away from the GOP, however, in 1976 Ford, as presidential candidate, showed that sometimes ethnicity itself still had incredible salience to the Polish-American electorate. In a televised debate with Georgia Governor Jimmy Carter, the Democratic challenger, the verbally inept Ford angered organized Polonia by saying "there is no Soviet domination in Eastern Europe." Ford, of course, meant that the Soviet Union had not bowed the will of the resolute Poles. The press jumped on Ford's clumsy remark and the Democrats made it out to be a sensational political gaffe. Indeed, many Polish-Americans believed that the president had insulted them by glossing over the plight of their ancestral homeland. On the effect of Ford's remark on the campaign, Mazewski, president of the Polish American Congress, observed, "Our people do usually vote Democratic, but we are aware that many of them were not enthusiastic about Carter and were going to vote for President Ford. I think many of them will go back to the Democratic side now." Buffalo's Polish-American mayor concurred. "Many were undecided. Sometimes it takes one thing that pushes them over the brink. This looks like it."[15] Whatever the cause, 60 percent of the Polish-American vote went to Carter, the strongest Democratic showing by group voters since the Johnson landslide of 1964.

Polish-Americans surely helped elect Jimmy Carter in 1976. Judging by the next two elections though, they had not so much voted for the Democratic candidate as against the Republican incumbent. Their political volatility had yet to reach a state of equilibrium. Though Carter, as chief executive, made a few dramatic appointments that lent national honor to the group—Zbigniew Brzezinski as national security adviser and Edmund Muskie as secretary of state— over the next four years Polish-American voters may have found it difficult to relate to the president's Southern accent and his pious, evangelical style, so culturally alien to them. More importantly, many doubtless shared the widespread sentiment that Carter seemed ineffectual and "weak," especially in comparison to conservative Ronald Reagan, the Republican party's 1980 presidential nominee. In Texas, Leon Jaworski organized a Democrats for Reagan unit. "Better to back a competent extremist than an incompetent moderate," Jaworski said.[16] As the election neared, a Polish-American electoral realignment once again seemed possible.

Whether they were realigning probably matters less to America's Poles than to the political leaders of both parties, for Polish-American ballots made up a hefty chunk of America's total vote. A review of the statistics is illuminating. Estimates place the size of the Polish-American population between 5 and 12 million.° Poles composed 5 percent of the population in seven large states with a total of 133 electoral votes—New York, Illinois, Pennsylvania, Connecticut, Massachusetts, Wisconsin, and New Jersey—and between 3 and 5 percent in four other populous states. In 1980, several metropolitan areas also had sizeable Polish blocs—1 million in metropolitan Chicago; some 300,000 to 400,000 in metropolitan Detroit; 200,000 in Buffalo; 200,000 in Milwaukee; and large concentrations in and around Pittsburgh, Philadelphia, Cleveland, and New York. According to one political analyst, "Because all ten states where [Polish-Americans] are concentrated are politically competitive, any shift in voting by a group as cohesive as the Poles in closely contested elections could mean victory or defeat to Democratic or Republican candidates for public office."[17]

In 1980, both President Carter and Republican challenger Ronald Reagan therefore went after the Polish vote. Reagan's anti-Soviet rhetoric, his attacks on Carter's economic policy, and his social conservatism were intended as a generic appeal to dissatisfied Demo-

°The discrepancy in figures relates to the method of estimation and, often, its purpose.

crats, including working-class and lower-middle-class ethnics like the
Poles. Carter, meanwhile, introduced specifically ethnic themes into
his campaign by strongly backing Solidarity, promising $670 million
in food credits to Poland, wooing Polish-American leaders at the centennial celebration of the Polish National Alliance in Chicago, and using the services of Muskie and Brzezinski on the campaign trail.
Though Reagan eventually won the contest with the help of 39 percent of the Polish-American vote, a plurality of 43 percent of the
group still backed Carter. GOP strategists once again failed to shift a
majority of Polish-Americans into the Republican column.

Like a traditional New Deal Democrat, however, Republican President Reagan pushed all the right ethnic buttons when he ran for re-
election in 1984 against Minnesota New Dealer Walter Mondale. One
typical day on the ethnic political stump had Reagan lunching with
125 Polish-Americans and veterans of the WW II Polish Home Army,
boasting of sanctions applied to Poland after the imposition of martial
law there in December of 1981, and announcing that he would seek a
$10 million congressional appropriation as a United States contribu-
tion to a new Polish farm improvement program administered by the
Roman Catholic Church, a non-Communist program. More graphic
still was a Reagan barnstorming trip to Polish America's shrine town
of Doylestown, Pennsylvania. There the president ate Polish pan-
cakes, excoriated the evils of abortion, and extolled the virtues of parochial school. He proudly declared, "Thank God for Pope John Paul
II," from whom he sought "advice and guidance on numerous occa-
sions." He also mentioned Yalta. For his trouble he received a wild
reception from an "exuberant" crowd that sang the traditional Polish
toast song, *"Sto Lat"*—"A hundred years. A hundred years. May you
live a hundred years."[18] Reagan's welcome followed a special coup:
Polish America's Cardinal Krol introduced the president and praised
his policies. In November 1984, Ronald Reagan got his Polish-
American majority, narrowly outpolling Mondale 51 to 49 percent.[19]

Clearly, Polish-Americans had ridden through a major political
groundswell during the past decade and a half that had a tremulous
impact on American politics. Had they also undergone a political realignment as predicted by GOP strategist Kevin Phillips? This question is important in determining the political ramifications of their
participation in the ethnic revival called the new ethnicity. In an-
swering, it becomes obvious that in the 1980s, the Polish-American
electorate—criss-crossed by divisions based upon occupation, resi-
dence, generation, education, ideology, and religion—was also divided into at least three segments, each exhibiting different voting
behavior.

First, despite stereotypes depicting the entire group as politically
moderate or even conservative, many Polish-Americans did not join

the so-called Reagan Revolution of the Right. During the years of "backlash" politics, Polish-American names have always graced the lists of backers—and sometimes leaders—of the era's progressive political and social causes. It might be hard to name prominent Polish-Americans among the leaders of the Republican party or the political Right, but Polish-Americans still figured prominently in the liberal wing of the Democratic party, though admittedly not in great numbers. Rep. Barbara Mikulski of Maryland remains a leading progressive in Congress.° Other prominent Polish-American politicians, like Rep. Roman Pucinski (D., Ill.) or Rep. Dan Rostenkowski (D., Ill.), the powerful chair of the House Ways and Means Committee,° may vote more eclectically than Mikulski but also share an essentially liberal political outlook. Polish-Americans have more visibly stamped their imprint on the American labor movement in the fifteen to twenty years leading up to the 1980s, fighting for union democracy and workers' rights. Until he and his family were brutally murdered, allegedly on order of his union opponents, Joseph (Jock) Yablonski spoke the voice of reform in the United Mine Workers Union. Twenty years later, in 1976–1977, Edward Sadlowski, Jr., another insurgent Polish-American labor leader, challenged union establishment candidate Lloyd McBride to succeed I.W. Abel as president of the United Steelworkers of America. Of some 577,000 ballots cast, Sadlowski's campaign to topple McBride fell only about 80,000 votes short. Polish-Americans also joined in causes more specifically identified with America's political Left. In 1985, for example, a Polish-American directed Amnesty International's Campaign to Abolish Torture in the World, while in 1986 a Polish-American School Sister of St. Francis was indicted for her work in the Sanctuary movement, assisting Central American refugees—"illegal aliens"—fleeing political repression in their homelands. When he died in 1982, Polish-American sculptor Korczak Ziolkowski had spent the last thirty-five years of his life carving a gigantic statue of the Sioux Indian Chief Crazy Horse out of a granite mountain in South Dakota's Black Hills at the request of tribal leaders who said they wanted "the white man to know the red man had great heroes too."[20]

As for rank-and-file Polish-American voters, while 51 percent had voted for Reagan in 1984, 49 percent had not! This was an impressive showing compared to the vote totals of, for example, Irish Catholics (56 percent to 44 percent) or Italian-Americans (58 percent to 41 percent). Less a part of the new ethnicity than the old, nearly a majority of Polish-Americans remained Democrats. Presidential balloting tells only part of the Polish-American political story and so tends to obscure it. While a slim majority of Polish-Americans were giving Rea-

° As of 1985.

gan their votes in 1984, in neither the 1982 nor the 1984 congressional races did Polish voters shift to the Republican party. According to American Broadcasting Company (ABC) News exit-polls among Poles and other Slavs, Democratic candidates polled about 63 percent in the 1982 election and outpolled the GOP 59 percent to 41 percent even during the 1984 Reagan landslide. Despite talk of realignment, most Polish-Americans remained Democratic and continued to poll liberal on a range of economic issues.

Second, despite the fact that Polish America remained Democratic, it was not as Democratic as it used to be. At one time as many as nine out of ten Polish-American voters backed FDR's party, and party leaders counted on this level of support for their overall majorities. In the early 1980s only five or six out of ten Polish-Americans backed the Democrats. This change constituted a major political event: it was a realignment. The meaning of this electoral movement bears further examination.

At the outset, for example, it is not clear that the Polish-American voters who switched to Reagan and the Republicans made that switch as Polish-Americans. While Reagan did use an ethnic appeal to win their support, his behavior as candidate and later as president also might have alienated group voters. Reagan's 1980 campaign featured the candidate telling a "Polish joke" to a group of newspaper reporters. In the White House, Reagan later moved ethnic matters to the nation's political backburners by closing the Office of Ethnic Affairs, perhaps a particular blow to the Poles given their record of interest in promoting ethnicity regardless of their own political affiliation. Democrat Roman Pucinski had led the fight to obtain passage of an Ethnic Studies Heritage bill in Congress in the early 1970s; the Polish American Congress also vigorously supported it. Finally, the president surrounded himself with "Born-Again" Christians of the so-called Moral Majority who, while they may have shared conservative ethnics' own dislike of feminists, homosexuals, atheists, and radicals, also scorned trade unionists, Roman Catholics, and the ethnics themselves.

Arguably, it was in their other identities and affiliations that Democratic voters who happened also to have Polish ancestry shifted to the Republican column. As third- and fourth-generation Polish-Americans entered middle-class occupations, earned larger incomes, and moved to the suburbs, they came more to resemble nonethnic Republican voters. As they moved to the GOP, they did so as middle-class suburbanites, not as members of an ethnic group. Voting Republican was thus another aspect of upward mobility and assimilation, of "having arrived." Declining Democratic totals among Americans of Polish descent thus might have more correctly represented a shrinkage in the size of the group.

Many blue-collar Polish-Americans who changed over to the Republican party also seem to have done so because their ethnicity had expired. Some of them voted for Ronald Reagan because they identified with this God-fearing, up-beat, mass-marketed, patriotic American. They voted not as ethnics, but as Americans. Others invoked the new ethnicity when they backed Reagan and the GOP, but for them new ethnicity no longer meant what it had in the 1970s. In the 1930s the Democratic party recruited ethnic working-class support by mobilizing the "have nots" against the "haves." In the early 1970s, Michael Novak, Barbara Mikulski, and other advocates of the new ethnicity tried to replicate this formula as a means of bringing ethnics and Blacks together again. But in forty years, "have nots" had disappeared. Public policy and pluralist politics instead pitted ethnic "have littles" against Black "want mores." Working- and lower-middle-class ethnics feared, with reason, that Black gains would not come at the expense of middle-class white, Anglo-Saxon Protestant suburbanites, but at their expense and that of their children. This sounded the death knell of coalition politics between the two groups. Michael Novak himself abandoned hope for progressive social change within the Democratic party and by the 1980s had taken up a place in the right-wing think-tank, the American Enterprise Institute; the new ethnicity also changed in meaning for many ethnic voters. Melding class and economic interests together, it soon had less to do with culture and group and more to do with race, color, and sometimes racism. Thus, some voters of Polish descent who left the Democratic party in the early 1980s and voted for Reagan were, in a sense, no longer "Polish-Americans": their "new ethnicity" was *white.*

A third segment of the Polish-American electorate in the 1980s was the "swing" voter. Swing voting was a new phenomenon in Polish America, where loyalty to party had been a moral duty. These voters—perhaps 20 percent of the Polish-American electorate—had not shifted to the Republican party but were willing to cast their ballots either for Republicans or Democrats. One aspect of the phenomenon in 1980 was that 15 percent of Polish-American voters chose Independent John Anderson, the third-party candidate for president, over both Carter and Reagan. Traditional voters, not unlike those who remained in the Democratic fold, responded favorably to Reagan when he praised hard work, promised lower taxes, and vowed to curtail "welfare" and other transfer payments to the poor. Whether they would stay in the Republican column probably depended upon whether—and how much—GOP economic policy benefited them, and whether the Democratic party could present candidates more dynamic than McGovern, Carter, or Mondale and a program that addressed their issues—economic fairness for tax-payers and working people and recognition of their social concerns and cultural values— as the old Democratic party had.

A comment made by one New Jersey working-class Polish-American woman of the second generation leads to the conclusion that Polish-American voters had grown disenchanted with the Democratic party not so much because they had changed but because party leaders and programs had. The party's platform had become diffuse and little resembled party principles of the Depression era. Many of its leaders were mealy-mouthed and distant from their local constituencies. A traditionalist on social and cultural issues, this Polish-American woman criticized Democrats Jimmy Carter and Walter Mondale, but not because they were too liberal. She also decried Republican President Ronald Reagan. No, she preferred Geraldine Ferraro, the 1984 Democratic vice-presidential candidate; Edward Kennedy, the Democrats' progressive champion; and Mario Cuomo, New York's liberal Democratic governor, the party's 1984 keynote speaker, FDR reincarnate.[21] Perhaps Democratic party strategists had a lot to learn about the enigmatic white ethnic vote. In fighting for cultural and social liberalism, a worthy goal in and of itself, the Democratic party had lost its concern for neighborhoods, communities, grass roots. But did that mean it had to ape the cultural conservatism of the Republicans? On economic issues, perhaps it simply had not gone Left enough.

The votes of culturally traditional men and women, those who still enjoyed strong ties to the ethnic community, the parishes, the social networks, the neighborhoods, the families, the values, and the traditions—ties to their ethnicity as daily lived—are not yet owned by the Republicans. Their support, though often alienated by recent Democratic candidates and programs, still hangs in the balance. One Polish-American working man in New Jersey, for example, in 1984 remarked, "Reagan is good for the rich."[22] If working- and lower-middle-class Polish-Americans conclude that Reaganomics has attacked middle-class entitlements like federal student aid and Social Security, has driven industry to the Sun Belt and jobs overseas, and has allowed interest rates on home mortgages to remain too high—all this while subvening upper-middle- and upper-class taxpayers through economic deregulation and retrogressive tax "reform"—they may shift political loyalties again. " . . . [T]he Slavic voter," political analysts Mark R. Levy and Michael S. Kramer wrote in the early 1970s, "can no longer be taken for granted by the Democrats or ignored by the Republicans as unimportant to their coalition. The Slavic voter is more discriminating than ever, and the politician who forgets this political axiom does so at his peril."[23] In short, the Republicans may lose them, or the Democrats win them back, by what they say and do after the 1980s.

The Polish-American political upsurge was therefore far more limited than Republican strategists like Kevin Phillips might have hoped. But it was also different. Focusing too narrowly on electoral politics misses an important facet of the ethnic revival of the 1970s. The new ethnicity also introduced—albeit often haltingly and tentatively—a "new politics." Similar to Black politicians who had been touched by the Black Power movement, Polish-American candidates occasionally used their ethnicity in what seemed to be an appeal directed specifically at Polish-American voters. In his unsuccessful 1982 Michigan gubernatorial primary bid, for example, Democrat David Plawecki used placards and bumper-stickers showing his name printed in a graphic style evocative of the unforgettable red and white *Solidarność* logo. But the new ethnic politics went far beyond style and also shaped political content.

The new ethnic politics produced a fresh wave of mobilization and organization among groups like the Poles. Some of it featured cooperation across ethnic lines, like the recently formed Slavic Caucus in the National Education Association, which in 1983 boasted 177 members. The caucus passed a resolution backing Solidarity, but it also considered progressive stands on a range of national and international issues like nuclear disarmament, health care, and apartheid.[24] More ethnic mobilization and organizing had taken place on the neighborhood, local, and community level. In early 1983, Buffalo Poles established a new *English*-language Polish-American newspaper, the *Polish American Voice*, and with it organized a grassroots neighborhood political movement. In 1985 its editor, David Franczyk, won election to the Buffalo City Council. In the Greenpoint section of Brooklyn, the Polish and Slavic Center encouraged advocacy and activism around neighborhood, social, and cultural issues. In 1979 in Detroit, six "Polish-American Slavic Parishes" joined together in the Poletown Inter-Parish Council, which, in addition to other goals, sought "to identify common problems[,] . . . to share resources . . . ," and " . . . to foster ethnically based community development."[25] These and other local efforts received national recognition and encouragement. Since its founding in 1970 by the late Monsignor Geno Baroni, the National Center for Urban Ethnic Affairs (NCUEA) in Washington, D.C., now headed by John Kromkowski, has lobbied on behalf of the old urban ethnic enclaves and has worked to aid ethnic neighborhood groups in waging their local political fights.

It is not clear whether such localism represented political proclivities that were Polish-American (ethnic) or more generically blue-collar/working-class. The National Center for Urban Ethnic Affairs, however, mingled class and ethnic positions together to sketch out a political vision that departed from both the reactionary politics of "backlash," which attempted to do the same thing, and the hierarchi-

cal, formalistic, bureaucratic pattern that has evolved since the New
Deal. The NCUEA newsletter, *Buildingblocks*, maintained

> Rightly nurtured, ethnicity is the bridge of community . . . not a code
> word of social divisiveness. . . . NCUEA will continue to aid the well
> launched neighborhood movement to organize transportation facili-
> ties, rebuild commercial areas, preserve and develop the particular
> character of the neighborhood, save and rebuild its stock of housing
> and get its share of services and resources from governing bodies.

Criticizing "narrow self-interest" and "selfish privatism," the
NCUEA advocated political cooperation among groups, "the negoti-
ation of ethnic alliances." "The urban ethnic working class," *Buildingblocks* concluded, "should champion the cause of cultural pluralism
built on the most generous and unselfish impulses of ethnic values
that have always sustained our people." This was a new politics.[26]

In some places, the new ethnic politics did revive interest in interracial coalition-building. The defeat of a Common Council scheme in
Buffalo, which would have wiped out the city's Fillmore district, traditionally a Polish-American seat, ignited a political scrap between
Poles and Blacks. Buffalo's *Polish American Voice* asked if a Black/
Polish political coalition were nonetheless possible. One writer for
the newspaper concluded that such a coalition was more desirable
than ever before and, indeed, quite possible, *if* Blacks "understand
how Poles feel about their neighborhoods" and Poles "respect the hu-
manity of their Black neighbors."[27] In 1984, the Black/Polish Coalition of Buffalo was formed in order to try to build bridges between
the two previously warring groups. Presumably some Blacks and
Polish-Americans realized that both groups shared common ground
around the issues of identity and powerlessness and that neither had
caused the other's problems.

The new ethnic politics also produced a new assertiveness, even a
stridency, among Polish-Americans whose political tactics had usually shown moderation and restraint. Polish-Americans and other ethnics squeezed concessions from the federal Census Bureau over the
planned method of enumeration in 1980, which would have drasti-
cally undercounted members of ethnic groups, diminishing their political clout. Polish-Americans also increasingly took to the courts.
Sometimes they used this means to fight defamation, a stronger approach than merely writing protest letters. The Polish Guardian Society, for example, sued actor Burt Reynolds for anti-Polish material
that appeared in *The End*, a motion picture in which he starred. In
1978, a second-generation Michigan Pole filed a $600,000 damage
suit against the Ford Motor Company for allegedly failing to stop
anti-Polish harassment perpetrated against him on the job. "I'm
proud of being Polish," the litigant said.[28] Though the suit was the

first of its kind in a Michigan court, similar action filed in the United States Supreme Court by a Mexican-American truck driver had set a precedent for such a complaint. After the Ford suit, a Polish-American General Motors Corporation employee took similar action against the giant automaker. Earlier, a Michigan compensation referee had ruled that quitting her job over anti-ethnic harassment did not disqualify her from receiving unemployment compensation payments.[29] Other Polish-Americans launched legal actions to protect the economic position of members of the group. Perhaps recalling the injunction of Eugene Kusielewicz, then president of the Kosciuszko Foundation—"We have to get ahead of our parents; our children have to get ahead of us. Only then will we count in America."[30]—the Polish American Congress in 1978 and 1979 supported the challenges to "affirmative action" in the Bakke and Weber "reverse discrimination" Supreme Court cases (clearly, they had yet to reach rapprochement with Black Americans on this point). Finally, and perhaps most uncharacteristically, a few Polish-Americans began to resort to direct action to stand up for their rights—not unlike their immigrant forebears had done during America's heroic labor organizing drives. Polish-Americans in Detroit's Poletown neighborhood staged a sit-in inside their church in 1981 to prevent it from being torn down to make way for a new Cadillac plant. They had to be hauled out by city police. In 1983, in Longmeadow, Massachusetts, Polish-Americans forced bicentennial committee officials to unearth a "time-capsule" in order to remove a book of anti-Polish jokes from it. One Polish-American woman had vowed to get the book removed, she said, even if "I have to get a shovel and do it myself."[31]

Most significant of all, however, the new ethnic politics criticized the middle-class Lockean individualism enshrined in American law, promoted new forms of social and economic organization, and advanced a new concept of rights. During the recent deindustrialization of many Snow Belt cities in the industrial Northeast and north central states, blue-collar Polish-Americans and other often ethnic working people condemned corporations for plant closings that destroyed their neighborhoods and took away their jobs. They challenged private enterprise assumptions about the American economy when they participated in employee buy-outs of the factories in which they worked—an effort to prevent them from being shut down. The Polish-Americans in Detroit, faced with the demolition of their neighborhood for a reindustrialization project, condemned General Motors Corporation officials who wanted the land on which their homes and church stood. Rev. Joseph Karasiewicz, the local pastor, and Thomas Olechowski, president of Detroit's Poletown Neighborhood Council, published the following statement in a Detroit Polish-American newspaper:

The use of eminent domain by Multi-National, private, Corporate powers, [sic] turns democracy into a sham and working people's property deeds into meaningless papers; lends sovereign state police power to secretive, anti-democratic, profit-centered corporations, who use the tax structure as just another vehicle and the government as its willing tool and accomplice.[32]

Would Republican strategists have believed ordinary Polish-Americans capable of such inflammatory language? These Polish-Americans argued that, while American law has recognized that individuals and "corporate persons" (corporations) have rights, neighborhoods and communities should have rights too. In addressing the issue of anti-Polish defamation Aloysius Mazewski, president of the Polish American Congress, remarked, " . . . maybe they should change the laws so that groups as well as individuals can sue for defamation. . . . "[33] In the view of this Polish-American, perhaps groups also should have rights.

Only time will tell whether the anti-individualistic, sometimes anticapitalistic, corporatist notions of these Polish-Americans would affect American political discourse in important and lasting ways. If they do, these Polish-American contributions to the new ethnic movement will have helped accomplish a veritable revolution in American law, politics, and life. In the words of Congresswoman Barbara Mikulski, they would outline "a whole new Agenda for America."[34] For individual Polish-Americans and for American society, it must finally be asked, would that be bad or good?

EPILOGUE

Polish-American Ethnicity— Its Meaning and Its Future

> . . . [I]t is the same old story over and over
> again, eh, Stanislaw? And it happens to all
> of us, only in different ways—a little joy, a
> little sorrow, and the hope for maybe just a
> little glory. And so many different things
> happen, in so many different ways, in so
> many different places; and still it is always
> the same story and it always ends the same
> way. . . . Tomorrow morning, I will throw
> a flower into your grave and maybe a
> handful of earth, and try to remember
> again how it was in the beginning . . . IS
> NOW AND EVER SHALL BE, WORLD
> WITHOUT END. AMEN.
>
> —Richard Bankowsky, *A Glass
> Rose* (1958)

During the mass migration years, it was not so hard to define the Polish immigrants who knocked at America's gates. They went to live in
Polish neighborhoods, which they called the *okolica.* They took the
term *okolica* from the Polish word for "eye." Their world was tangible
and immediate; they could touch it, hear it, see it.

The young Jan and Maria Kowalskis and most of their compatriots
—who would become the immigrant miners, millhands, and factory
workers—were rural people with country customs and values oriented toward stability and family, security and home. Most were also
Roman Catholics, but their religion was a distinctive blend of magic
and mysticism, rural superstition and orthodox belief. Fatalistic, pray-
erful, and hoping for a better afterlife, above all they venerated the
Blessed Virgin Mary—*Matka Boska*°—Poland's patroness. To this
they added characteristics derived from their world of work. Sheltered in patriarchal, matrifocal families—child-centered families
with strong fathers and venerated Polish mothers—these immigrant

°The Mother of God.

143

Poles prized steady, usually factory, work, saved their money, and gave generously to their nuns, their priests, and their parish. To them, "success" was quiet and simple enough: homes of their own, a beautiful church, and respectful, hard-working, dutiful children who would take care of them in their old age and follow in their footsteps. Finally, many of these immigrants glowed hot with a singular political passion. As they tried to resurrect their often martyred motherland, they lived the politics of Polish nationalism and imbibed its insurrectionary, romantic myths.

Compared to America's "Polish pioneers," the second—Polish-American—generation was harder to define. These mostly blue-collar ethnic Americans spoke an odd patois of peasant Polish and Polonized American words that mirrored the hybrid nature of their culture, but more often they spoke English. Their culture had Polish elements and American ones, but really it was a new Polish-American synthesis that resembled the cultures of America's other blue-collar, Catholic ethnic groups. Most second-generation Poles had divided loyalties and identities, which were still rooted in the parish, the family, and the neighborhood—the familiar workers' world. Already, however, some had begun to leave that world as they took better paying jobs, bought suburban homes, and left the urban ethnic enclave behind. How "Polish" were they? How "Polish-American"? Some were—as the sociologists would say—stereotypically marginal men and women, suspended between two social and cultural worlds. Others made the leap quite well and considered themselves nothing less than full-fledged Americans.

One could still plainly say who the men and women in both these groups were. In 1944, Rev. Joseph Swastek, the Orchard Lake priest and Polish studies founder, explained that the Polish-American " . . . is of common folk, peasant origin . . . for the most part Roman Catholic in belief. . . , " culturally shaped by four major formative influences: religious idealism; an agrarian, semifeudal peasant background; Poland's political and cultural bondage; and the American Dream.[1] With the coming of the third and fourth generations, however, defining what a Polish-American is became a far trickier matter, for ethnicity to them often seemed an intangible thing. Some, of course, remained snugly sheltered in the older, blue-collar Polish-American communities, living and working as their parents had done, marrying within the group. For all intents and purposes, they formed a kind of eddy in time, missing the major changes that were remaking the society and other Polish-Americans in their age cohort, reproducing the second-generation blue-collar world. The rest—probably a large majority—were more integrated into the larger society around them and perhaps geographically and occupationally more mobile. "Polish-American" was something that they called themselves—or that others called them—but only sometimes, if at all. Perhaps it did join them to customs, places, and other members of their group in ways that non-Poles could never be so joined. Altogether it was an occasional identity, one that coexisted with other, often more compelling, identities and the cultures and associations that accompanied them—musician, engineer, American, Democrat, socialist, writer, softball team member, or historian. Culturally, little about these young men and women was identifiably Polish or Polish-American. Homogenized—or, for the upwardly mobile, assimilated—they were Polish-Americans only when they wanted to be. Their Polish-American identity has persisted so long that there is no reason to suppose that it will expire, even among the grandchildren of the grandchildren of the immigrants—world without end. Amen.

Is the retention of ethnic identity important to Polish-American descendants? Does it mean anything? What good does it do young men and women to practice an occasional ethnic custom, to speak a few words of kitchen Polish, to visit a Polish parish at Eastertide or Christmas, to bear a Polish-sounding surname, or even to know that their distant forebears were immigrants? They would never know their parents for what they were, never know what they sacrificed—no more than the second-generation Polish-Americans had known their parents of the immigrant generation. In the end, all young Polish-Americans could do would be to clutch after a receding past and try to recover the fleeting history of yesterday's hopes and struggles and dreams. One Polish-American scholar called theirs "an adulterated, hollow sub-culture. . . . "[2] In the same vein, sociologist Stephen Steinberg more recently has asked: " . . . can ethnicity, especially in its attenuated forms, provide the nexus for social life that it did in another era for people quite unlike ourselves? Can it be more than a palliative for spiritual yearnings that are not fulfilled elsewhere?" In short, was it anything more than " . . . a comfortable illusion to shield us from present-day discontents?"[3]

In order to avoid precisely what Steinberg and others have criticized in the so-called ethnic revival, another scholar of the group proposed an overhaul in middle-class Polish-Americans' orientation to their ethnicity, which would bring them closer to a full participation in modern American life, but at the same time would make them more like urbane Poles in modern-day Poland.

> Change from the narrow in-group identity . . . based on isolated communities to broad concepts of direct involvement in the mainstream of American life. Change from the static base of folk-cultural identity to a dynamic . . . socio-cultural distinctiveness based on the conscious cultivation of unique values and patterns. . . . Change from exclusive emphasis on the past, to include the contemporary living Polish culture as it evolves in Poland and among Poles abroad. . . . [4]

Yet, unlike middle-class Black Americans, who are still in many ways forced to remain separate and apart, upwardly mobile and assimilable Polish-Americans are much less likely to develop a true biculturalism.[5]

It is too soon to gauge the broader cultural and political impact of the various manifestations of the new ethnicity among Polish-Americans. But we can, in the end, conclude that at the very least it has served personal and psychological purposes for the persons who have embraced it. In the 1970s, Rev. Leonard Chrobot, now president of St. Mary's College at Orchard Lake, tried to update and refine the definition of this elusive Polish-American identity. "Who am I," Chrobot asked, and what is a Polish-American?[6] Polish-American identity, he proposed, is a critical knowledge of the special heritage of one's Polish past that lets one overcome the pain of rootlessness and helps one become a better human being.

Some of the Polish-Americans who read this book will do so because they know who they are; others, because they want to find out. In doing so, they—we—may wish to reflect on the words of an essay written in the 1950s by a young Polish-American in Hamtramck, Michigan, who won a *Reader's Digest* sponsored essay contest on the theme, "Why I Am Proud of My Polish Ancestry:"

> I am proud that I am a Pole—and for good reasons. My Polish ancestry entitles me to a share in a history that is rich in God-fearing heroes and heroines, who have championed the cause of liberty, peace, and freedom; of honesty and justice; of equality and brotherhood.
>
> Polish descent offers a heritage of honor. . . .
>
> YES, I am proud I am a Pole—for a good Pole has every right and reason to be a good American.[7]

BIBLIOGRAPHICAL ESSAY

In their century-long struggle against statelessness and national oppression, Poles employed historical memory as a means of keeping Poland alive. There is, accordingly, a vast literature in several languages on Polish and Polish-American subjects. Because it is impossible to review all of it here, this bibliographical essay will attempt a far more modest task. As these pages will be of principal use to the beginning student of Polish and Polish-American history and to the general reader, I have decided to include works that are most accessible and available. Most of the writings discussed here are, therefore, books; most are in English. For a comprehensive bibliography of English and Polish citations on Polish immigration history, see Irena Paczyńska and Andrzej Pilch, eds., *Materiały do Bibliografii Dziejów Emigracji oraz Skupisk Polonijnych w Ameryce Północnej i Południowej w XIX i XX Wieku* (History of Polish Emigration and Polish Communities in North and South Americas in the 19th and 20th Century: Bibliographical Materials) (Warsaw: Państwowe Wydawnictwo Naukowe, 1979). For a brief review of the historiography, also see Andrzej Brożek, "Historiography of Polish Emigration to North America," *Immigration History Newsletter* 18 (May 1986): 1–4.

In addition to these references, there are numerous articles on the subject in several specialized publications: *Polish American Studies, Polish Review, Slavic Review,* the *Kosciuszko Foundation Newsletter,* the *Annals of the Polish Roman Catholic Archives and Museum.* There are, of course, also a wealth of competent unpublished master's theses and doctoral dissertations. The serious reader is directed to these useful sources, most of which, for the sake of brevity, I have chosen to omit here.

The following essay is organized by chapter in order to aid the reader with specific questions or specialized interests. Where appropriate, I have included a brief historiographical discussion.

1
From Hunger, "for Bread"
Rural Poland in the Throes of Change

In order to fathom the Polish-American experience, one must first understand the long and complicated history of Poland. The most available general history is Oscar Halecki, *A History of Poland,* translated by Monica Gardner and Mary Corbridge-Patkaniowska (New

York: David McKay Co., 1976). It was recently reprinted, but the
book may be of only limited utility to the novice because it assumes
prior familiarity with its subject and because it is stylistically dated.
Preferable is the massive tome authored by Stefan Kieniewicz, Alek-
sander Gieysztor, and a team of Polish scholars, *History of Poland*, 2d
ed. (Warsaw: PWN-Polish Scientific Publishers, 1979). Possible sub-
stitutes for the Kieniewicz volume, which is informed by a Marxist
historiographical perspective, include the older classic by William F.
Reddaway, *The Cambridge History of Poland, 1697–1935* (Cambridge:
Cambridge University Press, 1941) and the recently published, very
lively and readable two-volume work by Norman Davies, *God's Playground: A History of Poland* (New York: Columbia University Press,
1984).

As a supplement to these general histories, a large number of the-
matic and monographic works are also available, many of which are
first-rate. On the Polish feudal economy, one may read the rather
theoretical work by the outstanding Polish scholar, Witold Kula, *An
Economic Theory of the Feudal System: Towards a Model of the Polish
Economy, 1500–1800*, translated by Lawrence Garner (London: NLB,
1976), which establishes a background for understanding Polish agricultural change in the nineteenth century. Two works on agricultural
change have now become standard: Piotr S. Wandycz, *The Lands of
Partitioned Poland, 1795–1918* (Seattle: University of Washington
Press, 1974) and the more critical book by Stefan Kieniewicz, *The
Emancipation of the Polish Peasantry* (Chicago: University of Chicago
Press, 1969). A capable summary of the developments examined in
the above appears in Caroline Golab, *Immigrant Destinations* (Philadelphia: Temple University Press, 1977), while several works on special topics supplement these surveys. For an overview of the
historiography of the 1846 in Galician jacquerie, a central topic in the
history of class relations in the nineteenth-century Galician countryside, and of Polish nationalism, see Thomas W. Simons, Jr., "The Peasant Revolt of 1846 in Galicia: Recent Polish Historiography," *Slavic
Review* 30 (December 1971): 795–817. A further discussion of conditions in Galicia is found in the sympathetic classic by Emily Greene
Balch, *Our Slavic Fellow Citizens* (New York: Charities Publication
Committee, 1910). For contemporary eyewitness descriptions of conditions in Poland, the reader may wish to consult the novels of Władysław Reymont and Henryk Sienkiewicz; the travel account of Louis
E. Van Norman, *Poland the Knight Among Nations* (New York: Fleming H. Revell Co., 1907); and the fascinating and immensely colorful
document, Jan Słomka, *From Serfdom to Self-Government: Memoirs
of a Polish Village Mayor, 1842–1927*, translated by William John
Rose, English shortened edition (London: Minerva Publishing Co.,
1941). On the rise of Polish peasant politics through the modern pe-

riod the reader might wish to refer to Olga Narkiewicz, *The Green Flag: Polish Populist Politics, 1867–1970* (London: Croom Helm; Totawa, N.J.: Rowman and Littlefield, 1976).

Finally, the reader will want to turn to the rich, specialized literature on the migration process itself. The peerless classic is, of course, William I. Thomas and Florian Znaniecki, *The Polish Peasant in Europe and America*, 2 vols. (New York: Knopf, 1927), which, though principally a sociological examination of "disorganization" among uprooted peasant immigrants, is nonetheless an invaluable source for the history of Polish rural society during the mass migration years. This work is long out of print, but happily an abridged edition, edited and with a long introduction by sociologist Eli Zaretsky, has recently been published by the University of Illinois Press. For a statistical supplement, the reader should refer to the long article by Johann Chmelar, "The Austrian Emigration; 1900–1914," translated by Thomas C. Childers, *Perspectives in American History* 7 (1973): 273–378, which corroborates the findings of such scholars as Frank Thistlethwaite and John S. and Leatrice MacDonald on the push factors of emigration.

Looking at the human face of migration, the reader may wish to turn to Polish emigrant letters. Those contained in translation in the Thomas and Znaniecki volume, cited above, are more accessible than the letters assembled in the more recent Polish-language collection edited by Witold Kula and others, *Listy Emigrantów z Brazylii i Stanów Zjednoczonych* (Warsaw: Ludowa Spółdzielnia Wydawnicza, 1973). On the migration policy of the partitioning powers and Polish thought on the emigration question, an excellent work is Benjamin Murdzek, *Emigration in Polish Social-Political Thought, 1870–1914*, East European Monographs, No. 33 (Boulder, Colo.: East European Quarterly, 1977).

The last word on Polish emigration to the United States remains to be written. One concise work very worth consulting is Victor Greene's article on "Poles" that appears in *The Harvard Encyclopedia of American Ethnic Groups*, edited by Stephan Thernstrom (Cambridge, Mass.: Harvard University Press, 1980), pp. 787–803.

2

To Field, Mine, and Factory: Work and Family in Polish America

A good starting point from which to approach Polish-American history are two bibliographical aids that appeared in the 1970s: Joseph L. Zurawski, *Polish American History and Culture: A Classified Bibliography* (Chicago: Polish Museum of America, 1975) and the sociological compilation of Irwin T. Sanders and Ewa T. Morawska, *Polish American Community Life: A Survey of Research*, The Community Sociology Monograph Series, Vol. 2 (Boston and New York: Community Sociology Training Program, Dept. of Sociology, Boston University and the Polish Institute of Arts and Sciences in America, 1975).

Several scholars, like Wacław Kruszka, Stanisław Osada, Karol Wachtl, and Mieczysław Haiman, have written general histories and syntheses on the group in America that are now regarded both as secondary and primary sources. No recently published volume is satisfactory on all counts. An older, general treatment, the short review written by Rev. Paul Fox, a Protestant minister, *The Poles in America* (New York: George H. Doran Co., 1922), was recently made available again in a 1970 Arno Press reprint but is incomplete and dated. More recently still, Joseph A. Wytrwal has published a succession of long, detailed tomes on the subject, including *America's Polish Heritage* (Detroit: Endurance Press, 1961), *Poles in American History and Tradition* (Detroit: Endurance Press, 1969), and *Behold! the Polish-Americans* (Detroit: Endurance Press, 1977), but all take a filiopietistic, miscellaneous, antiquarian approach, which renders them of limited use to a scholastic audience. Similarly, the popular pictorial volume by W.S. Kuniczak, *My Name is Million* (Garden City, N.Y.: Doubleday and Co., 1978), while more accessible than Wytrwal's works, differs little in attitude and is most commended for its photographs and colorful, readable anecdotes. Written in the same vein as the Kuniczak volume, *Poles in America: Bicentennial Essays*, edited by Frank Mocha (Stevens Point, Wis.: Worzalla Publishing Co., 1978) also stresses Polish contributions to America. The Mocha collection, however, does contain several good essays and much useful information, even though it completely ignores some aspects of the Polish-American experience, like the history of the Polish-American family. Finally, there is Theresita Polzin's *The Polish Americans: Whence and Whither* (Pulaski, Wis.: Franciscan Publishers, 1973). It is more sociological than historical and makes for ponderous reading.

Recent Polish treatments of the history of Polish immigration have generally been more scholarly than the foregoing but have often been troubled by translation difficulties and problems of availability. Perhaps the best currently available treatment of the subject is Andrzej Brożek's *Polish Americans, 1854–1939* (Warsaw: Interpress, 1985), a 1977 work recently translated by Wojciech Worsztynowicz. It is, however, very detailed and the period it covers is limited. General historical material on the Polish-Americans appears in a more specialized work by Józef Miąso, *The History of the Education of the Polish Immigrants in the United States*, translated by Ludwik Krzyżanowski (New York and Warsaw: Kosciuszko Foundation and the PWN-Polish Scientific Publishers, 1977). Given the fervor of Polish emigration studies in the last ten or so years, we should expect more similar volumes soon, depending, of course, upon Poland's political and economic situation.

Four other general publications merit attention here. Frank Renkiewicz's thin volume, *The Poles in America: A Chronology & Fact Book* (Dobbs Ferry, N.Y.: Oceana Publications, 1973), a compilation of dates, facts, and documents, is useful as a research tool and introduction to the subject. Victor Greene's article, published in *The Harvard Encyclopedia of American Ethnic Groups*, edited by S. Thernstrom (Cambridge, Mass.: Harvard University Press, 1980), S.V. "Poles," remains the best and most recent, if brief, review of Polish-American history. It is widely available in libraries. Two recently published essay collections have added immensely to the general literature on the group: *Pastor of the Poles: Polish American Essays Presented to Right Reverend Monsignor John P. Wodarski in honor of the Fiftieth Anniversary of His Ordination*, edited by S. Blejwas and M.B. Biskupski, Polish Studies Program Monographs, No. 1 (New Britain: Central Connecticut State College, 1982), whose contents group around religious topics; and the more general book, *The Polish Presence in Canada and America*, edited by F. Renkiewicz (Toronto: Multicultural History Society of Ontario, 1982).

In addition to the foregoing, a broad literature has developed around specialized topics. For the period prior to the mass migration "for bread," the reader may consult several works. Miecislaus Haiman's *Polish Past in America, 1608–1865* (Chicago: Polish Roman Catholic Union Archives and Museum, 1939) is a filiopietistic but interesting review of the early years of Polish settlement in America. It can be supplemented with the work of Polish scholar Bogdan Grzeloński, *Poles in the United States of America, 1776–1865*, translated by R. Strybel (Warsaw: Interpress, 1976), which treats Polish-American cultural topics in greater detail. In addition to the many biographies of Kościuszko and Puļaski, a literature also exists on the Polish exiles of the Great Emigration. See, for example, Jerzy Jan Lerski, *A Polish Chapter in Jacksonian America* (Madison: University of Wisconsin Press, 1958) and Joseph W. Wieczerzak, *A Polish Chapter in Civil War America: The Effects of the January Insurrection on American Opinion and Diplomacy* (New York: Twayne Publishing Co., 1967).

Polish-American agriculture remains relatively uncharted country for recent scholars because relatively few Poles found occupations in it, but a small literature on this subject developed over the years. Works on Polish-American agricultural settlements include Merle Curti, *The Making of an American Community: A Case Study of Democracy in a Frontier County* (Stanford, Calif.: Stanford University Press, 1959) on Wisconsin's Trempeleau County; Richard H. Zeitlin's informative piece, "White Eagles in the North Woods: Polish Immigration to Rural Wisconsin, 1857–1900," *Polish Review* 25 (1980):

69–92; Theodore Abel, "Sunderland: A Study of Changes in the Group Life of the Poles in a New England Farming Community," *Immigrant Farmers and their Children*, edited by E. de S. Brunner (New York: 1929); Stefan Wloszczewski, *History of Polish American Culture* (Trenton, N.J.: White Eagle Publishing Co., 1946), which highlights Polish farmers in Southampton, Long Island; and, more recently, T. Lindsay Baker, *The First Polish Americans: Silesian Settlements in Texas* (College Station: Texas A & M University Press, 1979) and Richard M. Bernard, *The Poles in Oklahoma* (Norman: University of Oklahoma Press, 1980).

In contrast, the literature on Polish immigrant working people has grown measurably in the last ten years. While much remains to be written on the Polish immigrant family, until new research is done the reader can consult the articles of Helen Stankiewicz Zand, which appeared in *Polish American Studies* between the 1940s and 1960s; Helena Znaniecka Lopata, "Polish American Families," *Ethnic Families in America: Patterns and Variations*, edited by Charles H. Mindel and Robert W. Habenstein, 2d ed. (New York: Elsevier, 1981), pp. 17–42; Margaret Byington's classic work, *Homestead: The Households of a Mill Town* (New York: Russell Sage Foundation, 1910), which was recently reprinted by the University Center for International Studies at the University of Pittsburgh; and Tamara K. Hareven's recent study of Manchester, New Hampshire, *Family Time and Industrial Time: The Relationship Between the Family and Work in a New England Industrial Community* (New York: Cambridge University Press, 1982). On the more specialized topic of authority within immigrant families and domestic violence, the reader should see Elizabeth H. Pleck, "Challenges to Traditional Authority in Immigrant Families," *The American Family in Social-Historical Perspective*, ed. Michael Gordon, 3rd ed. (New York: St. Martin's Press, 1983), pp. 504–517, which contains some material on Poles.

On the subject of Polish immigrants as workers, readers should begin by consulting several general works such as Herbert G. Gutman's landmark article, "Work, Culture, and Society in Industrializing America, 1815–1919," *American Historical Review* 78 (June 1973): 531–588; John Bodnar, *Workers' World: Kinship, Community, and Protest in an Industrial Society, 1900–1940* (Baltimore: Johns Hopkins University Press, 1982), a book based upon extensive oral history interviews conducted throughout Pennsylvania; and three other articles by Bodnar: "Immigration and Modernization: The Case of Slavic Peasants in Industrial America," *Journal of Social History* 10 (Fall 1976): 44–67; "Migration, Kinship, and Urban Adjustment: Blacks and Poles in Pittsburgh, 1900—1930," *Journal of American History* 66 (December 1979): 548–565, coauthored with Michael Weber and

Roger Simon; and "Immigration, Kinship, and the Rise of Working-Class Realism in Industrial America," *Journal of Social History* 14 (Fall 1980): 45–65. Olivier Zunz wrote a more technical comparative look at the development of the immigrant working-class city, *The Changing Face of Inequality: Urbanization, Industrial Development, and Immigrants in Detroit, 1880–1920* (Chicago: University of Chicago Press, 1982). Ewa Morawska authored three works: "'For Bread with Butter': Life-Worlds of Peasant-Immigrants from East Central Europe, 1880– 1914," *Journal of Social History* 17 (1984): 387–404; "East European Labourers in an American Mill Town, 1880–1940: The Deferential–Proletarian–Privatized Workers?" *Sociology* 19 (August 1985): 364–383; and *For Bread with Butter: Life-Worlds of East Central Europeans in Johnstown, Pennsylvania, 1890-1940* (New York: Cambridge University Press, 1985).

A few works might be consulted that deal specifically with Polish workers. These include Victor Greene, "The Polish-American Worker to 1930: The 'Hunky' Image in Transition," *Polish Review* 21 (1976): 63–78; Frank Renkiewicz, "Polish American Workers, 1880–1980," *Pastor of the Poles*, cited above; John J. Bukowczyk, "Polish Rural Culture and Immigrant Working Class Formation, 1880–1914," *Polish American Studies* 41 (Autumn 1984): 23–44; and the classic article by Progressive Walter E. Weyl cited in the text, "Jan, the Polish Miner," *The Outlook* 94 (March 26, 1910). Other works treat the same workers as strikers: Donald B. Cole, *Immigrant City: Lawrence, Massachusetts, 1845–1921* (Chapel Hill: University of North Carolina Press, 1963); Henry B. Leonard, "Ethnic Cleavage and Industrial Conflict in Late 19th Century America: The Cleveland Rolling Mill Company Strikes of 1882 and 1885," *Labor History* 20 (Fall 1979): 524–548; Edward Pinkowski's colorful short pamphlet, *Lattimer Massacre* (Philadelphia: Sunshine Press, 1950); the pathbreaking work by Victor R. Greene, *The Slavic Community on Strike: Immigrant Labor in Pennsylvania Anthracite* (Notre Dame, Ind.: University of Notre Dame Press, 1968); and Donald Pienkos's study of Polish socialists, "Progressives, Socialists, and Milwaukee Poles," *Wisconsin Magazine of History* 61 (Spring 1978). As for why Poles often failed as strikers, two general works by Stephen Meyer III look at Americanization and shed light on the Polish experience: "Adapting the Immigrant to the Line: Americanization in the Ford Factory, 1914–1921," *Journal of Social History* 14 (1981): 67–82, and *The Five Dollar Day: Labor Management and Social Control in the Ford Motor Company, 1908–1921* (Albany: State University of New York Press, 1981). The failure of Polish immigrant working-class protest is linked both to Americanization and to the rise of the immigrant middle class in John J. Bukowczyk's "The Transformation of Working-Class Ethnicity: Corporate Control, Americanization, and the Polish Immigrant Middle Class in Bayonne, N.J., 1915–1925," *Labor History* 25 (Winter 1984): 53–82.

Finally, a few broad comparative studies examine immigrant social mobility. These include John Bodnar, Roger Simon, and Michael P. Weber, *Lives of Their Own: Blacks, Italians, and Poles in Pittsburgh, 1900–1960* (Urbana: University of Illinois Press, 1982); Stanley Lieberson, A *Piece of the Pie: Blacks and White Immigrants Since 1880* (Berkeley and Los Angeles: University of California Press, 1980); and Stephan Thernstrom, *The Other Bostonians: Poverty and Progress in the American Metropolis, 1880–1970* (Cambridge, Mass.: Harvard University Press, 1973).

3
Hands Clasped, Fists Clenched:
Unity and Strife in the Immigrant Community

In addition to the general works cited previously, a wide variety of sources are available on the topics treated in this chapter, owing to the extensive recent research on the institutional history of Polonia. For Polish immigrant demographic data, in addition to state and federal manuscript census schedules, the reader may wish to review two governmental reports from the period: the massive, biased study of the Dillingham Commission, *United States Senate, Immigrants in Industries: Reports of the Immigration Commission*, 61 Cong., 2 sess., Doc. no. 633, 41 vols. (Washington, D.C.: Government Printing Office, 1911); and Niles Carpenter, *Immigrants and Their Children, 1920*, Census Monographs, 7 (Washington, D.C.: Government Printing Office, 1927).

Because historians have yet to assemble a thorough account of the Polish immigrant middle class, glimpses of how small businesses and their proprietors operated must be gathered from community studies and from monographic literature on other topics. Among the specialized works on the topic that readers may consult are Sister Mary Remigia Napolska, *The Polish Immigrant in Detroit to 1914*, Annals of the Polish Roman Catholic Union Archives and Museum, vol. 10 (1945–1946) (Chicago: Polish Roman Catholic Union of America, 1946); John J. Bukowczyk, "The Immigrant 'Community' Re-examined: Political and Economic Tensions in a Brooklyn Polish Settlement, 1888–1894," *Polish American Studies* 37 (Autumn 1980): 5–16 and Bukowczyk's forthcoming monograph, tentatively entitled *Clerics and Shopkeepers: The Formation of the Immigrant Middle Class in Polish Brooklyn, 1880–1929;* Edward R. Kantowicz, *Polish-American Politics in Chicago, 1888–1940* (Chicago: University of Chicago Press, 1975); Victor Greene, "'Becoming American': The Role of Ethnic Leaders— Swedes, Poles, Italians, Jews," *The Ethnic Frontier: Essays in the His-

tory of Group Survival in Chicago and the Midwest, edited by Melvin
G. Holli and Peter d'A. Jones (Grand Rapids, Mich.: William B. Eerd-
mans Publishing Co., 1977), pp. 143–175. On status within Polonia, see
Ewa Morawska, "The Internal Status Hierarchy in the East European
Immigrant Communities of Johnstown, PA 1890–1930's," *Journal of
Social History* 16 (1983): 75–107.

An English-language history of Polonia's fraternals remains to be
written. Except for Donald E. Pienkos's excellent study, *PNA:A Centennial History of the Polish National Alliance of the United States of
America* (1984), at present we must rely upon dated Polish-language
works by such pioneers as Karol Wachtl, Mieczysław Haiman, and
Stanisław Osada and, of course, the organizations' own anniversary
albums. Readers may also wish to see Frank Renkiewicz, "The Profits
of Nonprofit Capitalism: Polish Fraternalism and Beneficial Insurance in America," *Self-Help in Urban America: Patterns of Minority
Business Enterprise,* edited by Scott Cummings (Port Washington,
N.Y.: Kennikat Press, 1980), pp. 113–129; and "An Economy of Self-
Help: Fraternal Capitalism and the Evolution of Polish America,"
Studies in Ethnicity: The East European Experience in America, edited
by Charles A. Ward et al. (Boulder, Colo.: East European Monographs, 1980), pp. 71–92, which examine the nexus between frater-
nalism and immigrant enterprise. Readers should also see Helena
Znaniecki Lopata, *Polish-Americans: Status Competition in an Ethnic
Community* (Englewood Cliffs, N.J.: Prentice-Hall, 1976), a sociological work which, despite its general title, largely examines the status
functions of organizational membership; Thaddeus Radzialowski's
treatment of a specific Polish women's organization, "'Let Us Join
Hands': The Polish Women's Alliance," *Immigrant Women,* edited by
Maxine Schwartz Seller (Philadelphia: Temple University Press,
1981), pp. 174–180; and, finally, the inventory article by Walter Zachariasiewicz, "Organizational Structure of Polonia," *Poles in America,* edited by F. Mocha (Stevens Point, Wis.: Worzalla Publishing
Co., 1978), pp. 627–670.

By far the richest literature on Polonia treats various aspects of
Polish America's organized religious life. The most indispensible reference work on Roman Catholicism in Polonia is Very Rev. F. Do-
mański et al., *The Contribution of the Poles to the Growth of
Catholicism in the United States, Sacrum Poloniae Millennium* (Rome:
Gregorian University Press, 1959), vol. 6, which surveys the parishes,
the sisterhoods, and the clergy. This, combined with anniversary volumes from the various parishes and female religious congregations,
form a good starting point for studying Polish-American Roman Catholic history. A number of works supplement these general treatments. Rev. John J. Iwicki studied the Resurrectionists in *The First
One Hundred Years: A Study of the Apostolate of the Congregation of*

the Resurrection in the United States, 1866–1966 (Rome: Gregorian University Press, 1966); Daniel Buczek examined an important Polonia pastorate in *Immigrant Pastor: The Life of the Right Rev. Msgr. Lucyan Bójnowski of New Britain, Connecticut* (Waterbury, Conn.: Heminway Corp., 1974); and Stanislaus Blejwas and M. B. Biskupski have compiled an important collection on religion in Polonia in *Pastor of the Poles: Polish-American Essays Presented to Right Reverend Monsignor John P. Wodarski in honor of the Fiftieth Anniversary of His Ordination*, Polish Studies Program Monographs, No. 1 (New Britain: Central Connecticut State College, 1982). On Polish immigrant Marianism, see John J. Bukowczyk, "Mary the Messiah: Polish Immigrant Heresy and the Malleable Ideology of the Roman Catholic Church, 1880–1930," *Journal of American Ethnic History* 4 (Spring 1985): 5–32.

Conflict within immigrant parishes forms the subject for some of the most interesting monographs on Polish-American history. The reader should first refer to several general studies on relations between Poles and the Church, notably Victor Greene, *For God and Country: The Rise of Polish and Lithuanian Ethnic Consciousness in America* (Madison: State Historical Society of Wisconsin, 1975); Daniel Buczek, "Polish-Americans and the Catholic Church," *Polish Review* 21 (1976): 39–61; and William Galush, "Faith and Fatherland: Dimensions of Polish-American Ethnoreligion, 1875–1975," *Immigrants and Religion in Urban America*, edited by R. M. Miller and T. Marzik (Philadelphia: Temple University Press, 1977). Many other good studies have now appeared that deal with specific local conflicts. On Detroit Polonia, readers should look at Eduard Adam Skendzel, *The Kolasinski Story: Priest-Protector of Detroit's Pioneer Polish Immigrants or Father of Polish-American Church Independentism* (Grand Rapids, Mich.: Littleshield Press, 1979); Lawrence D. Orton's lively and provocative *Polish Detroit and the Kolasiński Affair* (Detroit: Wayne State University Press, 1981); Leslie Woodcock Tentler's "Who Is the Church? Conflict in a Polish Immigrant Parish in Late 19th Century Detroit," a look at Polish immigrant women's involvement in the controversy, in *Comparative Studies in Society and History* 25 (1983): 241–276; and Rev. Earl Boyea's forthcoming study, the first to use Vatican archives, which is to appear in the *American Catholic Historical Review*. On Chicago Polish affairs, Joseph John Parot's *Polish Catholics in Chicago, 1850–1920: A Religious History* (DeKalb: Northern Illinois University Press, 1981) details the doings of the Resurrectionists and their opponents. John J. Bukowczyk's "Factionalism and the Composition of the Polish Immigrant Clergy," in *Pastor of the Poles*, cited above, looks at these conflicts in relation to clerical careerism. Anthony J. Kuzniewski's *Faith and Fatherland: The Polish Church War in Wisconsin, 1896–1918* (Notre Dame, Ind.: University of Notre Dame Press, 1980) treats the controversial Rev.

Wenceslaus Kruszka and Milwaukee Polonia and places intrachurch conflict in the context of the campaign for a Polish-American bishop.

While the foregoing studies often consider trusteeism and schism, they do not explore the history of the Polish National Catholic Church (PNCC), a subject in its own right. The English-language biography of Bishop Hodur, being written by Joseph Wieczerzak, is yet to appear. There are several histories of the PNCC including Theodore Andrews, *The Polish National Catholic Church in America and Poland* (London: SPCK, 1953); Rev. Paul Fox, *The Polish National Catholic Church* (Scranton, Pa.: School of Christian Living, 1961); Rev. Stephen Wlodarski, *The Origin and Growth of the Polish National Catholic Church* (Scranton, Pa.: Polish National Catholic Church, 1974)—all favorable. A critical treatment of its origins is included in Rev. John Gallagher's *A Century of History: The Diocese of Scranton, 1868–1968* (Scranton, Pa., 1968). Many articles on the PNCC have also appeared in *Polish American Studies;* and Hieronim Kubiak's study of the PNCC is now available in an English translation.

Polish nationalism as a political movement is a big topic that still needs its own history. Few English-language works have discussed the PNA-PRCU rift. Joseph A. Wytrwal has treated it in *America's Polish Heritage: A Social History of Poles in America* (Detroit: Endurance Press, 1961). Better, however, is Victor Greene's *For God and Country,* cited above. Miecislaus Haiman's *Polish Past in America, 1608–1865* (Chicago: Polish Roman Catholic Union Archives and Museum, 1939), reissued in 1974, presents a fine overview of early Polish nationalist activity by the insurrectionary émigrés of the early nineteenth century. Studies of special topics in this area abound in the early issues of *Polish American Studies* and in master's theses. In the absence of a complete English-language study of Polish nationalist political activity in the United States during the mass migration years, we are obliged to rely upon sections of general works on Polish America, like those cited earlier, and unpublished master's theses and doctoral dissertations, like Stanley R. Pliska, "Polish Independence and the Polish Americans" (Ed.D. diss., Columbia University, 1955); Rev. Casimir Stec, O.F.M., "The National Orientation of the Poles in the United States, 1608–1935" (Master's thesis, Marquette University, 1946); and Stanley Bruno Stefan, "The Preparation of the American Poles for Polish Independence, 1880–1918" (Master's thesis, University of Detroit, 1939).

Some material on special topics concerning the study of Polish nationalism has appeared, though none is completely satisfactory. On the Polish Falcons, the works of Arthur Waldo, including his five-volume Polish-language history of Falconism, are well known. The reader may also wish to look at Joseph A. Borkowski's pamphlet, *The Role of Pittsburgh's Polish Falcons in the Organization of the Polish*

Army in France (Pittsburgh: Polish Falcons of America, 1972). Because of the reputation of the author, John Dewey's brief *Conditions among the Poles in the United States, a Confidential Report* (n.p., 1918) is of general interest. This government report reviews and assesses Polish political activities during the war years and represents one of the few English-language treatments of the Committee for National Defense (Dewey shows a pro-KON bias). The Polish press in America and its role during the nationalist years merits more attention than it has received. For these and other press-related topics, a good starting point is Edmund G. Olszyk's *The Polish Press in America* (Milwaukee, Wis.: Marquette University Press, 1940) and Jan Wepsiec's indispensible reference work, *The Polish American Serial Publications, 1842–1966: An Annotated Bibliography* (Chicago, 1968), a union list. An accessible essay on the development of the Polish immigrant press by Bernard Pacyniak also appears in *Poles in America,* cited above.

4
Continuity and Change in the 1920s and 1930s: From Polish to Polish-American

The English-language literature on postwar re-emigration and Polonia's relations with postwar Poland is not extensive. A good and accessible starting point for readers interested in exploring Polonia's postwar turn inward is William J. Galush, "Faith and Fatherland: Dimensions of Polish-American Ethnoreligion, 1875–1975," *Immigrants and Religion in Urban America,* edited by R. M. Miller and T. Marzik (Philadelphia: Temple University Press, 1977), pp. 84-102. The reader also may wish to consult Galush's doctoral dissertation, "Forming Polonia: A Study of Four Polish-American Communities, 1890-1940" (University of Minnesota, 1975).

Since the American Poles' reorientation came in response not only to Polish developments, but also in reaction to events in America, readers will want to consult the general literature on American attitudes toward immigrants during the 1910s and 1920s. Serious students of nativism and immigration restriction might start by looking through the massive report of the Dillingham Commission, United States Senate, *Immigrants in Industries: Reports of the Immigration Commission,* 61 Cong., 2 sess., Doc. no. 633, 41 vols. (Washington, D.C.: Government Printing Office, 1911). Those with more general interests should see John Higham, *Strangers in the Land: Patterns of American Nativism, 1860–1925* (New Brunswick, N.J.: Rutgers University Press, 1963), available in an inexpensive Antheneum paperback edition, and may also wish to consult Glenn C. Altschuler, *Race, Ethnicity, and Class in American Social Thought, 1865–1919* (Arlington Heights, Ill.: Harlan Davidson, 1982).

For information on the relationship between the Roman Catholic Church and "new" immigrants like the Poles, readers should avoid the standard histories of the American Church, which largely ignore the topic, and instead consult Richard M. Linkh's *American Catholicism and European Immigrants (1900–1924)* (Staten Island, N.Y.: Center for Migration Stuidies, 1975), a modest, useful volume; or monographic works, like Edward R. Kantowicz's *Corporation Sole: Cardinal Mundelein and Chicago Catholicism* (Notre Dame, Ind.: University of Notre Dame Press, 1983).

Study of a related subject, assimilation, should begin with Milton Gordon's *Assimilation in American Life: The Role of Race, Religion, and National Origins* (New York: Oxford University Press, 1964) for background. Those interested will also find a wide literature of the community study genre that reviews conditions in Polish-American communities between the 1920s and 1950s. For a comparative review of the findings of these works, the reader would do best to consult Irwin T. Sanders and Ewa T. Morawska, *Polish-American Community Life: A Survey of Research,* Community Sociology Monograph Series, vol. 2 (Boston and New York: Community Sociology Training Program, Dept. of Sociology, Boston University and Polish Institute of Arts and Sciences in America, 1975). Among the works they survey are, for the twenties, Niles Carpenter's and Daniel Katz's classic study based upon questionnaire data, *A Study of Acculturization in the Polish Group in Buffalo, 1926–1928,* Monographs in Sociology, No. 3, *The University of Buffalo Studies* 7 (June 1929): 103–133; for the thirties, Peter Ostafin, "The Polish Peasant in Transition: A Study of Group Integration as a Function of Symbiosis and Common Definitions" (Ph.D. diss., University of Michigan, 1948) and the volumes that appeared in the "Yankee City" series, authored by William Lloyd Warner and colleagues; for the forties, Arthur Evans Wood, *Hamtramck, Then and Now: A Sociological Study of a Polish-American Community* (New York: Bookman Associates, 1955); and for the fifties, Stanley Mackun, "The Changing Patterns of Polish Settlement in Greater Detroit" (Ph.D. diss., University of Michigan, 1964). For a general and comparative treatment of immigrant social conditions relating to the subject of assimilation, see Niles Carpenter, *Immigrants and Their Children, 1920,* Census Monographs, 7 (Washington, D.C.: Government Printing Office, 1927).

Polish resistance to assimilation, on the other hand, awaits a comprehensive treatment. By far the largest literature covers Polish-American education. For a general overview of this important subject, reference should be made to Józef Miąso, *The History of the Education of Polish Immigrants in the United States*, translated by L. Krzyżanowski (New York and Warsaw: Kosciuszko Foundation and Polish Scientific Publishers, 1977); Ellen Marie Kuznicki, CSSF, "The

Polish American Parochial Schools," *Poles in America: Bicentennial Essays*, edited by F. Mocha (Stevens Point, Wis.: Worzalla Publishing Co., 1978), pp. 435–457; and Anthony J. Kuzniewski, S.J., "The Catholic Church in the Life of the Polish-Americans," also in the Mocha volume, pp. 399–422. For a more specialized examination of the Polish sisterhoods' educational work in the context of their religious mission, also see, for the Felicians, *Magnificat: A Centennial Record of the Congregation of the Sisters of St. Felix (The Felician Sisters), 1855 Nov.–1955* (n.p., n.d.) and, for the Nazareth Sisters, Sr. M. DeChantal, *Out of Nazareth: A Centenary of the Holy Family of Nazareth in the Service of the Church* (New York: Exposition Press, 1974); Francis A. Cegielka, *"Nazareth" Spirituality*, translated by Sr. M. Theophame [sic] and Mother M. Laurence (Milwaukee, Wis.: Bruce Publishing Co., 1966), and Cegielka, *Reparatory Mysticism of "Nazareth"*, translated by a Sister of the Holy Family of Nazareth (Philadelphia, Pa.: Star Printers, 1951). Finally, the reader should also consult Frank Renkiewicz, *For God, Country, and Polonia: One Hundred Years of the Orchard Lake Schools* (Orchard Lake, Michigan.: Center for Polish Studies and Culture, 1985).

On the accommodation that middle-class Polish immigrants made with Americanization in the 1910s and 1920s, see John J. Bukowczyk, "The Transformation of Working-Class Ethnicity: Corporate Control, Americanization, and the Polish Immigrant Middle Class in Bayonne, N.J., 1915–1925," *Labor History* 25 (Winter 1984): 53–82. Also see Stanislaus A. Blejwas, "Old and New Polonias: Tensions Within an Ethnic Community," *Polish American Studies* 38 (Autumn 1981): 55–83; Eugene Kusielewicz, "The Kosciuszko Foundation: A Half Century of Progress," *Poles in America*, cited above, pp. 671–686; and Konstantin Symmons-Symonolewicz, "The Polish-American Community—Half a Century after 'The Polish Peasant'," *Polish Review* 11 (Summer 1966): 67–73.

This is not the place to review the general literature on the causes and consequences of the Great Depression of the 1930s, and a definitive treatment of Polish working people during the period remains to be written. Good—sometimes excellent—monographs on social conditions among working-class Polish-Americans in the 1930s, however, have recently appeared. There is the excellent book by John Bodnar, Roger Simon, and Michael P. Weber, *Lives of Their Own: Blacks, Italians, and Poles in Pittsburgh, 1900–1960* (Urbana: University of Illinois Press, 1982), which has the advantage of being comparative and may therefore remain the most valuable work on the subject for some time. In addition, there are Bodnar's provocative *Workers' World: Kinship, Community, and Protest in an Industrial Society, 1900–1940* (Baltimore, Md.: John Hopkins University Press, 1982), a study based upon extensive Pennsylvania oral history sources that also examines organized working-class responses to the crises at hand, and Thaddeus C. Radzialowski's excellent, pathbreaking article "Ethnic Conflict and the Polish Americans of Detroit, 1921–42," *The Polish Presence in Canada and America*, edited by F. Renkiewicz (Toronto: Multicultural History Society of Ontario, 1982), pp. 195–207.

To date, there is no specific treatment of the role that Poles—and other "new" immigrants—played in the founding of the CIO or the rise of industrial unionism in the 1930s. Accordingly, information must be gleaned from various general labor histories, as well as articles and monographs dealing with specialized labor and labor-related subjects during the period. Readers may find useful material in Frank Renkiewicz, "Polish American Workers, 1880–1980," in *Pastor of the Poles: Polish American Essays Presented to Right Reverend Monsignor John P. Wodarski in honor of the Fiftieth Anniversary of His Ordination*, edited by S. Blejwas and M. B. Biskupski, Polish Studies Monographs, No. 1 (New Britain: Central Connecticut State College, 1982), pp. 116–136; Steve Babson et al., *Working Detroit: The Making of a Union Town* (New York: Adama Books, 1984); Jeremy Brecher et al., editors, *Brass Valley: The Story of Working People's Lives and Struggles in an American Industrial Region* (Philadelphia: Temple University Press, 1982); Tamara K. Hareven and Randolph Langenbach, *Amoskeag: Life and Work in an American Factory-City* (New York: Pantheon Books, 1980); and Frank Serafino's journalistic *West of Warsaw* (Hamtramck, Mich.: Avenue Publishing Co., 1983), which looks at Poles in Hamtramck. For a biographical sketch of a Polish-American labor leader, see Eugene Miller, "Leo Krzycki—Polish American Labor Leader," *Polish American Studies* 33 (Autumn 1976). Readers may soon consult the forthcoming autobiography of organizer Stanley Nowak.

If there is little published on Polish-American unionism in the 1930s, there is even less available on social protest in the Poles' neighborhoods and communities during the period. Readers interested in this fascinating and virtually undocumented dimension of ethnic life may wish to look at Georg Schrode, "Polonia's Working-Class People and Local Politics" (Master's essay, Wayne State University, 1985), a treatment of Mary Zuk and the Hamtramck, Michigan, meat boycott of 1935.

While the definitive study remains to be written, plentiful works exist on Polish-American involvement in American party politics since the Great Depression. These include Edward R. Kantowicz's interesting study of Chicago Polonia, *Polish-Amerian Politics in Chicago, 1888–1940* (Chicago: University of Chicago Press, 1975) and a recent collection of articles edited by Angela Pienkos, *Ethnic Politics in Urban America: The Polish Experience in Four Cities* (Chicago: Polish American Historical Association, 1978).

Probably the most controversial subject treated in this chapter—and the one treated most speculatively—is the matter of class formation among Polish-American and other working people in the 1930s and the development of an ethnic blue-collar subculture or, as I have termed it, "way of life." Establishing that it happened is difficult, but dating it as an "event" is more difficult still. Several important works address this question: John Bodnar's *Workers' World,* cited earlier; Thaddeus Radzialowski, "The View from a Polish Ghetto: Some Observations on the First One Hundred Years in Detroit," *Ethnicity* 1 (1974): 125–150; Charles Keil, "Class and Ethnicity in Polish-America," *Journal of Ethnic Studies* 7 (Summer 1979): 37–45; and Olivier Zunz, *The Changing Face of Inequality: Urbanization, Industrial Development, and Immigrants in Detroit, 1880–1920* (Chicago: University of Chicago Press, 1982). Readers might also wish to compare the conclusions reached in Paul Wrobel, *Our Way: Family, Parish, and Neighborhood in a Polish-American Community* (Notre Dame, Ind.: University of Notre Dame Press, 1979) with the analysis presented in Herbert J. Gans, *The Urban Villagers: Group and Class in the Life of Italian-Americans* (New York: Free Press, 1962). The reader should also refer to Thaddeus Radzialowski's review essay on the Wrobel book, which appeared in *Polish American Studies* 37 (Spring 1980): 42–51.

5
The Decline of the Urban Ethnic Enclave:
Polish America Transformed, WW II–Present

A large literature has developed on Polish history in the interwar years, and on Polish/Soviet, Polish/German relations. The general histories of Poland edited, respectively, by W. Reddaway and by Stefan Kieniewicz et al., and the one written by Norman Davies (cited in the first section of this essay) are a good place to begin the study of this difficult period. Specific works that the general reader also might find interesting include Piotr S. Wandycz, *Soviet-Polish Relations, 1917–1921* (Cambridge, Mass.: Harvard University Press, 1969); and M. K. Dziewanowski's *Communist Party of Poland: An Outline of History* (Cambridge, Mass.: Harvard University Press, 1959) and *Joseph Pilsudski: A European Federalist, 1918–1922* (Stanford, Calif.: Stanford University Press, 1969).

Accessible, good literature on Polish-Americans in the days before the Second World War and during the actual conflict is relatively lacking. Joseph Wytrwal's works, *America's Polish Heritage* (Detroit: Endurance Press, 1961), *Poles in American History and Tradition* (Detroit: Endurance Press, 1969), and *Behold! the Polish-Americans* (Detroit: Endurance Press, 1977), though filiopietistic, still make up much of what is available. Frank Renkiewicz's *The Poles in America, 1608–1972: A Chronology & Fact Book* (Dobbs Ferry, N.Y.: Oceana Publications, 1973) presents a clear and succinct summary of events during the period. For a look at the Polish-American press, the reader should leaf through Bernard Pacyniak, "An Historical Outline of the

Polish Press in America," *Poles in America: Bicentennial Essays*, edited by F. Mocha (Stevens Point, Wis.: Worzalla Publishing Co. 1978), pp. 509–530. The general surveys cited above offer adequate coverage on the course of the war in Poland. As the Kieniewicz volume excludes all mention of Soviet participation in the invasion of Poland, the reader should also consult Davies's volumes and Oscar Halecki's *A History of Poland*, translated by Monica Gardner and Mary Corbridge-Patkaniowska (New York: David McKay Co., 1976).

Scattered articles and monographs on special themes and topics in Polish-American history of the 1940s and early 1950s have appeared, but not a comprehensive general work. For wartime anecdotes, largely of Michigan veterans, the reader might see Joseph A. Wytrwal, *Behold! the Polish-Americans* cited earlier. No similar material yet exists for Polish-Americans on the "home front." The literature on the period, however, does feature an excellent introduction to developments within Polonian politics and the growing split between old and new Polonia in Stanislaus A. Blejwas's "Old and New Polonias: Tensions Within an Ethnic Community," *Polish American Studies* 38 (Autumn 1981): 55–83, which carries on where an older piece by Konstantin Symmons-Symonolewicz, "The Polish-American Community —Half a Century after 'The Polish Peasant'," *Polish Review* 11 (Summer 1966): 67–73, left off. A sweeping article, the Blejwas piece deals with many of the topics treated in the early part of this chapter.

On the Polish American Congress and its role in Polonia, the reader should consult, in addition to Blejwas, Richard C. Lukas, "The Polish American Congress and the Polish Question, 1944–1947," *Polish American Studies* 38 (Autumn 1981): 39–53; Donald E. Pienkos, "The Polish American Congress—An Appraisal," *Polish American Studies* 36 (Autumn 1979): 5–43; and, for a look at a regional branch of the Polish American Congress in action, Blejwas's "The Local Ethnic Lobby: The Polish American Congress in Connecticut, 1944–74," *The Polish Presence in Canada and America*, edited by F. Renkiewicz (Toronto: Multicultural History Society of Ontario, 1982), pp. 305–325.

On the various Polish-American cultural organizations founded by war refugees, the reader should see pieces by Michael Budny and by Frank Mocha in *Poles of America*, edited by F. Mocha (Stevens Point, Wis.: Worzalla Publishing Co., 1978), pp. 687–708 and pp. 709–724, respectively, and also consult appropriate sections of Wytrwal's Polish-American histories, all cited earlier. A number of works set a broader context for institutional developments during the period. For a look at the problems of the Polish soldier-refugee, consult Sarah Van Aken-Rutkowski, "Integration and Acculturation of the Polish Veteran of World War II to Canadian Society" (Master's thesis, University of Windsor, 1982). See the summary review by Walter Zachariasiewicz in *Poles in America* on the various Polish-American veterans organizations. The reader will find a number of interesting studies on the Polish displaced person. Two general introductions are

Memo to America: The DP Story: The Final Report of the United States Displaced Persons Commission (Washington, D.C.: Government Printing Office, 1952) and the more critical survey by Maria Barbara Korewa, "Casework Treatment of Refugees: A Survey of Selected Professional Periodicals for the Period from January 1, 1939 to January 1, 1956" (Master's thesis, Wayne State University, 1957). For studies that specifically treat the Poles, the reader should refer to Rev. Stanislaus T. Sypek's dated "The Displaced Person in the Greater Boston Community" (Ph.D. diss., Fordham University, 1955); Danuta Mostwin's "Post–World War II Polish Immigrants in the United States," *Polish American Studies* 26 (Autumn 1969): 5–14 and "The Profile of a Transplanted Family," *Polish Review* 19 (1974): 77–89; Alicja Iwańska, "Values in Crisis Situation" (Ph.D. diss., Columbia University, 1957); and, on displaced Poles in agriculture, Rudolf Heberle and Dudley S. Hall, *New Americans: A Study of Displaced Persons in Louisiana & Mississippi* (Baton Rouge, La.: Displaced Persons Commission, 1951).

The Blejwas article, cited earlier, does not of course deal with developments remaking old Polonia from within, like changes in the wartime and postwar economy and the rise of the American-born generation. These subjects have yet to receive a full treatment by historians. Polish-American occupational mobility is one area burdened by methodological problems but greatly in need of further study. Thus far, readers must rely on monographic works like John Bodnar, Roger Simon, and Michael Weber, *Lives of Their Own: Blacks, Italians, and Poles in Pittsburgh, 1900–1960* (Urbana: University of Illinois Press, 1982), excellent but geographically specific, or Thomas Sowell's attempt to be more general and comparative, *Essays and Data on American Ethnic Groups* (n.p.: Urban Institute, 1972), which contains interesting data, much of which is difficult to use because of missing information, the incompatibility of information available on different groups, and its inability to control for crucial variables. Stephan Thernstrom's *The Other Bostonians: Poverty and Progress in the American Metropolis, 1880–1970* (Cambridge, Mass.: Harvard University Press, 1973) and Stanley Lieberson's *A Piece of the Pie: Blacks and White Immigrants Since 1880* (Berkeley and Los Angeles, Calif.: University of California Press, 1980), both quantitative works, also contain material on Polish-Americans.

Charting changes in the Polish-American family, women's roles, fertility, and demographics remains to be done. For the time being, students of these subjects can glean information from the various sociological treatments of the group and, in particular, from two specialized articles: Helena Znaniecka Lopata, "Polish American Families," *Ethnic Families in America: Patterns and Variations*, edited by Charles H. Mindel and Robert W. Habenstein (New York: Elsevier, 1981), pp. 17–42; and Theresita Polzin's informative piece, "The Polish American Family—I; the Sociological Aspects of the Families of Polish Immigrants to America before World War II, and Their Descendants," *Polish Review* 21 (1976): 103–122.

Good studies on Polish-Americans in the suburbs, white-collar Polish-Americans, and Polish-American farmers in the postwar period are lacking. Those interested in the last topic, however, might refer to Richard M. Bernard, *The Poles in Oklahoma* (Norman: University of Oklahoma Press, 1980) and to a dated but interesting small book by Stefan Wloszczewski, *History of Polish American Culture* (Trenton, N.J.: White Eagle Publishing Co., 1946), which focuses especially on Long Island's Polish farmers.

On the special topics covered in this chapter, probably the best literature exists on Polish/Black relations, even though a definitive work has yet to be written. Several books treat the subject in passing: St. Clair Drake and Horace R. Cayton's classic work, *Black Metropolis: A Study of Negro Life in a Northern City*, revised and enlarged edition, 2 vols. (New York: Harper & Row, 1962), on Chicago; Allan H. Spear, *Black Chicago: The Making of a Negro Ghetto, 1890–1920* (Chicago: University of Chicago Press, 1967); and William M. Tuttle, Jr., *Race Riot: Chicago in the Red Summer of 1919* (New York: Antheneum, 1977). Others focus more specifically on it, like Joseph A. Wytrwal's *Behold! the Polish-Americans*, cited earlier; Thaddeus Radzialowski, "The View From a Polish Ghetto: Some Observations on the First One Hundred Years in Detroit," *Ethnicity* 1 (1974); Joseph Parot, "Ethnic versus Black Metropolis: The Origins of Polish-Black Housing Tensions in Chicago," *Polish American Studies* 29 (Spring–Autumn 1972): 5–33; and Paul Wrobel's recent study of a Detroit neighborhood, *Our Way: Family, Parish, and Neighborhood in a Polish-American Community* (Notre Dame, Ind.: University of Notre Dame Press, 1979). In particular, for information on the Sojourner Truth episode in Detroit, the reader should examine Thaddeus C. Radzialowski's excellent article, "Ethnic Conflict and the Polish Americans of Detroit, 1921–42," *The Polish Presence in Canada and America*, cited earlier; Dominic J. Capeci, Jr., *Race Relations in Wartime Detroit: The Sojourner Truth Housing Controversy of 1942*; and August Meier and Elliott Rudwick, *Black Detroit and the Rise of the UAW* (New York: Oxford University Press, 1979).

General treatments on change in—and decline of—the Polish urban ethnic enclave include Wrobel's book and Radzialowski's "View From a Polish Ghetto," both cited earlier. Those interested in the impact of deindustrialization on a Polish-American neighborhood should also read John J. Bukowczyk, "The Decline and Fall of a Detroit Neighborhood: Poletown vs. G.M. and the City of Detroit," *Washington and Lee Law Review* 41 (Winter 1984): 49–76.

While the last word on the immigrant aged has yet to be written, two works merit attention. They are Roman L. Haremski's *The Unattached, Aged Immigrant: A Descriptive Analysis of the Problems Experienced in Old Age by Three Groups of Poles Living Apart from Their Families in Baltimore* (Washington, D.C.: Catholic University of America Press, 1940); and Helena Znaniecka Lopata, "Widowhood in Polonia," *Polish American Studies* 34 (Autumn 1977): 7–25.

6

What Is a Polish-American?
The Revival of Ethnic Identity

In approaching the history of Polish America in the postwar period, the reader should first consider the structural position the group occupies in American society. Useful census data are available in Frank Renkiewicz's *The Poles in America, 1608–1972: A Chronology & Fact Book* (Dobbs Ferry, N.Y.: Oceana Publications, 1973). Economic and occupational statistics can be found in a number of books and articles. Thomas Sowell's *Essays and Data on American Ethnic Groups* (n.p.: Urban Institute, 1972); Harold J. Abramson, *Ethnic Diversity in Catholic America* (New York: John Wiley and Sons, 1973); E.P. Hutchinson, *Immigrants and Their Children, 1850–1950* (New York: John Wiley and Sons, 1956); and the excellent recent United States Commerce Department Bureau of Census Current Population Report, *Ancestry and Language in the United States: November 1979* (Series P–23, No. 116; March 1982), offer comparative figures for various ethnic groups, including the Polish-Americans. Russell Barta's pamphlet, *The Representation of Poles, Italians, Hispanics and Blacks in the Executive Suites of Chicago's Largest Corporations: A Progress Report, 1972–1983*, Minority Report No. 2, prepared by the Institute of Urban Life, Chicago, Illinois for the National Center for Urban Ethnic Affairs (1984), shows how little progress minority groups like the Poles have made in penetrating the upper reaches of the American economy. The reader can find other relevant statistics in two articles in *Polish Review* 21 (1976): Theresita Polzin, "The Polish American Family—I; The Sociological Aspects of the Families of Polish Immigrants to America before World War II, and Their Descendants" (pp. 103–122) and Eugene Obidinski, "Polish American Social Standing: Status and Stereotypes" (pp. 79–102). Also see Kazimierz Olejarczyk, "Some Groups that Don't Make It: The Polish Community," *Ethnic Groups in the City: Culture, Institutions, and Power*, edited by Otto Feinstein (Lexington, Mass.: D.C. Heath and Co., 1971), pp. 315–316.

The reader may wish to review the rather extensive literature on the social and cultural assimilation of the group. By way of general introduction, the reader should begin with Milton M. Gordon's *Assimilation in American Life: The Role of Race, Religion, and National Origins* (New York: Oxford University Press, 1964). Several books deal specifically with the Polish-American group including Theresita

Polzin, *The Polish Americans: Whence and Whither* (Pulaski, Wis.: Franciscan Publishers, 1973) and Irwin T. Sanders and Ewa T. Morawska, *Polish-American Community Life: A Survey of Research*, Community Sociology Monograph Series, vol. 2 (Boston and New York: Community Sociology Training Program, Dept. of Sociology, Boston University and Polish Institute of Arts and Sciences in America, 1975), both of which review the sociological literature; Helena Znaniecki Lopata, *Polish Americans: Status Competition in an Ethnic Community* (Englewood Cliffs, N.J.: Prentice-Hall, 1976); and Neil C. Sandberg, *Ethnic Identity and Assimilation: The Polish-American Community: Case Study of Metropolitan Los Angeles* (New York: Praeger, 1977), an interesting study, which is troubled by methodological and theoretical weaknesses, of a "newer" Polonia.

As for specialized topics, on Polish-American intermarriage, the reader should see Ruby Jo Reeves Kennedy, "Single or Triple Melting Pot? Intermarriage Trends in New Haven, 1870–1940," *American Journal of Sociology* 49 (January 1944): 331–339 and "Single or Triple Melting Pot? Intermarriage in New Haven, 1870–1950," *American Journal of Sociology* 58 (July 1952): 56–59; Helena Znaniecka Lopata, "Polish American Families," *Ethnic Families in America: Patterns and Variations*, edited by Charles H. Mindel and Robert W. Habenstein, 2d ed. (New York: Elsevier, 1981), pp. 17–42; and, finally, the Abramson volume and the census report, both cited earlier. On language maintenance, in addition to the special census report cited above, reference should be made to Joshua A. Fishman et al., editors, *Language Loyalty in the United States: The Maintenance and Perpetuation of Non-English Mother Tongues by American Ethnic and Religious Groups* (London: Mouton and Co., 1966). Finally, for a glimpse of the personal side of the assimilation process, the reader should see "The Pasciak Family of Chicago" in Paul Wilkes, *Six American Families* (n.p.: Seabury/Parthenon Press, 1977), pp. 21–39.

Several books by Rev. Andrew M. Greeley present data gathered by the National Opinion Research Center of the University of Chicago on Polish-American attitudes and social practices, compared to those of other groups. These include *The American Catholic: A Social Portrait* (New York: Basic Books, 1977); *Why Can't They Be Like Us? America's White Ethnic Groups* (New York: E.P. Dutton & Co., 1971); and *Why Can't They Be Like Us? Facts and Fallacies About Ethnic Differences and Group Conflict in America* (New York: Institute of Human Relations Press, American Jewish Committee, 1969).

Despite the importance of the topic and its relationship to assimilation, the literature on Polish-American social standing is still fairly slim. Despite its title, Obidinski's article "Polish American Social Standing: Status and Stereotypes," cited above, only briefly reviews the cultural aspects of the issue and moves on to structural matters. Studies on special topics in the area are also few in number. Of these, work on the "Polish joke" is probably best represented. The reader might wish to look at Alan Dundes, "A Study of Ethnic Slurs: the Jew and the Polack in the United States," *Journal of American Folklore* 84 (April 1971): 186–203, which contains some interesting material on the origins of anti-Polish stereotypes. Anti-Polish defamation in film is discussed in Caroline Golab's essay, "Stellaaaaaa......!!!!!!!!: the Slavic Stereotype in American Film," *The Kaleidoscopic Lens: How Hollywood Views Ethnic Groups*, edited by Randall M. Miller (Englewood Cliffs, N.J.: Jerome S. Ozer, Publisher, 1980), pp. 135–155. Those interested in a discussion of Polish-American/Jewish-American relations, still rather unexplored territory, should read Joseph L. Lichten, "Polish Americans and American Jews: Some Issues Which Unite and Divide," *Polish Review* 18 (1973): 52–62, and the chapter entitled "Polish-Jewish Relations in America" in Joseph A. Wytrwal's *Behold! the Polish-Americans* (Detroit: Endurance Press, 1977), pp. 497–523.

Bridging the distance betwen discussions of the culture of the old urban ethnic enclave and the so-called new ethnicity are several works that point out the persistence of traditional ethnic culture. These include Rev. Joseph Swastek's "What Is a Polish American?" *Polish American Studies* 1 (Jan.–Dec. 1944); Thaddeus Radzialowski's "The View from a Polish Ghetto: Some Observations on the First One Hundred Years in Detroit," *Ethnicity* 1 (July 1974): 125–150, a perceptive review of Polish-American social and cultural subjects; W.S. Kuniczak's *My Name Is Million* (Garden City, N.Y.: Doubleday, 1978), a popularized and rather filiopietistic rendition of group achievements; Paul Wrobel's *Our Way: Family, Parish, and Neighborhood in a Polish-American Community* (Notre Dame, Ind.: University of Notre Dame Press, 1979), which gives a glimpse of Polish-American ethnicity as lived in a Detroit blue-collar neighborhood; and, on middle class/working class differences, Charles Keil, "Class and Ethnicity in Polish America," *Journal of Ethnic Studies* 7 (Summer 1979): 37–41.

Little scholarly interest has focused on ethnic pride and Polish-American antidefamation efforts in the 1950s and 1960s. The reader may wish to browse Olgierd Budrewicz, *The Melting-Pot Revisited: Twenty Well-Known Americans of Polish Background*, translated by E.J. Czerwiński and A. Makarewicz (Warsaw: Interpress, 1977), a charming collection of journalistic essays. Despite the journalistic attention attracted by the new ethnicity, the subject has received little scholarly attention. For the classic prediction of the third generation's return to ethnicity, see Marcus Lee Hansen, *The Problem of the Third Generation Immigrant* (Rock Island, Ill.: Augustana Historical Society, 1938). A recent classic statement is Michael Novak's *The Rise of the Unmeltable Ethnics: Politics and Culture in the Seventies* (New York: Macmillan Co., 1971). Polish-American treatments of the subject, with the exception of Feliks Gross, "Notes on the Ethnic Revolution and Polish Immigration in the U.S.," *Polish Review* 21 (Fall

1976): 149–176, are mostly personal reflections, like Eugene Kusielewicz's *Reflections on the Cultural Conditions of the Polish American Community* (New York: Czas Publishing Co., 1969); Rev. Leonard E. Chrobot's *Who Am I? Reflections of a Young Polish American On the Search for Identity*, Monograph No. 4 (Orchard Lake, Mich.: Orchard Lake Center for Polish Studies and Culture, St. Mary's College, 1971); and *Ethnic Awareness and Self-Identity*, Monograph No. 6 (Orchard Lake, Mich.: Orchard Lake Center for Polish Studies and Culture, St. Mary's College, 1971); Paul Wrobel, "Becoming a Polish American: A Personal Point of View," *White Ethnics: Their Life in Working Class America*, edited by Joseph Ryan (Englewood Cliffs, N.J.: Prentice-Hall, 1973), pp. 52–58; and Alfred F. Bochenek, editor, *American Polonia: The Cultural Issues* (Detroit: American Council of Polish Cultural Clubs, 1981).

For balance, the reader should see several works critical of the ethnic revival. These include Konstantin Symmons-Symonolewicz, "The Polish-American Community—Half a Century after 'The Polish Peasant'," *Polish Review* 11 (Summer 1966): 67–73; and the more general works by Gunnar Myrdal, "The Case Against Romantic Ethnicity," *The Center Magazine* 7 (1974): 26–30; and Stephen Steinberg, *The Ethnic Myth: Race, Ethnicity, and Class in America* (New York: Antheneum, 1981). For a criticism of the polka mass, the reader should see Regina Koscielska, "Polka Mass: Ethnic Liturgy?" *Pastoral Music: National Association of Pastoral Musicians* 8 (Feb.–Mar. 1984): 27–29.

7
Vanguard or Rearguard?
Ethnic Politics in Mass Society

A definite study of Polish-American political behavior—before and after the new ethnicity— remains to be written, but several books, articles, and essays, some fairly recent, give the reader a good general introduction to the subject. The best overviews have been written by Donald E. Pienkos, "Research on Ethnic Political Behavior among the Polish Americans: A Review of the Literature," *Polish Review* 21 (1976): 123–148 and "Polish-American Ethnicity in the Political Life of the United States," *America's Ethnic Politics* edited by Joseph S. Roucek and Bernard Eisenberg, Contributions in Ethnic Studies, No. 5 (Westport, Conn.: Greenwood Press, 1982), pp. 273–305. The reader will also find material of a general nature in Feliks Gross, "Notes on the Ethnic Revolution and the Polish Immigration in the U.S.A.," *Polish Review* 21 (1976): 149–176; Victor Greene's essay on the "Poles" in the *Harvard Encyclopedia of American Ethnic Groups*, edited by S. Thernstrom (Cambridge, Mass.: Harvard University Press, 1980), pp. 787–803; Frank Renkiewicz's always useful volume, *The Poles in*

America, 1608–1972: A Chronology & Fact Book (Dobbs Ferry, N.Y.: Oceana Publications, 1973); and Joseph A. Wytrwal's *Poles in American History and Tradition* (Detroit: Endurance Press, 1969) and *Behold! the Polish-Americans* (Detroit: Endurance Press, 1977).

While there are not a lot of good items that treat specific aspects of traditional Polish-American party politics, several pieces are well worth consulting. On Polish-American participation in urban electoral politics, Edward R. Kantowicz's *Polish-American Politics in Chicago, 1888–1940* (Chicago: University of Chicago Press, 1975) remains without a doubt the best work, but the reader should also see Angela T. Pienkos, editor, *Ethnic Politics in Urban America: The Polish Experience in Four Cities* (Chicago: Polish American Historical Association, 1978), which contains essays on Chicago, Buffalo, Milwaukee, and Detroit; and Donald Pienkos, "Politics, Religion, and Change in Polish Milwaukee, 1900–1930," *Wisconsin Magazine of History* 61 (Spring 1978): 178–209. For biographical sketches of Polish-American political figures, the generalist may wish to look through Marek Święcicki and Róża Nowotarska, *The Gentleman from Michigan*, translated by Edward Cynarski (London: Polish Cultural Foundation, 1974), a popularly written account of the life of Thaddeus M. Machrowicz, a Michigan congressman and judge; Olgierd Budrewicz, *The Melting-Pot Revisited: Twenty Well-Known Americans of Polish Background*, translated by Edward J. Czerwiński and Andrzej Makarewicz (Warsaw: Interpress, 1977), which features short pieces on Edmund Muskie, Leon Jaworski, and Roman Gribbs; and Steven V. Roberts, "A Most Important Man on Capitol Hill," *New York Times Magazine*, September 22, 1985, a look at Rep. Dan Rostenkowski of Illinois.

There have not, however, been many prominent Polish-American political figures. On the underrepresentation of Polish-Americans in American political life, see Kazimierz J. Olejarczyk, "Some Groups That Don't Make It: The Polish Community," *Ethnic Groups in the City: Culture, Institutions, and Power*, edited by Otto Feinstein (Lexington, Mass.: D.C. Heath and Co. 1971), pp. 315–316; Eugene Kusielewicz, "Reflections on the Political Condition of the Polish American Community," *Kosciuszko Foundation Newsletter* 30 (October 1975): 1–4. Alternatively, on attempts by organized Polonia —the Polish American Congress—to have an impact in the American political arena, the reader should see Joseph A. Wytrwal, "The Changing Role of the Polish American Congress," *Ethnic Groups in the City*, cited above, pp. 165–173; Richard C. Lukas, "The Polish American Congress and the Polish Question, 1944–1947," *Polish American Studies* 38 (Autumn 1981): 39–53; Stanislaus A. Blejwas, "The Local Ethnic Lobby: The Polish American Congress in Connecticut, 1944–74," *The Polish Presence in Canada and America*, edited by Frank Renkiewicz (Toronto: Multicultural History Society of Ontario, 1982), pp. 305–325; and the informative piece by Donald E. Pienkos, "The Polish American Congress—An Appraisal," *Polish American Studies* 36 (Autumn 1979): 5–43.

Polish-American politics since the ethnic revival of the late 1960s and early 1970s suffers from a paucity of serious studies. On the ethnics' proposed New Political Agenda, the interested student will find Michael Novak, *The Rise of the Unmeltable Ethnics: Politics and Culture in the Seventies* (New York: Macmillan Co., 1971); Barbara Mikulski, "Who Speaks for Ethnic America?" in Colin Greer, editor, *Divided Society: The Ethnic Experience in America* (New York: Basic Books, 1974), pp. 355–358; and, on Polish/Black cooperation in Detroit, Perry L. Weed, *The White Ethnic Movement and Ethnic Politics* (New York: Praeger Publishers, 1973), pp. 106–111. On the predicted political realignment of groups like the Poles there is Kevin P. Phillips's prescient volume, *The Emerging Republican Majority* (New Rochelle, N.Y.: Arlington House, 1969).

Manifestoes and predictions notwithstanding, actually establishing Polish-American political tendencies since the late 1960s has been a murky chore because of the contradictory trends and themes observed in a nuanced and still highly tentative literature. On Polish-American political attitudes, the reader may wish to consult Robert Coles's impressionistic but fascinating volume, *The Middle Americans: Proud and Uncertain* (Boston: Little, Brown and Co., 1971), pp. 43–49; and three volumes by Rev. Andrew M. Greeley that present data—sometimes of questionable usefulness—assembled by the University of Chicago's National Opinion Research Center, *Why Can't They Be Like Us? Facts and Fallacies About Ethnic Differences and Group Conflict in America* (New York: Institute of Human Relations Press, American Jewish Committee, 1969); *Why Can't They Be Like Us? America's White Ethnic Groups* (New York: E.P. Dutton & Co., 1971); and *The American Catholic: A Social Portrait* (New York: Basic Books, 1977). For an examination of Polish-American political behavior, readers should return to the Pienkos essay in *America's Ethnic Politics* and *The White Ethnic Movement*, both cited above. Jules Witcover's *Marathon: The Pursuit of the Presidency, 1972–1976* (New York: Viking Press, 1977) discusses Polish-American reactions to Ford's famous gaffe on Poland. The excellent and provocative volume by Mark R. Levy and Michael S. Kramer, *The Ethnic Factor: How America's Minorities Decide Elections* (New York: Simon and Schuster, 1972), is a sober corrective to the Phillips thesis. Finally, the serious student of ethnic politics will want to analyze exit-poll data compiled by the various television news organizations—ABC, NBC, and CBS.

Thematically and stylistically less conventional than electoral politics, the so-called new ethnic politics has received far skimpier treatment. On the organization of the Poletown neighborhood of Detroit, see John J. Bukowczyk, "The Decline and Fall of a Detroit Neighborhood: Poletown vs. G.M. and the City of Detroit," *Washington and Lee Law Review* 41 (Winter 1984): 49–76. Readers may also wish to view a documentary film made during the controversy, *Poletown Lives!* For an example of one kind of local new ethnic lobbying activ-

ity undertaken by a Brooklyn ethnic center, refer to Leslaw Jurewicz,
editor, *Polish-Americans in the City of New York: An Outline of Socio-
economic and Cultural Needs* (New York: Polish and Slavic Center,
1979). No examination of local ethnic organizing can be complete
without making reference to *NCUEA Buildingblocks*, the newsletter
of the National Center for Urban Ethnic Affairs. The reader, however, may also wish to consult the *Polish American Journal* and the
now defunct *Polish American Voice* for activities in Buffalo.

NOTES

In line with the format of the series, the following citations only credit the sources for quoted material included in the text. Most of the remaining historical detail and evidence has been drawn from the secondary works cited in the bibliographical essay, and I am deeply grateful to their authors. The interpretive synthesis presented herein, however, is my own. All interviews were conducted by the author.

I. From Hunger, "for Bread"

1. Louis E. Van Norman, *Poland the Knight Among Nations* (New York: Fleming H. Revell Co., 1907).
2. Oscar Halecki, *A History of Poland* (New York: David McKay Co., 1976), p. 217.
3. Stefan Kieniewicz, *The Emancipation of the Polish Peasantry* (Chicago: University of Chicago Press, 1969), p. 193.
4. Ibid., p. 204, quoted in Caroline Golab, *Immigrant Destinations* (Philadelphia: Temple University Press, 1977), p. 84.
5. William I. Thomas and Florian Znaniecki, *The Polish Peasant in Europe and America* (New York: Alfred E. Knopf, 1927), I: 147.
6. T. Lindsay Baker, *The First Polish Americans: Silesian Settlements in Texas* (College Station: Texas A & M University Press, 1979), pp. 8, 20.
7. Benjamin P. Murdzek, *Emigration in Polish Social-Political Thought, 1870–1914*, East European Monographs, no. 32 (Boulder, Colo.: *East European Quarterly*, 1977), pp. 45, 55, 60.
8. Baker, *First Polish Americans*, p. 21.

II. To Field, Mine, and Factory

1. T. Lindsay Baker, *The First Polish Americans: Silesian Settlements in Texas* (College Station: Texas A & M University, 1979), p. 37.
2. Ibid., pp. 47, 51.
3. John Bodnar, Roger Simon, and Michael P. Weber, *Lives of Their Own: Blacks, Italians, and Poles in Pittsburgh, 1900–1960* (Urbana: University of Illinois Press, 1982), p. 59.
4. Caroline Golab, *Immigrant Destinations* (Philadelphia: Temple University Press, 1977), p. 61.
5. John Reed, "Industrial Frightfulness in Bayonne," *Metropolitan Magazine* (January, 1917), n.p., clipping in Bayonne Public Library Clipping File.
6. Bodnar et al., *Lives of Their Own*, p. 18.
7. *New York State Department of Labor Annual Report*, Vol. 3, Part 3 (Albany: State Department, 1903), pp. xxv–xxvii.
8. Herbert G. Gutman, "Work, Culture, and Society in Industrializing America, 1815–1919," *American Historical Review* 77 (1973): 533.
9. Change-of-name petitions, 1927, 8108, in City Court Record Room, Brooklyn, N.Y.
10. David Brody, *Labor in Crisis: The Steel Strike of 1919* (Philadelphia: Lippincott, 1965), p. 155; quoted in Joseph A. Wytrwal, *Behold! the Polish-Americans* (Detroit: Endurance Press, 1977), p. 542.

III. Hands Clasped, Fists Clenched

1. *Brooklyn Eagle*, December 28, 1919.

2. Niles Carpenter, *Immigrants and Their Children, 1920*, Census Monographs, 7 (Washington, D.C.: Government Printing Office, 1927), p. 286.

3. Interview with Casimir Tokarski (Bayonne, N.J., July 23, 1980).

4. Description of the Association of Polish Women of Our Lady of Czestochowa, Group 53, Polish Roman Catholic Union, excerpted from the fiftieth anniversary album of St. Stanislaus Kostka parish, Chicago, and quoted in *The Poles in America, 1608–1972: A Chronology & Fact Book*, ed. F. Renkiewicz (Dobbs Ferry, N.Y.: Oceana Publications, 1973), p. 62.

5. Thaddeus C. Radzialowski, "'Let Us Join Hands': The Polish Women's Alliance," *Immigrant Women*, ed. Maxine Seller (Philadelphia: Temple University Press, 1981), pp. 177, 179.

6. Interview with Frank Laukaitis (Brooklyn, N.Y., August 24, 1977).

7. *Ognisko* [The hearth] (New York), February 7, 1889.

8. Lawrence D. Orton, *Polish Detroit and the Kolasiński Affair* (Detroit: Wayne State University Press, 1981), p. 34.

9. Daniel S. Buczek, *Immigrant Pastor: The Life of the Right Reverend Monsignor Lucyan Bójnowski of New Britain, Connecticut* (Waterbury, Conn.: Heminway Corp., 1974), p. 144.

10. Rev. Lucyan Bójnowski, quoted in Stanislaus A. Blejwas, "A Polish Community in Transition: The Origins of Holy Cross Parish, New Britain, Connecticut," *Polish American Studies* 34 (Spring 1977): 33.

11. Eduard Adam Skendzel, *The Kolasinski Story* (Grand Rapids, Mich.: Littleshield Press, 1979), p. 6.

12. Theodore Andrews, *The Polish National Catholic Church* (London: SPCK, 1953), p. 29.

13. Paul Fox, *The Polish National Catholic Church* (Scranton, Pa.: School of Christian Living, 1961), p. 78.

14. Franciszek Hodur, *Our Faith*, trans. Theodore L. Zawistowski and Joseph C. Zawistowski, mimeographed (n.p., 1966), p. 13.

15. Anthony J. Kuzniewski, *Faith and Fatherland: The Polish Church War in Wisconsin, 1896-1918* (Notre Dame, Ind.: University of Notre Dame Press, 1980), p. 46.

16. Sister Mary Remigia Napolska, O.S.F., *The Polish Immigrant in Detroit to 1914*, Annals of the Polish Roman Catholic Union Archives and Museum, Vol. 10 (1945–1946) (Chicago: Polish Roman Catholic Union of America, 1946), p 46.

17. F. Bujak, *Zmiaca Wieś Powiatu Limanskiego: Stosunku Gospodarcze i Spoleczne* (Cracow, 1903), p. 13, quoted in Vladimir C. Nahirny and Joshua A. Fishman, "Ukrainian Language Maintenance Efforts in the United States," *Language Loyalty in the United States: The Maintenance and Perpetuation of Non-English Mother Tongues by American Ethnic and Religious Groups*, ed. Joshua A. Fishman (London: Mouton & Co., 1966), p. 345.

IV. Continuity and Change in the 1920s and 1930s

1. Walter E. Weyl, "Jan, the Polish Miner," *The Outlook* 94 (March 26, 1910): 716.

2. Louis E. Van Norman, *Poland the Knight Among Nations* (New York: Fleming H. Revell Co., 1907), pp. 243–244.

3. Maldwyn Allen Jones, *American Immigration* (Chicago: University of Chicago Press, 1960), p. 268.

4. Eugene Obidinski, "American Polonia: Sacred and Profane Aspects," *Polish American Studies* 32 (Spring 1975): 12.

5. Adam Urbanski, "Immigration Restriction and the Polish American Press: the Response of *Wiadomosci Codzienne, 1921–1924,*" *Polish American Studies* 28 (Autumn 1971): 18.

6. From the report of a Philadelphia socialworker, quoted in *The Poles in America, 1608–1972: A Chronology & Fact Book,* ed. F. Renkiewicz (Dobbs Ferry, N.Y.: Oceana Publications, 1973), p. 80.

7. Edward R. Kantowicz, *Corporation Sole: Cardinal Mundelein and Chicago Catholicism* (Notre Dame, Ind.: University of Notre Dame Press, 1983), p. 75.

8. Joseph A. Wytrwal, *Behold! the Polish-Americans* (Detroit: Endurance Press, 1977), p. 243.

9. Edward R. Kantowicz, *Polish-American Politics in Chicago, 1888–1940* (Chicago: University of Chicago Press, 1975), p. 105.

10. Stanislaus A. Blejwas, "Old and New Polonias: Tensions Within an Ethnic Community," *Polish American Studies* 38 (Autumn 1981): 57.

11. Ibid.

12. *Brooklyn Daily Times,* July 5, 1921.

13. Harriet Pawlowska, "'The Lessons Which Most Influenced My Life Came from My Parents,'" *Immigrant Women,* ed. Maxine Schwartz Seller (Philadelphia: Temple University Press, 1981), p. 217.

14. Mary B. Kedzierska, "The Polish Family—Problems of Adjustment" (Unpublished project, Fordham School of Social Service, 1936), p. 13.

15. Theodore F. Abel, "The Poles in New York: A Study of the Polish Communities in Greater New York" (Master's thesis, Columbia University, 1924), ms. p. 29.

16. Joseph A. Wytrwal, "The Changing Role of the Polish American Congress," *Ethnic Groups in the City: Culture, Institutions, and Power,* ed. Otto Feinstein (Lexington, Mass.: D.C. Heath & Co., 1971), p. 170.

17. Anthony J. Kuzniewski, S.J., "The Catholic Church in the Life of the Polish-Americans," *Poles in America: Bicentennial Essays,* ed. F. Mocha (Stevens Point, Wis.: Worzalla Publishing Co., 1978), p. 410.

18. Urbanski, "Immigration Restriction and the Polish American Press," p. 15.

19. Pawlowska, "'The Lessons Which Most Influenced My Life,'" p. 218

20. John Bodnar, *Workers' World: Kinship, Community, and Protest in an Industrial Society, 1900–1940* (Baltimore: Johns Hopkins University Press, 1982), pp. 22, 73, 135.

21. An Ex-Leatherneck to Harry L. Hopkins, August 12, 1935, quoted in *Down & Out in the Great Depression: Letters from the "Forgotten Man",* ed. Robert S. McElvaine (Chapel Hill: University of North Carolina Press, 1983), pp. 152–153.

22. Anonymous interview 1 (Brooklyn, N.Y., July 22, 1981).

23. Bodnar, *Workers' World,* p. 22.

24. Anonymous interview 2 (Perth Amboy, N.J., n.d.).

25. Jeremy Brecher et al., eds., *Brass Valley: The Story of Working People's Lives and Struggles in an American Industrial Region* (Philadelphia: Temple University Press, 1982), p. 107.

26. Anonymous interview 3 (Perth Amboy, N.J., n.d.).

27. Bodnar, *Workers' World,* pp. 16, 22, 55.

28. Frank Serafino, *West of Warsaw* (Hamtramck, Mich.: Avenue Publishing Co., 1983), p. 46.

29. *Detroit News*, August 4, 1935.

30. Eugene Miller, "Leo Krzycki—Polish American Labor Leader," *Polish American Studies* 33 (Autumn 1976): 54, 56.

31. *New York Times*, October 10, 1938.

V. The Decline of the Urban Ethnic Enclave

1. Joseph A. Wytrwal, *Poles in American History and Tradition* (Detroit: Endurance Press, 1969), p. 387.

2. *Czas* (Brooklyn, N.Y.), November 24, 1939.

3. Arthur L. Waldo, *Sokolstwo: Przednia Straż Narodu: Dzieje, Idei i Organizacji w Ameryce* (Pittsburgh, Pa.: Sokolstwo Polskie w Ameryce, 1953), I: 242.

4. Norman Davies, *God's Playground: A History of Poland* (New York: Columbia University Press, 1984), II: 477.

5. *New York Times*, August 18, 1984.

6. Peter H. Irons, "'The Test is Poland': Polish Americans and the Origins of the Cold War," *Polish American Studies* 30 (Autumn 1973): 54, 60.

7. *The Citizen* (Hamtramck, Mich.), March 2, 1945.

8. *Detroit Free Press*, March 17, 1955, in Hamtramck Public Library Clipping File, hereafter cited as HPLCF.

9. *New York Times Magazine*, August 3, 1952, HPLCF.

10. From a Polish American Congress statement, quoted in Irons, "'The Test is Poland'," p. 60.

11. Frank Mocha, "The Polish Institute of Arts and Sciences in America; Its Contributions to the Study of Polonia: The Origins of the Polish American Historical Association (PAHA)," *Poles in America: Bicentennial Essays*, ed. F. Mocha (Stevens Point, Wis.: Worzalla Publishing Co., 1978), p. 709.

12. Sarah Van Aken-Rutkowski, "Integration and Acculturation of the Polish Veteran of World War II to Canadian Society" (Master's thesis, University of Windsor, 1982), pp. 59, 65.

13. Maria Barbara Korewa, "Casework Treatment of Refugees: A Survey of Selected Professional Periodicals for the Period from January 1, 1939 to January 1, 1956" (Master's thesis, Wayne State University, 1957), ms. pp. 58–59.

14. Rudolph Heberle and Dudley S. Hall, *New Americans: A Study of Displaced Persons in Louisiana and Mississippi* (Baton Rouge, La.: Displaced Persons Commission, 1951), p. 3.

15. Danuta Mostwin, "Post-World War II Polish Immigrants in the United States," *Polish American Studies* 26 (Autumn 1969): 9.

16. Heberle and Hall, *New Americans*, p. 87.

17. Ibid., p. 47.

18. Ibid., p. 45.

19. *The Displaced Persons Commission; Sixth Annual Report to the President and the Congress, August 1951* (Washington, D.C.: Government Printing Office, 1952), p. 61.

20. Stanislaus A. Blejwas, "Old and New Polonias: Tensions Within an Ethnic Community," *Polish American Studies* 38 (Autumn 1981): 76–77, quoting Alicja Iwańska, "Values in Crisis Situation" (Ph.D. diss., Columbia University, 1957), pp. 63–64.

21. Ibid.

22. Blejwas, "Old and New Polonias," p. 79, quoting Iwańska, "Values in Crisis Situation," pp. 57, 66–67.

23. Thomas Sowell, ed., *Essays and Data on American Ethnic Groups* (n.p.: Urban Institute, 1978), p. 378.

24. Joseph Parot, "Ethnic versus Black Metropolis: The Origins of Polish-

Black Housing Tensions in Chicago," *Polish American Studies* 29 (Spring-Autumn 1972): 27.

25. Niles Carpenter and Daniel Katz, "A Study of Acculturization in the Polish Group of Buffalo, 1926–1928," *The University of Buffalo Studies* 7 (June 1929): 129.

26. St. Clair Drake and Horace R. Cayton, *Black Metropolis: A Study of Negro Life in a Northern City*, revised and enlarged edition (New York: Harper and Row, 1962), I: 180, 181.

27. Joseph A. Wytrwal, *Behold! the Polish-Americans* (Detroit: Endurance Press, 1977), pp. 471–474.

28. From a conversation with Sister Ellen Marie Kuznicki, CSSF.

29. Dominic J. Capeci, Jr., *Race Relations in Wartime Detroit: The Sojourner Truth Housing Controversy of 1942* (Philadelphia: Temple University Press, 1984), p. 78.

30. Frank Serafino, *West of Warsaw* (Hamtramck, Mich.: Avenue Publishing Co., 1983), p. 50.

31. Paul Wrobel, *Our Way: Family, Parish, and Neighborhood in a Polish-American Community* (Notre Dame, Ind.: University of Notre Dame Press, 1979), pp. 128–129.

32. Anonymous interview (Perth Amboy, N.J., August 14, 1984).

33. Jeremy Brecher et al., eds., *Brass Valley: The Story of Working People's Lives and Struggles in an American Industrial Region* (Philadelphia: Temple University Press, 1982), p. 228.

34. Historian Rudolph Vecoli made this important semantic distinction in "'Ethnic versus Black Metropolis': A Comment," *Polish American Studies* 29 (Spring– Autumn 1972): 37.

35. Roman L. Haremski, *The Unattached, Aged Immigrant: A Descriptive Analysis of the Problems Experienced in Old Age by Three Groups of Poles Living Apart from Their Families in Baltimore* (Washington, D.C.: Catholic University of America Press, 1940), p. 82.

36. *The Immigrant Experience: The Long Long Journey*, 16 mm. documentary film produced by Linda Gottlieb, written by Joan Micklin Silver, Learning Corporation of Amcrica (1972).

37. Helen Znaniecki Lopata, "Widowhood in Polonia," *Polish American Studies* 34 (Autumn 1977): 19, 20.

38. Conversation with the author's grandmother, n.d.

VI. What Is a Polish-American?

1. Anonymous interview (Perth Amboy, N.J., n.d.).

2. *New Horizon: Polish American Review* (New York), 13 (June 1985): 4.

3. *The Immigrant Experience: The Long Long Journey*, 16 mm. documentary film produced by Linda Gottlieb, written by Joan Micklin Silver, Learning Corporation of America (1972).

4. Russell Barta, *The Representation of Poles, Italians, Hispanics and Blacks in the Executive Suites of Chicago's Largest Corporations: A Progress Report, 1972–1983*, Minority Report No. 2 (typewritten draft), prepared by the Institute of Urban Life, Chicago, Illinois, for the National Center for Urban Ethnic Affairs, 1984, ms. pp. 4ff.

5. Paul Wrobel, "Some Discontinuities in Becoming Polish American: A Personal Point of View," unpublished paper (August 1973), ms. p. 4, in the Hamtramck Public Library Clipping File, hereafter cited as HPLCF.

6. Paul Wilkes, *Six American Families* (n.p.: Seabury/Parthenon Press, 1977), p. 35.

7. Ibid., pp. 34, 35.

8. August B. Hollingshead, *Elmtown's Youth: The Impact of Social Classes on Adolescents* (New York: John Wiley and Sons, 1949), p. 62.

9. Remark made in one of the author's Wayne State University history classes (April 9, 1985).

10. Andrew M. Greeley, *Why Can't They Be Like Us? Facts and Fallacies About Ethnic Differences And Group Conflicts in America* (New York: Institute of Human Relations Press, American Jewish Committee, 1969), p. 47.

11. Thaddeus Radzialowski, "The View from a Polish Ghetto: Some Observations on the First One Hundred Years in Detroit," *Ethnicity* 1 (1974): 138–139.

12. See Caroline Golab, "Stellaaaaaa.......!!!!!!!!: The Slavic Stereotype in American Film," *The Kaleidoscopic Lens: How Hollywood Views Ethnic Groups*, ed. R.M. Miller (Englewood, N.J.: Jerome S. Ozer, 1980), p. 148.

13. *Polish American Voice* (Buffalo, N.Y.), November 1984.

14. Conversation with the author.

15. *New York Times*, July 30, 1983.

16. *Detroit News*, December 26, 1971, HPLCF.

17. This incident involved the author.

18. *Polish Daily News* (Detroit), June 18–19, 1977, HPLCF.

19. See Frank R. Walczyk, "The Walczyk Family in America," *Polish American Studies* 18 (1961): 43–62.

20. *National Observer* (Silver Spring, Md.), April 15, 1972, HPLCF.

21. *Detroit News*, December 5, 1974, HPLCF.

22. Joseph A. Wytrwal, *Behold! the Polish-Americans* (Detroit: Endurance Press, 1977), p. 503.

23. Gary Deeb, "'Polish jokes' called 'scandalous'," *Polish Daily News* (Detroit), April 13–14, 1974, reprinted from the *Chicago Tribune*, n. d., HPLCF.

24. Michael Durham, "One-man crusade against the Polish joke," *Life* 72 (January 14, 1972): 70.

25. Wrobel, "Some Discontinuities in Becoming a Polish American," ms. p. 5.

26. Jeremy Brecher et al., eds., *Brass Valley: The Story of Working People's Lives and Struggles in an American Industrial Region* (Phildelphia: Temple University Press, 1982), p. 21.

27. Marcus Lee Hansen, *The Problem of the Third Generation Immigrant* (Rock Island, Ill.: Augustana Historical Society, 1938), pp. 9–10.

28. *The Polish American Archives Project at the University of Wisconsin-Milwaukee*, brochure (n.d.).

29. P. Taras, A.T. Pienkos, and T. Radzialowski, "Paul Wrobel's *Our Way* —Three Views," *Polish American Studies* 37 (Spring 1980): 43.

30. *New York Times*, August 28, 1983.

31. *Detroit Free Press*, August 19, 1985.

32. *New York Times*, June 22, 1984.

33. *New Horizon*, 2.

VII. Vanguard or Rearguard?

1. Statement from the Orchard Lake Center for Polish Studies and Culture, quoted in Michael Novak, *The Rise of the Unmeltable Ethnics: Politics and Culture in the Seventies* (New York: Macmillan Co., 1971), p. 235.

2. Donald Pienkos, "Polish-American Ethnicity in the Political Life of the United States," *America's Ethnic Politics*, ed. Joseph S. Roucek and Bernard Eisenberg, Contributions in Ethnic Studies, No. 5 (Westport, Conn.: Greenwood Press, 1982), p. 288.

3. Richard C. Lucas, "The Polish American Congress and the Polish Question, 1944–1947," *Polish American Studies* 38 (Autumn 1981): 40.

4. Ibid., p. 43.

5. Donald E. Pienkos, "Research on Ethnic Political Behavior Among the Polish-Americans: A Review of the Literature," *Polish Review* 21 (1976): 136.

6. Barbara Mikulski, "A Young Polish American Speaks Up: 'The Myth of the Melting Pot' (1970)," *The Poles in America, 1608–1972: A Chronology & Fact Book,* ed. F. Renkiewicz (Dobbs Ferry, N.Y.: Oceana Publications, 1973), p. 110.

7. Robert Coles, *The Middle Americans: Proud and Uncertain* (Boston: Little, Brown and Co., 1971), pp. 43–46.

8. Mikulski, "A Young Polish American Speaks Up," p. 110.

9. Ibid., p. 111.

10. Joseph A. Wytrwal, *Behold! the Polish-Americans* (Detroit: Endurance Press, 1977), p. 495.

11. Congressional Record-House, 90 Cong., 2 sess., H7871, 30 July 1968.

12. Unidentified clipping dated July 11, 1970, from the files of Regina Koscielska, Detroit. The author wishes to thank Ms. Koscielska for her assistance.

13. Kevin B. Phillips, *The Emerging Republican Majority* (New Rochelle, N.Y.: Arlington House, 1969), p. 170.

14. Perry L. Weed, *The White Ethnic Movement and Ethnic Politics* (New York: Praeger Publishers, 1973), pp. 165–166.

15. Jules Witcover, *Marathon: The Pursuit of the Presidency, 1972–1976* (New York: Viking Press, 1977), pp. 597, 603, 607.

16. Pienkos, "Polish-American Ethnicity in the Political Life of the United States," p. 289.

17. Ibid., p. 278.

18. *New York Times,* September 10, 1984.

19. ABC News exit-poll statistics tabulating Poles and other Slavs.

20. *New York Times,* October 22, 1982.

21. Anonymous interview 1 (Perth Amboy, N.J., August 14, 1984).

22. Anonymous interview 2 (Perth Amboy, N.J., August 14, 1984).

23. Mark R. Levy and Michael S. Kramer, *The Ethnic Factor: How America's Minorities Decide Elections* (New York: Simon and Schuster, 1972), p. 158.

24. See *New York Times,* July 7, 1983.

25. POLETOWN Inter-Parish Council (January 20, 1979), flier in Hamtramck Public Library Clipping File, hereafter cited as HPLCF.

26. National Center for Urban Ethnic Affairs *Buildingblocks* (Washington, D.C.) (Spring 1982): 1–2.

27. Bill Falkowski, "Is a Black/Polish Coalition Now Possible?" *Polish American Voice* (Buffalo, N.Y.) 2 (January 1984): 6.

28. *Detroit News,* February 1, 1978, HPLCF.

29. Ibid., September 27, 1978.

30. Olgierd Budrewicz, *The Melting-Pot Revisited: Twenty Well-Known Americans of Polish Background,* trans. E.J. Czerwiński and A. Makarewicz (Warsaw: Interpress, 1976), p. 158.

31. *Detroit Free Press,* October 13, 1983.

32. *Dziennik Polski* (Polish Daily News) (Detroit), May 8–9, 1981.

33. *New York Times,* July 30, 1983.

34. Ibid., September 28, 1970.

Epilogue: Polish-American Ethnicity

1. Rev. Joseph Swastek, "What Is a Polish American?" *Polish American Studies* 1 (Jan.–Dec. 1944): 35.

2. Professor Tymon Terlecki, quoted in Helen K. Wojniusz, "Ethnicity and Other Variables in the Analysis of Polish American Women," *Polish American Studies* 34 (Autumn 1977): 28.

3. Stephen Steinberg, *The Ethnic Myth: Race, Ethnicity, and Class in America* (New York: Atheneum, 1981), p. 262.

4. Proposal made by Professor Richard Kolm, quoted in *Polish American Journal* (Buffalo, N.Y.), October 11, 1969, in Hamtramck Public Library Clipping File, hereafter cited as HPLCF.

5. Cf. Glenn Collins, "A Study of Blacks in White Suburbia," *New York Times,* July 30, 1984.

6. See Rev. Leonard F. Chrobot, *Who Am I? Reflections of a Young Polish American On the Search for Identity,* Monograph No. 4 (Orchard Lake, Mich.: Orchard Lake Center for Polish Studies and Culture, St. Mary's College, 1971).

7. Robert W. Kopek, quoted in *The Citizen* (Hamtramck, Mich.), June 9, 1955, HPLCF.

INDEX

JOHN J. BUKOWCZYK (Northwestern University, B.A., 1972; Harvard University, A.M., 1973; Ph.D., 1980) is Associate Professor of History at Wayne State University in Detroit, where he teaches immigration and ethnic history. The recipient of research grants from the American Council of Learned Societies, the National Endowment for the Humanities, the New Jersey Historical Commission, and the Kosciuszko Foundation, Bukowczyk has published articles in *Labor History*, the *Journal of American Ethnic History*, and *Polish American Studies*.